Astad Deboo

AN ICON OF CONTEMPORARY INDIAN DANCE

Astad Deboo (1947–2020), widely considered a pioneer of modern dance in India, was globally renowned for his distinctive style, characterized by meditative minimalism, gravity-defying backbends and signature whirls that defined his innovative approach to form and content. In this first biography and book-length appreciation of Deboo's work, Ketu H. Katrak unveils the remarkable life, choreography and legacy of this ground-breaking figure in Indian modern dance.

Divided into four parts, this biography sheds light on various aspects of Deboo's life and career: his youth and schooling in Jamshedpur, and the friendships that shaped him; his solo choreography, which boldly addressed social issues and fused modern dance with traditional elements; his humanitarian spirit, showcasing group choreography with deaf performers and Manipuri drum dancers; and his mastery in collaborating with artists from India and abroad.

From receiving prestigious awards to transforming lives through dance, travelling around the world for over five decades yet being firmly rooted in Indian soil, Deboo left an indelible mark on contemporary Indian dance. This volume pays homage to the dancer's legendary status, emphasizing his unparalleled dedication and resilience—a guiding light for aspiring dancers striving to realize their artistic visions. It is a valuable addition to scholarship on dance studies, performance studies and South Asian studies.

KETU H. KATRAK is professor emerita of drama at the University of California, Irvine. She is the author of *Jay Pather: Performance and Spatial Politics in South Africa* (2021); *Contemporary Indian Dance: New Creative Choreography in India and the Diaspora* (2011); and *Politics of the Female Body: Postcolonial Women Writers* (2006), as well as other publications on African and postcolonial writers, performance and feminist theory. Katrak is a recipient of a Fulbright Research Award to India and the Bunting Institute Fellowship.

Astad Deboo

AN ICON OF CONTEMPORARY INDIAN DANCE

KETU H. KATRAK

LONDON NEW YORK CALCUTTA

Seagull Books, 2024

Text © Ketu H. Katrak, 2024
Photographs © Individual photographers

Hardback ISBN 978 1 80309 429 8
Paperback ISBN 978 1 80309 430 4

British Library Cataloguing-in-Publication Data
A catalogue record for this book is available from the British Library

Typeset by Seagull Books, Calcutta, India
Printed and bound by WordsWorth India, New Delhi, India

__For Astad__
In reverence for his devotion to dance.
And for the dancers he nurtured and inspired whose bodies
carry Astad's legacy.

FIGURE 1. Astad's legendary chakkar. *Photograph by Farrokh Chothia.*

Contents

PART IV

Collaborations with Artists in India and Beyond

A Journey in Dance

'Our contemporary dance in India has to evolve and be Indian contemporary.'—Astad Deboo

Astad holds his audience with his eyes as he glides across the stage, unfolding a dance work that links his heartstrings to those of his rasikas. His charismatic presence on stage exudes rasas embedded deeply in his muscles and bones. He is a delight to behold—his winning smile and twirling costume, his hands weaving magical patterns in the air. Astad is a dancer who belonged to Indian soil even as he travelled, arguably more than any other Indian dancer, across 72 countries over 51 years. In 1995 Astad received the Sangeet Natak Akamedi's Creative Dance Award, and in 2007 the Government of India's Padma Shri as a pioneer of modern dance in India.

Astad evolved his signature style—meditative, minimalist, slow, with gravity-defying backbends and balancing poses—from his roots in the classical Indian dance styles of Kathak and Kathakali, along with dance and musical inspirations from Southeast Asia, Korea, Japan, Brazil, Europe and the US. Astad describes his style as 'contemporary in vocabulary and traditional in restraints'. His body of work is original, Astad pushed boundaries of movement in his choreography—both solo and for groups; he adapted his style in creative ways in his collaborations with musicians and dancers.

Astad's memorable chakkars stopped as if midway with his untimely passing on 10 December 2020, leaving the dance world bereft of his impeccable artistry, humanitarian spirit and warm friendship with many across India and the world. Mumbai-based Astad, even at age 73, remained a force in contemporary Indian dance as he was still choreographing digitally with artists in Delhi during the Covid-19 pandemic lockdown in 2020.

I am honoured and humbled by the invitation from Astad's family to write his biography—a role I recognize as daunting, indeed, formidable. I agreed hesitantly, knowing that it would be challenging to capture Astad's charm and loyalty, his personal journey and his range and accomplishments as a dancer. How was I to capture the essence of Astad the man, the one who persevered against steep odds, never giving up his devotion to dance? His generous heart treated anyone who crossed his path as an equal, as a human being, never judging their social or financial backgrounds which were irrelevant to him. My writing has been fuelled by loving Astad as a friend and as a scholar of dance who has written about his work over the years. As such, my writerly tone is infused with both my warm feelings for Astad and my engagement with a wide range of his dance works from the 1970s until his passing in 2020.

Indeed, it was Astad who instigated and encouraged my scholarly pursuits when he invited me in 2015 to be his co-editor on *Marg* magazine's special issue, 'Contemporary Dance in India'. Initially, I was in two minds since I thought that an artist or scholar living in India would be better suited for the task. But Astad, as a visionary, believed that through his contacts and knowledge on the one hand and my scholarly abilities on the other, we would create a valuable product. And we did! This 2017 *Marg* issue finely complemented my 2011 book, *Contemporary Indian Dance: New Creative Choreography in India and the Diaspora*.

We had a fabulous time collaborating from 2015 to 2017, a period characterized above all by Astad's generosity of spirit. He was discerning in his selection of artists, companies and thinkers on Indian dance. Wherever in the world Astad was, he responded to emails, remaining connected with the project as we structured the sections, keeping contributions lively and thought-provoking, discussing the parameters and challenges faced by contemporary Indian dancers. We co-wrote the Introduction and Conclusion, exploring key challenges in contemporary dance in India. We raised questions about its identity, differences from Western contemporary dance, the integration of classical Indian styles, training, funding and originality. We also discussed innovations in movement, music, costuming and staging. Prominent dance writers and dancers like Leela Venkataraman, Ranjana Dave, Vikram Iyengar and Anita Ratnam contributed essays. We also compiled photographs of iconic dancers, including Chandralekha, Mrinalini and Mallika Sarabhai, Sanjukta Wagh, Bharat Sharma and Santosh Nair, among others.

We chose Bharatanatyam exponent Ramaa Bharadvaj to write about Astad's journey as a dancer, and her insightful essay, 'Astad Deboo: Pilgrim, Pathfinder, Protagonist', beautifully captures his spirit and dedication to dance. Ramaa mentioned to me that Astad had travelled to Bengaluru, where she is based, and they spent a few 'unforgettable days together and developed a special friendship based on trust, and admiration for each other'. She noted that Astad

> knew how to make himself comfortable around you and thus made you feel comfortable around him. He would just spread out on the floor as if we were having a pajama party, and when I cooked, he would perch on the counter and chat . . . As an artist, his quest was less about finding a place for himself in the art world, and more about shaping a life-purpose for himself through his art. (interview with the author, August 2021; henceforth referred to as *int.*)

Major support for the publication and distribution of this *Marg* issue was provided by BNP Paribas, a France-based bank that has been in Mumbai for nearly 160 years. I learnt from Anjali Patil, head of brand and communications for BNP Paribas India, about their support to Astad in 2017 for the launch event of this *Marg* issue at Mumbai's G5A space. Anjali noted that BNP Paribas also funded the creation of new work such as Astad's collaboration with rudra veena player Bahau'd-din Dagar in 2018 as well as *Unbroken Unbowed* at NCPA in 2019 (int., February

2022). Under their 'Corporate Social Responsibility (CSR)' programme, BNP supported Astad's work with St Stephen's School for the Deaf in Worli, Mumbai, for nearly 18 months, with a culminating grand finale of the students' performance on 27 March 2020.

Shankar Ramakrishnan, the head of BNP Paribas India, told me that he always pushed for the Bank to support those who are 'very passionate about their work' (int., February 2022). He certainly found that in Astad who left 'no stone unturned' when he committed to a project. Having followed his work for some years, Shankar was struck by Astad's humanity that aimed 'to uplift mankind'. Astad had many projects in mind that he had shared with Shankar, but they were not to happen due to his untimely death. On 10 January 2021, one month after Astad's passing, Shankar and BNP Paribas fully funded the event 'Remembering Astad' held at G5A in Mumbai.

Astad's collaborative spirit that met others halfway and worked hard to reach the finish line of a project in dance, music or publication saw *Marg*'s special issue on contemporary dance in India from its inception to fruition. As his co-editor, I had no idea of his diligent efforts behind the scenes in getting key sponsorship from BNP Paribas to cover part of the production expense (keeping the price to a modest 350 Indian rupees for a beautifully produced, glossy volume with colour photographs) as well as its distribution across India. This edition of *Marg* remains a testament to Astad's legacy in contemporary Indian dance.

* * *

Astad's family and mine were acquainted in Bombay—as the city Mumbai was called at the time—as we visited between my home in Dadar Parsi Colony, and his in Shapur Baug off Lamington Road, also a colony for Parsees, that is, the Indian term for Zoroastrians.[1] We share the same

---

1 Fleeing religious persecution by Muslims, the Parsee community migrated to India from Iran by sea between the eighth and tenth centuries CE to preserve their Zoroastrian faith. The Zoroastrians first came to Sanjan in Gujarat, seeking asylum

mother tongue, Gujarati, which was spoken by Astad with delicious mischief, wonderful rhyming phrases and nuances imbibed from the Gujarati spoken by his mother Rhoda who grew up in Navsari, Gujarat.

We also share the ancient Zoroastrian religion, with its central tenets of 'good thoughts, good words, and good deeds'—in that order. In this religion, young boys and girls are initiated into the Zoroastrian fold with the Navjote ceremony by reciting the primary prayers. Zoroastrians practice charity to anyone in need. Astad lived this aspect of his religion by giving liberally of his dance style in training various groups—deaf actors and dancers in Kolkata and Chennai, street youth in New Delhi and neglected Manipuri dancers and martial artists with whom he cultivated a 16-year working relationship. I interviewed some from these groups who revered Astad, not only as a guru imparting dance and discipline but also as a caring elder who taught them life skills in their interactions with the public both on and off stage. His caring for these groups consumed him for years, especially during India's strict Covid-19 lockdown in 2020 when Astad supported 25–40 families in Delhi, Mumbai and Imphal. He had said to me in a WhatsApp call that he lay awake many nights thinking of how he could raise funds to support so many talented dancers and to provide daily sustenance for their families.

Astad founded the Astad Deboo Dance Foundation in 2002 to realize his dream of providing training and financial assistance to marginalized groups in India and to make the road easier for current and future contemporary Indian dancers than it had been for him. As Mumbai-

---

from the ruler there. As the legend goes, when asked by the ruler how they would fit into Indian society, the Zoroastrian priest asked for a cup of milk and some sugar; he mixed them and told the ruler that that was how the Zoroastrians would mingle with the local community—they would only make life sweeter rather than cause any bitter conflict. Once they adopted India as their home, Zoroastrians imbibed several local customs such as wearing the saree, and adopting the Gujarati language as their mother tongue, giving it a distinctive inflection and tone, different from the language spoken by the majority Gujarati Hindus.

based journalist and Astad's friend Carol Andrade remarks in 'About a Dream', the Foundation's goals included cultivating an appreciation of modern dance in India, building audiences, fund-raising and fostering the future of this Indian dance style (Andrade 2017).

In writing this biography, a labour of love, I have interviewed, with valuable contacts from Astad's sister Gulshan Deboo, many of Astad's friends, colleagues, interlocutors, collaborators, photographers, costume designers and classical Indian dancers; some of the latter regretted that they had not expressed their appreciation of Astad's art while he was alive.

Although Astad was always clear that his dance be viewed and evaluated on its own artistic merit and not through any other prism, it is important to recognize that he transgressed many boundaries in his personal and professional life. He traversed geographical borders with his extensive travels, also crossing borders of movement, music, costume and gender. While being totally dedicated to dance as his first love, Astad's personal life as a gay man was discreet, though as Sunil Shanbag, one of Astad's longtime friends and interlocutors noted, 'He never denied it to himself and in fact allowed it to flow into his creative work. The male body was very much present in his work and it was present in a loving and dignified manner' (int., July 2021). Astad did not publicly share his relationships (except with a few trusted friends), nor did he comment on gay issues. When Astad began performing in the 1970s, being gay was not widely accepted in India nor was it in most parts of the world—today dancers can be more open about their sexuality.

As a male dancer in India in the 1970s and 80s, Astad was unique in a field dominated by female, heterosexual Indian classical dancers. Astad remained boldly single, 'married' to his dance. Some of Astad's friends noted in interviews that he shared personal matters of the heart about his relationships. Astad mentioned to me on a WhatsApp call in 2016, that he had a partner, Rahul (aka Amit) Kumar and I was delighted for him. This personal relationship for around the last ten years of

Astad's life was perhaps the longest that Astad had. Kumar, a professional photographer, travelled with him, including in 2019 when Astad collaborated with the Chicago-based Indian classical dancer Hema Rajagopalan and her troupe.

Astad's prodigious talent as a dancer and choreographer was matched by his enormously giving heart. I feel fortunate to have been his friend. As many testify in this biography, he had an uncanny ability to cultivate and nurture friendships, always being the one to take the initiative to keep in touch via phone calls, visits and greeting cards for birthdays in the days before email and WhatsApp calls. He loved many who reciprocated his affection—this included artists, collaborators and ordinary people with whom he created magical connections on and off stage. A special place in Astad the foodie's heart was always reserved for family cooks who delighted in pleasing his palate and would look forward to his visits! Astad loved food and willingly explored different cuisines, also encouraging his dancers when they travelled with him across India and abroad, to be adventurous about food unfamiliar to them!

Astad leaves behind a formidable and undying legacy, as much for his exquisite artistry as for his special humanity, recalled in vivid memories shared by many. This biography traces that legacy via his life, his work and his caring for his dancers and ordinary people, including the younger generation of contemporary Indian dancers for whom he paved the way as a pioneer in this style. I include testimonies from those who knew him for 50 years, others for shorter amounts of time who recall fondly his impact on their lives. I also rely on media reviews and interviews with those who knew Astad from his earliest works in the 1970s, such as Ratan Batliboi and Sunil Shanbag; and more recent collaborators among Indian, Japanese and Korean musicians and theatre-makers.

Sunil Shanbag shared that a significant challenge facing Astad in his early work was that there was no context in which Astad was dancing, no discussion of the body, of movement, or contemporary dance that had a completely different vocabulary from Indian classical dance.

'There was a lot of pressure on him', Shanbag noted, adding forthrightly that 'In India, to be in the arts is heroic. I'm telling you, nothing short of that' (int., July 2021). Astad was courageous in taking risks with representing unusual and bold social issues such as drug addiction in his early works and with formal innovations in his use of lighting, props and space.

Ramaa Bharadvaj recalled lovingly that although she met Astad in 2002, she had 'met' him earlier emotionally via an interview in which she had been captivated by one sentence, namely, that to Astad, 'every performance was like a penance and so on that day he fasted. This fascinated me, and an intense longing swelled up in me to meet him' (int., August 2021).

A similar response as Ramaa's—that Astad enabled a collaborator or the audience to touch a realm beyond the physical—was expressed by Yukio Tsuji, a Japanese Shakuhachi flautist and percussionist who collaborated with Astad and adored him as a person and as an artist. Their collaboration entitled *Eternal Embrace* performed initially at the Metropolitan Museum of Art in New York City (later also performed across India), transported Yukio to a transcendent realm. What Yukio described to me was reminiscent of ancient Indian philosopher Abhinavgupta who stated that the experience of 'chamatkar' is similar both within a spiritual realm as in a heightened artistic communion experienced by a performer and transmitted to an audience.

This biography is one step towards paying homage posthumously to Astad's legendary status, as well as his exceptional tenacity in remaining faithful to his art through many struggles, which serves as a model for artists striving to realize their own visions. Six months after his passing, on 13 July 2021, Astad's birthday, Chennai-based performing artist, art entrepreneur and producer Anita Ratnam put together an incredible remembrance titled 'Amazing Astad' (the event was held online, and can be viewed in entirety on YouTube [Ratnam 2021]). Ably assisted by Ramaa Bharadvaj and Ratnam's technical team, this was an ambitious day-long event, 13-and-a-half hours that included 19 guest speakers with engaging, amusing and moving 15-minute stories with Anita as a brilliant host in 19 avatars or costume changes. Anita, with her engaging camera presence and insightful questions for Astad's friends, collaborators, curators and photographers, made his 74th birthday truly unforgettable, announcing: 'Watch out for the all-day tribute to icon ASTAD DEBOO on his 74th birthday—July 13th with conversations and reminiscences of the mercurial iconoclast whose legacy and stamp on India's contemporary dance scene is unquestionable' (Ratnam 2021). Astad was in the vanguard of innovative contemporary Indian dance; indeed, his life story encapsulates and traces the history and development of this style.

This biography is divided into four parts. Part I traces Astad's childhood and youth through dance. Part II discusses Astad's early solo choreography of the 1970s, 80s and 90s along with his signature style. Part III explores Astad's choreography for marginalized groups—the deaf, Manipuri drum dancers and martial artists, as well as the street youth from Salaam Baalak Trust. Part IV discusses this maestro's unique collaborations—with top-ranking artists in India and transnationally from Korea, Japan and the Indian diaspora; with costume designers, photographers and with spatial boundaries. Astad takes his final bow in a Conclusion with tributes by India's dance and media fraternity.

I conclude this Preface with a poem I wrote for Astad, the creation of which helped me through my initial process of mourning him.

> *For Astad, with love from biographer Ketu*
> *From you, dear friend*
> *I have learnt friend*
> *ship.*
> *You boarded a ship*
> *in the affordable lower deck*
> *with goats.*

The year was 1969
You were 22.
    You travelled courageously
to further your dance education
traversing 72 countries
in 51 years
crossing borders
of movement, cultures, cuisines.
You carried handwritten addresses
to send birthday cards to friends by post
in pre-internet days
Your loyalty to many resonates with
memorable words in Shakespeare's Hamlet:
'Those friends thou hast, and their adoption tried,
grapple them to thy soul with hoops of steel.'
Your name Astad means a star
    now, in your otherworldly abode
    I imagine you dancing freely,
    nonstop chakkars
    Flying like the cranes
    embroidered on your deep-blue angarkha.
Let me part the curtain, go backstage
Witness the sweat still gleaming on your brow.
Then see you in the lobby
A vision in white
In an immaculate white kurta and churidar
simple and elegant.
Join us, dear Astad
On this journey of your life in dance

FIGURE 2. 'Amazing Astad!': A 13-hour online celebration of Astad's life held on 13 July 2021, with 19 speakers comprising friends, family and collaborators; produced and hosted by Dr Anita Ratnam with Ramaa Bharadvaj as event manager. Photograph of Astad with joined hands by Sreekumar Krishnan. Composite images of Ratnam (from screenshots of interview videos) by Bharadvaj. *Courtesy Sreekumar Krishnan and Ramaa Bharadvaj.*

Acknowledgements

This book owes much gratitude to many who have shed light on Astad's personality, his indomitable spirit and his distinguished dance career. First, my sincere thanks to Astad's family, especially his sister Gulshan Deboo, who invited me to write the story of his life in dance and provided me with numerous contacts of Astad's friends, designers, collaborators and supporters within and outside India. I am also grateful to Astad's sister Kamal Antia, nephews Xerxes and Danesh Antia, who shared their own memories of a loving brother and uncle. I thank the family for the many photographs in this biography. Xerxes had sent me many newspaper reviews and other materials that Astad himself was compiling for his archive—a collection that would be useful to dancers and performing artists interested in learning about Astad's legacy—that still needs to find a home.

I owe a huge debt of gratitude to my friend and colleague at the University of California, Irvine, Professor Ngũgĩ wa Thiong'o, an internationally renowned writer, who introduced me most generously to Naveen Kishore, the founder-publisher of Seagull Books. That led to a contract for this publication. I am also very grateful to my excellent editor, Bishan Samaddar at Seagull Books, for his astute editing that has made this a readable and engaging book.

Astad's generosity and his ability to make and retain friends was legion. I am most grateful to the many who communicated with me and shared memories and anecdotes. I spoke to Astad's Jamshedpur friends: Jeelu Billimoria, Rohini Desai Mulchandani, Dinyar Divitre, Ashok Chirayath, Orville Domingo, Farrukh Dhondy and Ronald D'Costa.

I thank Soli Surti, Vidhya Gajapathi Singh, Bharti Patel, George Michell, Yasmine Stafford, Phainie Xydis, Kharmeen Ginwalla, Prabha Rao, Satya Achayya, Pheroza Modi, Yezdi Unwala and others. I thank

Jeelu Billimoria and Deena Haque, who spoke warmly about their parents, Homi and Khorshed Vakil, who supported Astad in significant ways. I thank Shanoo Bhatia of EuMo Design and Shernaz Cama of Parzor for sharing their remembrances of Astad.

I had extremely useful discussions about Astad's early works with Sunil Shanbag and Ratan Batliboi. Sunil was instrumental in bringing key publications to my attention: *Beyond the Proscenium: Reimagining the Space for Performance*, edited by Anmol Vellani; and Astad's interview, 'I Am Still Exploring . . .', for the *Seagull Theatre Quarterly* (1995).

I thank Rani Nair, based in Sweden, for sharing with me her role as biographer/archivist in creating *An Evening with Astad* about his early works.

I thank Astad's costume designers for their contributions to this biography—Archana Shah, Monica Jade and Ashdeen Lilaowala. I thank Astad's photographers—Farrokh Chothia, Ritam Banerjee and Sreekumar Krishnan, who very kindly made their images available for this project. Astad also worked with other photographers, including Neelesh Kale and Shantanu Shenoy.

I thank Dadi Pudumjee of Sutra Puppet Theatre for his collaborative work with Astad and for his interview with me. Among dancers trained by Astad, I thank Shamshul Mohamed (of Salaam Baalak Trust) and Narendra Chakpram (from Manipur), who shared with me their life-transforming experiences as disciples of Astad, their guru and mentor. I thank Astad's collaborators, some of whom I interviewed: Hyoung-Taek Lim (Korea), Yukio Tsuji (Japan/US), Bahau'd-din Dagar (India), Hema Rajagopalan (India/US).

I thank classical Indian dancers Alarmel Valli, Malavika Sarukkai, Aditi Mangaldas, Ramaa Bharadvaj, Chitra Sundaram and Anita Ratnam for interviews. My thanks to Uttara Asha Coorlawala for an interview and for sharing early photographs of dancing with Astad. I thank Anita Ratnam for her insightful interviews with Astad's family, friends, collaborators, producers and photographers over a 13-hour period celebrating Astad's 74th birthday on 13 July 2021.

Among foundations and corporate supporters of Astad's work, I thank Anuradha Parikh of Mumbai's G5A: Foundation for Contemporary Culture, who made this space available for the commemoration of Astad's one-month death anniversary on 10 January 2021. I thank Shankar Ramakrishnan and Anjali Patil of BNP Paribas for interviews and their support of Astad's vision. Mr Ramakrishnan and BNP Paribas funded the G5A event and supported the publication and distribution of *Marg*'s special issue, co-edited by Astad and me. BNP Paribas was supporting Astad's work with the Worli School for the Deaf in Mumbai during 2020 and had agreed to fund the dancer's future projects in 2021. I thank Rathi Jafer of InKo Centre for facilitating Astad's India–Korea collaborations, and for help with sources from the Centre's archive. My thanks to Mary Ann Whitten for sharing brochures of Astad's performances and correspondence.

I am grateful to my friends in the US—Arlene Avakian, Beheroze Shroff, Gabriele Schwab and Daniel Gary Busby—for valuable guidance and support of the project during certain challenges. I thank Leslie Blough for her professional editing of the manuscript and other research assistance. I thank my friend Arlene Avakian who stepped in with timely help with her keen editorial eye. I am grateful to my sister, Silloo Marker, for her support of the project, editing a few sections, and for coming up with the title of the book.

I thank the Clare Trevor School of the Arts at the University of California, Irvine for a research grant that supported this project. This grant enabled me to hire doctoral students for the transcription of interviews on Zoom. I thank Stephanie Lim, who did the bulk of interview transcriptions, and Deni Li, who assisted with a few.

For emotional support, I thank my daughter Roshni and my friend Beheroze Shroff, both of whom knew and loved Astad and his dance.

Ketu H. Katrak
Irvine, California, 13 July 2024

Chronology of Astad Deboo's Work

1978–79: *Space Odyssey* (*Zontus*)

1980: *Ritual*

1980s (in general): *Basics*

    Endless

    Search

    Asylum

1982: *Broken Pane*

    Insomnia, also performed as part of *Quintet* (1987).

1984: *Mangalore Street*, a theatre work with Astad as an actor.

1984: The East–West Dance Encounter

1987: *Aahavan* (The Challenge), with Sunil Shanbag's Arpana Theatre Group.

    Vicissitudes

    Oasis Disco Opening at the Hyatt Regency, Delhi, with Yasmine Stafford.

1988: *En Counterpoint*, with a jugalbandi between Astad and sarod maestro Pandit Brij Narayan.

    Duel

    Vissititudes

    Disquietude, selected for the International Choreographers Competition, Bobigny, Paris.

1989: *Chrysalis*

1990: *Confluences* featuring *Friends*, with Dadi Pudumjee.

    Passage of Life

    Lakdi ka Ravan, at Khajurao Dance Festival.

1991: *Thanatomorphia*, with Dadi Pudumjee.

1992: *Aahavan* (An Invocation), with Gundecha Brothers.

1993: *Dancing Dolphins*, with Kolkata's Action Players, a theatre company with deaf actors.

1995: Sangeet Natak Akademi Award for Creative Dance.

1998: Performances with deaf actors/dancers from Gallaudet University, Washington DC.

War, with dancers from Manipur.

1999: Performances with the Action Players at Gallaudet University, Washington DC.

Celebration, with dancers from Manipur.

2002: Establishment of the Astad Deboo Dance Foundation (ADDF).

Circle of Feelings by the Action Players at International Deaf Way II Arts Festival, Gallaudet University, Washington DC.

First Step, featuring R. Karthika, Clarke School for the Deaf, Chennai.

2004: *ContraPosition*, with Chennai School for the Deaf. Travelled across India and parts of Europe (2004–2007), with 75 performances.

Solo dance for the Jahan-e-Khusrau festival, New Delhi.

Solo at high elevation, Second Champaner Festival, Gujarat.

Solo at high elevation, National Institute of Design, Ahmedabad, Gujarat.

Five Minus Three, solo at high elevation, National Gallery of Modern Art, Mumbai.

2005: *ContraPosition*, opening for the 20th Summer Deaflympics, Melbourne, Australia.

Rhythm Divine I, with dancers from Manipur.

2007: Padma Shri from the Government of India.

ContraPosition, Rashtrapti Bhavan, New Delhi, on the occasion of Astad receiving the Padma Shri.

Excerpts from *Celebration* and *Rhythm Divine I* performed in Belgium and Spain.

2008: Performance at the coronation of the King of Bhutan, commissioned by the Government of India, featuring 30 dancers from Manipur.

2009: *Breaking Boundaries*, with Salaam Baalak street youth, New Delhi; travelled across India—Mumbai, Kanpur, Chennai, Kolkata and Bangalore.

2011: *Interpreting Tagore*, with Salaam Baalak street youth, Mumbai.

2012: *Interpreting Tagore*, with Salaam Baalak street youth, New Delhi.

2014: *Interpreting Tagore*, with Salaam Baalak street youth, Chennai.

Rhythm Divine II, with dancers from Manipur. Travelled across India—Delhi to Pondicherry, Kolkata, Mumbai, Jamshedpur, Bengaluru and Chennai; internationally, presented in European and South African cities.

2015: *Eternal Embrace*, with Japanese flautist Yukio Tsuji, at Metropolitan Museum of Art, New York.

Solo at high elevation, Mehrangarh Fort, Jodhpur, Rajasthan.

2015–16: *Hamlet_Avataar*, with Hyoung-Taek Limb, Seoul Factory, South Korea. Premiered at the Hindu Theater Festival, Chennai, 2015; performed at the Seoul Performing Arts Festival, South Korea, October 2015; performed in Bengaluru and Chennai in 2016.

2016: *Eternal Embrace*, with Japanese flautist Yukio Tsuji, performed across India–Mumbai, New Delhi, Chennai, Bengaluru and Ahmedabad.

Performance with Manipuri dancers, Opera Bastille, Paris.

2017: *Same Same but Different*, with Korean and Indian musicians, premiered at the National Theatre of Korea, Seoul.

Liminal, Late October on Jeju Island in South Korea, solo performance.

2018: Yagnaraman Living Legend Lifetime Achievement Award from Sri Krishna Gana Sabha, Chennai.

Rhythm Divine II, with dancers from Manipur, in Santiago, Chile, and Sao Paulo, Brazil.

Inter Connect, with rudra veena player Bahau'din Dagar, Mumbai.

2019: *Unbroken Unbowed*, with Salaam Baalak street youth, Mumbai.

Inai (*The Connection*), with Hema Rajagopalan, Chicago, USA.

2019–2020: *Same Same but Different*, with Korean and Indian musicians; travels across India.

2020: *Unbroken Unbowed*, with Salaam Baalak street youth, New Delhi and Bhubaneshwar, Odisha.

Inter Connect, with rudra veena player Bahau'din Dagar, Mumbai.

Video works during Covid-19 lockdown—*Boundaries*; *Boundaries 1.1*; and *Boundaries 2*.

FIGURE 3. Astad in his signature white kurta and churidar. *Photograph by Sreekumar Krishnan.*

PART I

Enter Astad Deboo

FIGURE 4. Astad (in the doorway) with his parents Rhoda and Adarbad Deboo. *Courtesy Deboo family.*

CHAPTER 1

Childhood, Youth and Family in Jamshedpur

The sound of ankle bells wafted in the air outside Jamshedpur's United Club. Kathak lessons were in progress. The year was 1952. Astad, though only six years old, was intently following Guru Prahlad Das' taal as he absorbed the North Indian classical dance style Kathak into his young body and mind. Astad was born on 13 July 1947, about a month prior to India's Independence from British colonial rule. His birth fell on Astad Roj—Astad translates as 'a star in the sky'—in the Zoroastrian calendar. It seems prophetic that a dance star was born with his gift for dancing on this very auspicious day.

Astad grew up in a close-knit and loving middle-class family. He recalled his childhood as 'a sweet memory', born in his Nani's house in Navsari, Gujarat. The family moved to Calcutta (now Kolkata) when Astad was five (Sawhney 2002). Astad and his two sisters with their parents relocated to Jamshedpur since their father got a job with the Tata Iron and Steel Company. The family lived there through the children's high school along with their masi's (mother's sister) son who grew up with the siblings.[1]

Adarbad and Rhoda Deboo, Astad's parents, were distinctive in supporting their son's passion for dance, a rare stance for parents raising

---

1 This cousin Cawas, born in Mombasa, Kenya, was sent to live with the Deboos at age five and considered Astad a brother. Cawas admitted in an interview that he was very naughty and that Astad's mother was very strict. However, Cawas felt closer to the Deboo siblings than he did to his own in Kenya.

a male child in India during the 1940s and 50s. 'Off to dance school you go,' Astad recalled his parents saying to their only son, who adds: 'It was probably to get me out of their hair!' (Sawhney 2002). Astad spoke of how his 'twinkle toes' were ever ready to dance for even a small audience of one or two. He never minded that he was the only boy in a dance class of 10 to 15 girls including his sisters Gulshan and Kamal. Astad had told me how much he valued his parents' unwavering emotional support throughout his life as a dancer, an unusual choice for boys from his social and religious background. Astad's open-minded parents, according to Gulshan, did not distinguish between girl-child and boy-child, hence the siblings could pursue any activity they desired, not guided by stereotypical expectations of daughters training to be teachers and sons to be doctors or engineers.

Astad was moulded from a young age in a Zoroastrian household that followed the tenets of this ancient religion—good thoughts, good words and good deeds, along with honesty, moral courage and generosity to help those in need. From childhood, Astad embodied these values, and as an adult he gave abundantly, sharing his dance skills with the deaf and with youth surviving on the streets. Astad was a humanitarian who cared especially for gifted dancers with limited means. From the 1990s until his passing in 2020, Astad devoted considerable time, resources and talent in showcasing some of Indian society's artists, marginal to the mainstream. Indeed, what Kamal loved about her brother was that he helped many and did not act as a celebrity with his family, friends, or even strangers he encountered. Her favourite memory of Astad as 'a loving, caring brother' is in his white kurta, churidar and Pathan sandals.

The flourishing dancer inherited his mother Rhoda's creative talents. She was interested in music, played the veena and worked as a secretary at Jamshedpur's United Club where her children took dance classes. Her dexterous and gifted hands designed and crafted torans with glass beads that adorned doorways in many Zoroastrian homes. Like his mother,

Astad had strong and flexible hands; his fingers created memorable patterns in mudras when he danced. 'He was very proud of his mother,' remarked Shernaz Cama (int., August 2021), director of Parzor UNESCO project, an organization that promotes Zoroastrian history and heritage in embroidery and toran-making. Shernaz shared a 2005 photograph with Astad and Rhoda who had brought her hand-made torans to Parzor's embroidery workshop. Rhoda was equally talented at weaving the sacred thread made of sheep's wool called kusti that Zoroastrians wear around their waist. Rhoda had gifted me one of her woven kustis, as also to Yasmine Stafford, a friend of Astad's who was delighted that we were both part of 'Rhoda's kusti brigade!' (int., July 2021).

Rhoda believed in lifelong learning; hence, she was keen to learn swimming at the age of 30 when she came to Jamshedpur after marriage. Later, Kamal recalled that at the advanced age of 90, her mother again wished to swim in the pool when she visited Jamshedpur where Kamal lives. A truly gutsy woman who fulfilled this wish! Astad's personality demonstrates this same determination and perseverance in his life and in realizing his dance vision against several setbacks. He was also adventurous like his mother in undertaking travels to new places, trying different cuisines and taking risks. Astad's personality was quite a combination of his father's affectionate and gentle nature and his mother's artistic talents along with her no-nonsense attitude—she did not suffer fools lightly!

Astad's father, Adarbad, and my father, Homi Katrak, were friends. Both worked for the Tata Iron and Steel Company. I recall, as a child, Adarbad's visits to our flat in Dadar Parsi Colony in Bombay (now Mumbai) and his memorable tight hugs. We also went over to the Deboo residence in Shapur Baug, another residential enclave for Parsees in Bombay. I remember meeting Rhoda, a strong and outspoken woman and an excellent cook, who treated us to many wonderful meals. We heard both parents express great pride in their son's achievements in dance and performance. During those visits in the 1960s and 70s, we did not see Astad at home in Bombay; he was always travelling for work, whether to Delhi or Tokyo.

Astad's sister Gulshan shared one disturbing memory about my father. Astad's father looked up to mine as a mentor. My father, a traditionalist, advised his friend to get his son to stop dancing and settle into a 'proper' career. Gulshan recalled that this disturbed Adarbad; nonetheless, he refused to waver from supporting his son's choice to be a professional dancer. Yet, even my father was a non-traditionalist—after all, he encouraged higher education for both his sons and daughters.

Jamshedpur: The Deboos' Beloved City

Astad and his siblings loved Jamshedpur, the small town in eastern India where they spent their early years. For further university studies, the Deboos, like other families, sent their children to urban centres such as Bombay and Delhi. Their father, like many of their neighbours and friends who came from across India—Bengalis, Gujaratis, Tamils—worked for the Tata Group of companies.

Jamshedpur, also called Tatanagar, was established in 1919 during the British Raj. This planned, industrial city was the vision of Jamshedji Nassarwanji Tata, a Zoroastrian who established India's first Tata Iron and Steel Company (TISCO) there, a major step forward in India's industrial modernization. He also developed other industries such as Tata Motors which built heavy machinery for construction and passenger cars and trucks. J. N. Tata's plan for Jamshedpur included workers' housing with modern conveniences. The urban environment had wide roads with shady trees, parks for sports and the well-known Jubilee Park and Sir Dorabji Tata Park. Certain areas of the city were earmarked for temples, mosques, and churches.

The Deboo family's Jamshedpur address was 10 Central Avenue. Gulshan recalled that there were no walls between houses and they could easily enter the next plot or house by simply crossing a hedge. The neighbours in several houses had kids the same age as the Deboos, in particular a Bengali family with nine children. The Deboo kids were often there, playing and enjoying Bengali cuisine, especially Astad, who was a foodie from a young age. Both sisters recalled their parents being strict about finishing everything on their plate during meals; if the food was not to Astad's liking, he cycled off to one of the neighbours' homes. His family joked that Astad must be visiting his Bengali *sasural* (in-laws)! From these Bengali neighbours, Astad developed his lifelong love for Bengali food and mishti or sweets.

Astad's sisters fondly remembered him as always ready to dance and act (int., June 2021). Gulshan recalled a fancy-dress party where he went dressed as Raj Kapoor from the Hindi film, *Shree 420*; Gulshan was Puss in Boots. Kamal narrated a charming anecdote from when Astad was around eight years old. An American family visiting Jamshedpur to work with Tata Steel had a young daughter interested in learning Indian dance. Astad danced as Krishna, his body painted blue, with the American girl playing Radha. Kamal found a beautiful photograph displaying innocent expressions on both their faces. I have a rather grainy photo of Astad as Krishna but not with the American girl. Along with such dancing and acting, Kamal recalled that their parents enforced discipline by requiring their children to be home by 7.30 p.m. If they came home late, they were punished by not being allowed to go swimming for one week. When they were teenagers, their curfew was extended to 11.00 p.m.

One memory of Astad, recalled differently by his two sisters, illuminates one of his personality traits: his fearlessness to climb heights and balance in risky spaces. As a youngster, Astad had climbed a guava tree, balanced on a branch, when he fell and broke his arm. This happened during the summer holidays when the family travelled by train from Jamshedpur to visit relatives in Mhow, a town near Indore in Madhya Pradesh. Gulshan recalled that Astad fell off the tree branch; according to Kamal, there was a pond underneath the guava tree and Astad tried to jump into it but missed. Either way, he did break his arm.

Astad's proclivity for heights, for balancing dangerously with a dare-devil attitude, continued in his later dance works—he danced on the Great Wall of China, on the Champaner Fort in Gujarat, on the staircase of the National Gallery of Modern Art (NGMA) in Mumbai. Whether on stage or at risky heights, Astad had an incredible ability to think on his feet and adjust even to a crumbling surface as on some of the forts he danced on.

There are stories of Astad's climbing adventures while dancing in people's homes—in a friend's courtyard in Madras, he performed on the roof, recalled Vidhya Gajapthi Singh, a friend of Astad's for 47 years. On another occasion, recalled Vidhya, at a lovely home on the beach in Chennai for the International Women's Association, Astad left the stage and climbed up on a water tank (int., July 2021).

Apart from his dancing on high surfaces, Astad took risks in many aspects of his life—his travels included hitch-hiking across Europe, unsure where he would stay for the night or get his next meal. In Astad's pioneering early choreography, his chosen costume was a unitard or leotard that proudly showed his male body; he also transgressed norms of heteronormativity. Although he was discreet about being gay, especially with his close family, he was not dishonest.

Astad's schoolmate Orville Domingo recalled that at Loyola School, Astad was teased by bullies because he looked effeminate and liked to dance (int., July 2021). However, Orville noted, Astad was undeterred. In fact, he laughed it off and was never apologetic about taking Indian dance classes. Orville remembered Astad's remarkable physical agility; he even practised stretches in class when the teacher was facing the blackboard! Another schoolmate, Ashok Chirayath, credited Astad for fighting many odds, including being gay during the 1970s and 80s (int., July 2021); Astad had shared his sexuality also with another friend, Sahadev Chirayath. Being gay never set Astad back; he remained defiant. He relished being ostracized—with aplomb.

Astad's gift both for dance and for making friends throughout his life began with his Loyola School classmates who remember him as friendly, warm, easy-going, quick to smile and share a hearty laugh. Even in school, he gravitated to dance and drama since, in his own words, he 'never liked studying'. Whenever there was a function, people would say that Astad would dance. His willingness to dance continued in later life when Astad performed at friends' weddings, openings of exhibitions and other artistic events (Cama 2016).[2]

After completing high school at Loyola in Jamshedpur, Astad went to Bombay for university studies in 1965. Although both parents encouraged Astad to pursue his love of dance, his father insisted that he first complete his Bachelor of Commerce degree at R. A. Poddar College, Bombay, before following his dream. After all, at that time as today, parents regarded a college degree as a safety net for someone seeking a career as an artist. Astad admitted that he was not rebellious— that was Gulshan's domain, as I learned through my interviews with both sisters—so he followed his father's advice, even though he found studying commerce boring.

During his days at university in Bombay, Astad moved in a circle of artist friends, some 'lovely Parsee men' as Astad's friend George Michell remarked. Among my conversations with many of Astad's friends, UK-based Michell noted that while travelling in Britain in 1978,

---

2 Shernaz Cama, Astad's friend for over 30 years, shared that he had danced at the Indira Gandhi National Center for the Arts (IGNCA) lawn in New Delhi with his Manipuri dancers for the opening ceremony of the exhibition *Threads of Community: Zoroastrian Life and Culture* on 21 March 2016 (int., August 2021). Another friend of Astad's since 1992, Shanoo Bhatia, director of EuMo: Making Intelligence Visible, a design firm in Mumbai, narrated that Astad had danced 'at the inauguration of [their] furniture brand AMAZNG' (int., July 2021). Shanoo, with Gulshan and family, curated an exhibition 'Astad—The Star' in Mumbai that documented his life and work, showcasing some of Astad's costumes and other family mementoes in December 2022. The curators were Poulomi Das of Varnika Designs and designers Shanoo Bhatia and Gary Grewal of EuMo.

Astad had told him he was gay and shared his private relationships. This experience might resonate with other artists who find it easier to discuss their homosexuality while they are away—perhaps in a different city and not necessarily always abroad—distancing themselves from their tradition-bound homes.

Although Astad did not come out to his family, he remained very close to them and to his nephews, Xerxes and Danesh, the sons of Kamal and Jimmy Antia. Xerxes recalled that when he was growing up in Jamshedpur, Astad would make time to undertake a 30-hour train journey from Bombay to regale him and his family with stories of his travels; he was like a loving Santa bearing gifts (int., June 2021). He used to reply to Xerxes' letters with handwritten ones. Xerxes moved to Bombay from Jamshedpur and lived with Astad, Gulshan and the family in their Shapur Baug flat. In 2002, Astad took 21-year-old Xerxes and his 18-year-old brother Danesh to Netherlands and the US.

Xerxes appreciated Astad's work, travelled with him to Russia, and started to help wherever he could with production and technical elements. He also assisted Astad with his interest in fashion and participation in fashion shows. He could not remember seeing Astad practise dance but recalled that his uncle listened to a lot of music and appeared to choreograph through music. Astad loved to spend time with his parents, Xerxes recalled, even playing cards with his mother at teatime.

He recalled Astad's quick temper. For instance, Astad always carefully taped his handwritten, complicated travel itinerary on a cupboard at home and expected his family to remember where he was on any given day. If they had forgotten when he called them, Astad would get angry. Astad's temper would boil over also when he was teaching groups whom he expected to deliver the most challenging poses and synchronized patterns. He was also known to shout at thoughtless photographers who used a flash that could blind an artist during performance. He would stop performing and call out the offending person; although this was frowned upon by some spectators, one can understand why Astad was infuriated since he could lose his balance on stage when disturbed in that harsh way.

Danesh had started a stamp collection from his uncle's correspondence from different parts of the world. He recalled a soft board at their Jamshedpur home where they would display Astad's letters. Danesh mentioned Astad's enormously thick address book in the days before the internet days; it looked swollen since other pieces of paper had been added to it. Astad's friend Prabha Rao recalled his leatherbound diary, about an inch and half thick, which he said held more than a thousand phone numbers and addresses.

Danesh moved to Bombay for college to study applied arts and visual design, during which he lived first in a hostel. After his studies, he moved to the family home in Shapur Baug with Astad's parents and Gulshan. Danesh noted that Astad loved his nephews unconditionally, giving them emotional support as if they were his own children. He described his feeling of living with 'a giant shadow of [his] uncle, with his big personality as a person, as a dancer' (int., June 2022). He looked up to Astad as someone who introduced him to new ideas and expanded his horizons.

Danesh was struck by Astad's habit of walking long distances in Bombay, such as from Shapur Baug to Bandra—a distance of 13 kilometres. He recalled that once when Astad was returning from a walk, he was bathed in sweat! 'Did you run?' asked Danesh. 'No, I just walked,' responded Astad. This inspired Danesh to take up the practice of such long walks in the city. Danesh found slow walks helped him in his visual arts work. Now an environmental scientist in Australia, Danesh told me over a WhatsApp call how difficult it was for him not to be in Bombay with his family when Astad passed away.

Whenever Astad was in Bombay, on a break from his hectic travels, he loved to go to discotheques to meet friends and dance; in fact, it was amid the lights and music in discos that he discovered he could twirl for a long time! On one occasion in the 1970s, on a dance floor, Astad accidentally stomped on his foot, remembered Jehangir Patel, the editor of the Bombay-based *Parsiana* magazine that carries news and features about Parsees in India and in the diaspora. When Jehangir turned around to see who the offending person was, Astad at once bowed and apologized. Jehangir did not know Astad then, but the bow gave the impression of someone who had spent time in Japan. Jehangir could not recall if Astad introduced himself. But when he read about him later, he recognized him from that disco encounter!

I close this chapter with Astad's words: 'I believe in destiny: as a child, I was exposed to the prayers of three religions—"Our father who art in heaven" at my Catholic Missionary school, "Raghupati Raghav" in my dance class, and Zoroastrian prayers at home. I am a believer in destiny. What has to happen will happen. God helps those who help themselves.' He then states unequivocally that dance is his 'everlasting love' and that he would never stop dancing. He wanted to perform in the smallest corners of India. 'Each time I am even near throwing in the towel, a stimulus comes my way and I begin with a renewed sense of energy. Dance I will, dance I do, dance I shall' (Sawhney 2002).

Dance permeated Astad's life. Indeed, his deep devotion to dance was unflinching even in his early career when he was in the minority as a male dancer in India. From one of his early innovative choreographies, *Ritual*, in which he carried lit candles in his hands and danced with them even as the hot wax fell on his bare palms, to his final group choreography with the youth of New Delhi's Salaam Baalak Trust in *Unbroken Unbowed*, inspired by Gandhi's sayings, Astad had a distinctive creative vision. It took him years to gain an audience willing to engage with his work and even longer to gain recognition for his art in India.

We shall now follow Astad's dedication to his dance, his undeterred resilience in keeping faith in his art, and his many special qualities as a friend to many.

CHAPTER 2

Astad's Gift of Friendship: Greeting Cards, Dhanshak and a Love for Food

Astad had a remarkably vast network of friends from all walks of life. Indeed, he was gifted not only as a dancer but in his personal life as one who made and cultivated friends with ease. He loved his friends who reciprocated his affection. In this chapter, I include anecdotes and memories shared with me by several of this remarkable man's friends whom I interviewed for this biography. At times, friends would repeat certain traits of Astad's personality such as his generous and caring nature; I have tried to honour what they remember about their dear friend. They were themselves very giving in sharing with me via phone calls, Zoom interviews and email correspondence what Astad meant to them as someone they could depend on and who stood by them in times of need. Above all, they relished his affection for them, and the care with which he was always the one to initiate contact and keep in touch. I too was the happy recipient of Astad's phone calls to simply catch up, to inquire how I was, how my work was going, how my daughter Roshni (of whom he was very fond) was doing in school, as well as our dog Charlie who loved to lick Astad's face when he visited my home in Irvine. Astad was a night bird; he stayed up way past midnight, so he would call from Bombay when it was still afternoon in California.

The seeds of friendship sown in his youth with Loyola School buddies blossomed with many of them living in the US. From his college days in Bombay, he cultivated deep and abiding connections for over 30 years—several not in the dance world—including his friends' family cooks who delighted in pleasing his palate! Bombay was Astad's base. He had told me in an interview that he was very grateful to have a loving home to return to from wherever his travels took him and, of course, to savour a delicious home-cooked meal.

Astad loved food as much as he loved his friends. He enjoyed a happy alliance between friendship and food throughout his life. A foodie from youth, he delighted in sampling different cuisines in India and abroad during his travels. He also shared his love of Parsee cuisine with friends abroad—akoori (eggs with onions, tomatoes, fresh coriander and spices), curry and rice and on birthdays, celebratory sev (vermicelli fried in ghee with sugar) eaten with sweetened dahi. Dhanshak is the pièce de resistance of Parsee cuisine that Astad revelled in cooking and teaching many friends to cook![1] During his travels, Astad loved to invite folks to his hosts' homes and cook meals for them as a way of giving back the generosity he enjoyed. Astad's friends will recall how, over the last few months of his life, Gulshan and Astad shared on a WhatsApp group chat what he ate for breakfast or lunch. Gulshan often had a tough time keeping Astad-the-foodie satisfied!

One hallmark of the way Astad expressed his love for his friends was to remember to greet them on their special days—a remarkable use

---

1 Dhanshak is a Parsee speciality with slightly different recipes among various families. I adapted the recipe followed by my Parsee family in Bombay. The process begins with boiling five types of dals (or even two, as available) with vegetables such as squash, eggplant, spinach, onion, green onion, green chilli and fresh coriander along with salt, turmeric, ginger, garlic and cooking oil. After the dals and vegetables are cooked, I would either mash the mixture manually or in a blender. In a separate pan, a vaghar (also called tarka) is prepared with dhanshak masala (a blend of different spices such as garam masala, coriander, cinnamon and cloves) fried in oil until the aromas emerge. I then add freshly chopped tomatoes to this and when well blended, mix it with the cooked dal. I squeeze in fresh lime or lemon to taste. This dal is eaten with rice, flavoured with cumin seeds, jaggery and cinnamon sticks.

of his time and energy, his memory and a testament to his obliging nature. Before iPhones and emails, Astad used to send handwritten cards, relying on his capacious address book, which was also his travel companion. In an interview with me on 1 July 2021, noted theatre personality Sunil Shanbag narrated a telling anecdote about encountering Astad in the 1970s in Paris. During their meeting, Astad made an unusual request for Sunil to carry a suitcase to London. Sunil agreed; to his utter amazement, the weighty bag turned out to be filled with a year's supply of greeting cards that Astad meant to send to his friends!

From Jamshedpur to the United States

Characteristically, Astad kept in touch with several Jamshedpur friends and delighted in connecting them with one another. He played the role of 'informal head of the Jamshedpur Alumni Association' as Jeelu Billimoria, now in New York City, teasingly called him (int., June 2021). With his talent for friendship, Astad threaded the past with the present.

Rohini Desai Mulchandani knew Astad since Jamshedpur days. Desai, now living in Columbus, Ohio, met Astad in the 1970s. She recalled excitedly that he taught her 'how to make Dhanshak!' (int., 26 June 2021). Rohini had a lasting memory of young Astad dancing at Jamshedpur's United Club; at that time, she could not imagine how far Astad would go with his unusual talent, especially as a Parsee youth. Astad also made dhanshak for his schoolmate Orville Domingo in 1983—a delicious memory that Orville relishes!

Orville remarked affectionately that many of Astad's classmates, including the late Anup Mody, loved to host Astad in New York City and Washington DC (int., July 2021). Ashok Chirayath, another schoolmate, noted that Astad connected with Ashok's brother Pratap (who passed away in 2016) who had hitchhiked from Delhi to London and had many stories to share with Astad such as staying at a castle in Yugoslavia (int., June 2022).

Furrokh Dhondy, now a well-known commissioning editor for Channel 4 in Britain, was a Jamshedpur acquaintance who later became Astad's good friend. They met occasionally in Britain or in India. Furrokh, who regarded Astad as a unique choreographer, had commissioned a Channel 4 documentary on Astad's life and art.

Another Loyola classmate, Ronald D'Costa, knew Astad from 1954 to 1964. D'Costa believed that Astad had chosen a lonely, albeit committed, path as a male dancer. D'Costa paid tribute to Astad's work with the deaf Manipuri drummers and street youth. Astad's genuine humanity was such that he would go the extra mile to support a cause that he believed in. Hence, D'Costa was touched that Astad had agreed to return to Jamshedpur to perform in 2005 for the programme organized by the NGO SEEDS (*News Desk* 2020).

Astad sustained his friendship with Dinyar Devitre from Jamshedpur days to different continents—Australia, the US and Europe—wherever Dinyar and his family moved. Dinyar had seen Astad perform in India from 1975 to 1980; he admired Astad's courage and confidence as a male dancer in a sea of female dancers. Astad had made the time and effort, as he did for other friends, to attend the wedding of Dinyar's son in Bombay in 2007, and then the Navjote of Dinyar's grandchild in Goa in 2015. Dinyar found Astad a pleasure to have around; his distinctive laugh and fascinating stories lit up every occasion.

Many friends admired Astad's resilient spirit, his persistence in not losing faith in his art, and fighting many rejections in India during his early career. Despite disappointments, Astad forged ahead. He took this same spirit to fighting his illness, remaining hopeful that he would eventually beat lymphoma. Dinyar recalled that even during his last conversation with Astad, the latter's fighting spirit was alive. Astad took this spirit of battling odds in his personal and professional life to the end.

From Jamshedpur to Bombay

Astad's friends in Bombay all paint a portrait of a warm and friendly man, full of entertaining tales from his travels and always ready to enjoy food when he visited them. He had a reputation for being a loveable 'fridge raider', as known among his close friends—some of whom Astad had known for half a century and others whom he had kept in touch with for over 30 years. Only an exceptional human being like Astad could accomplish this feat of sustaining friendships across long periods and vast geographical distances.

Soli Surti—whom Astad also called Sola, or Sorabjee—was one such friend: a fellow Zoroastrian who spoke Gujarati and shared community lore including favourite dishes, he was Astad's friend for 50 years. He painted an endearing picture of Astad as a down-to-earth, kind and food-loving person who took time to be supportive when needed. Soli recounted charmingly their fond friendship and Astad's love of food (int., August 2021). He recalled vividly that when Astad visited his apartment, he would strike a dance pose when Soli opened the door and, with his two hands clasped in the back and a twinkle in his eye, conceal a slab of chocolate that he had brought for Soli. After spending a few minutes on the sofa, Astad would make a beeline for the fridge looking for Mrs Daruwalla's homemade raspberry sherbet—a brand very commonly found in Parsee homes—and mutton or chicken cutlets! He would ask in his distinctive Parsee Gujarati, 'Ketchup kaha mukyoch?' [Where have you put the ketchup?]. Astad was particularly fond of snacky food like samosas.

Soli appreciated that Astad always kept in touch from wherever he was, at times visiting on his way to the airport or on his return. Astad's travels and complicated itinerary made it almost impossible, Soli admitted, for anyone to remember the details, but Soli recalled receiving handwritten letters on thin blue aerogramme paper with Astad's signature and a loving smiley. He also sent photographic prints of performances in envelopes with 'please do not bend' carefully written on the front. Soli cherished Astad's special *kotis*—'Koti dabine kare' [He gave tight hugs]—and his fragrant colognes (int., August 2021).

Kharmeen Ginwalla, a friend of over 30 years in Bombay, shared her memories of Astad as a very helpful friend and one who loved food. She recalled affectionately that when Astad dropped in at her place, the first thing he would do was go into the kitchen, check what had been cooked and often eat it up! He had a sweet tooth as well and loved ice creams and desserts. Astad also brought back from his travels special foods that his friends desired. Once he surprised Kharmeen by bringing raw pork chops from Australia (int., July 2021). In 2008, when I was in Delhi, Astad had also graced me with homemade akoori and Parsee-style curry that he had hand-carried carefully on his flight from Mumbai. He delighted in pleasing me with this cuisine close to both our hearts. He was full of such gestures since he loved to spoil his friends.

Astad would go out of his way to support a downcast friend, recalled Kharmeen. He would stand by a friend, call and meet every day if he knew that the person needed a kind listener for their problems (int., July 2021). This special quality of Astad's—to care for and follow up with a friend—had moved Bharatanatyam dancer Hema Rajagopalan. When Hema was in Chennai with her ailing father, Astad used to call almost daily to check on how she was and how her father was faring. 'People who lived right in Chennai did not call me, but Astad did,' remarked Hema, 'I was really touched' (int., July 2021).

Kharmeen recognized that life was tough for Astad, as he did a lot singlehandedly. He did not have a manager to organize his travels, hotel bookings and other details, partly because he was a perfectionist and partly because he had little patience to let someone else do these tasks that he could accomplish. So, tough as it was, he was his own manager—scheduling his performances in India and abroad, coordinating costumes and conducting rehearsals with his dancers when he choreographed for groups. When he took fellow dancers abroad, he himself took care of bookings for hotels, visas, airline tickets and other details as a tour manager. Kharmeen noted that Astad was a one-man enterprise who multitasked and did everything on his own. (int., July 2021). Sunil Shanbag expressed exasperation that Astad insisted on doing all the organizational and management work for his tours with dancers; he refused to get help, hence, he took on stress.

Astad the person and Astad the dancer were so integrally linked, almost like two sides of the same coin, that when Kharmeen asked Astad how he was, he would respond by telling her about his work. Even when she pressed him to talk about himself rather than his work, 'He could never really reply.' Kharmeen realized that his work was his life; there was no division between how he felt about himself and his work at any given time. He was immersed and truly passionate about what he did.

Kharmeen affectionately noted that as Astad's biographer, 'I had quite a story', since his life was full of unusual experiences. During his numerous journeys, Astad encountered a harrowing incident in South America, which he recounted to Kharmeen. While checking out of a Sao Paulo hotel, Astad and his dancers faced a life-threatening situation as gunmen entered the lobby. Forced to lie on the floor during the armed robbery, they escaped unharmed, though Astad's camera was stolen (int., July 2021).

Astad had a love-hate relationship with his Parsee community. A number of Parsees, as members of the National Centre for Performing Arts (NCPA), would be in the auditorium when Astad performed but many of them left early and did not engage with his dance.[2] They were

---

2 Astad had a long and positive connection with Mumbai's NCPA where he often premiered his shows. NCPA was the visionary cultural institution co-founded by Parsee industrialist J. R. D. Tata, head of the Tata Iron and Steel Company, and arts promoter Dr Jamshed Bhabha. This premier cultural institution has had a formidable legacy over the past five decades. It began humbly in 1969 in a small, rented space in the Akash Ganga building on Bhulabhai Desai Road. Today, the

'proud' of him as a famous dancer who happened to be Parsee, but they did not discuss Astad's work nor his vision of getting modern dance recognized in India. They would get excited at the news that Astad was selected as one of the Indian dancers to meet the Queen of England— 'Aapri rani ne malyo' [he met 'our' Queen]—but they did not care too much when Astad received the Padma Shri as a dancer (Masih 2017).[3]

Prabha Rao, who had known Astad since 1965, observed a comforting trait in his personality: Astad effortlessly made friends feel at ease by exuding a sense of being at home wherever he went (int., February 20220. There were times when Astad would come over to Prabha's for lunch and take a short nap. Prabha knew that this meant Astad was completely relaxed in her home and this made her happy. Astad had danced at her elder brother's wedding in Amravati in 1968. Even though their friendship was not a professional one, Prabha remarked insightfully that Astad's performances were 'experiences, not just visual, but a treat for all the senses'—a sentiment echoed by professional Indian dancers whom I interviewed.

Delhi-based Dr Anjali Raina, who had known Astad since the 1980s, enjoyed Astad's culinary prowess, as right after their initial meeting, Astad offered to cook dhanshak. Anjali knew Astad offstage first, then she had a great connection with him for over 40 years. Having witnessed numerous performances, she admired the versatility of his style, seamlessly transitioning from profound introspection to boldly unconventional expressions, like the piece *Chewing Gum*. His later work, she believed, became increasingly minimal and philosophical.

NCPA houses five theatres sprawled across eight acres on the southern tip of Nariman Point and hosts over 600 events each year spanning all art forms, to promote and preserve India's heritage of music, dance, theatre, film, literature and photography.

3 On 27 February 2017, Astad met Queen Elizabeth II at Buckingham Palace during the inauguration of the India–UK Year of Culture.

For Vidhya Gajapathi Singh, another good friend since 1974, Astad was her entry into modern dance. Her children, Viraj and Vasundhara, loved Uncle Astad who would go the extra mile to help sort out their 'serious squabbles' by driving 16 kilometres to their home in Juhu from Shapur Baug. After Vidhya and her family moved to Chennai, Astad would stay with them when he visited the city. For Vidhya, Astad was like a brother with whom she could share personal worries; a sympathetic listener, he always offered sound advice. Astad the foodie, Vidhya recalled, had his favourite culinary haunts in Chennai too: The Amethyst, Chamiers and Madras Club, where they enjoyed coffee or lunch (int., July 2021).

Bharti Patel, who closely knew Astad for 35 years, had a curious story to share: in their youth, she only met Astad when her father was not at home—because, as she writes humorously, 'Any boy not ready to marry his daughter was on his hit list.' Astad would show up surreptitiously after Bharti's dad had left, and while the cook Sheila-bai was ever-ready to 'ply him with stuff to eat [. . .] my shoulder [was] ready for him to cry on' (int., July 2021).[4] Bharti, under her name Bati Patel, published her autobiography called *My Kahaani* [My story] in which she includes an endearing photo of Astad embracing her. For Bharti, Astad was '[t]he recipient of all my whining and wailing, my raves and rants. He [was] intensely aware of the fact that if he ever spill[ed] my secrets, the dry cleaner will have a tough time getting the blood off his Parsi Persian carpet' (Patel 2013: 68). Bharti stayed in touch with Astad after she got married and had children. 'We met in different cities, NYC, San Francisco, London. I loved his work . . . I would tease him about counting how many times he could twirl round and round. I had counted 22, he said, "Darling, way more than that." ' Bharti noted: 'I

---

4 Astad's easy bonding with cooks in families he visited is noted by many friends whom I interviewed. Vidhya noted Astad's connection with her cook Laxmi as does Bharti about her cook.

miss him every day ... and expect a call with Brattteeee ... or Bha-rah-tee (when he is serious)' (int., July 2021). As with other friends, Astad made time and effort to attend his friends' children's weddings. In a sense, he had a vast and loving family of friends along with his own loving parents, sisters and extended family of nephews and cousins.

In the 1970s, whenever Astad was in India, he was fortunate to have the support of Homi and Khorshed Vakeel, whom he considered his godparents and who introduced Astad to people who could understand his creative vision and advance his dance career. They were the generous and open-minded parents of Jeelu and Deena, who had offered the living room of their bungalow to Astad for dance practice; the room was not generally in use and usually kept locked. Astad would arrive, polish off a snack, then begin his practice. He allowed them to watch him dance and they were struck by his bizarre music. Jeelu recounts:

> Mum and Dad loved Astad and he always made time to visit them. They were proud and protective of Astad. To be gay and not out was difficult for a male dancer. They introduced him to people and helped sponsor some of his shows. He was like their son. Our parents were amazing people; they had this gift to love everyone like their own. Astad gave back by always being grateful, kind, loving, loyal and very respectful. It was a nice relationship. (int., August 2021)

During his college days in 1967, Astad met dancer-choreographer Uttara Coorlawala who was auditioning dancers for her choreographed work entitled *The Joyous Cosmology* at Sardar Vallabhbhai Patel Auditorium, Bombay, to be performed over Christmas. Coorlawala described Astad as one who stood out among the applicants for his 'spinning with total abandon', utterly immersed and uninhibited. Astad spoke directly to Uttara's heart. 'As it turned out,' writes Uttara, 'spinning, sometimes Dionysiacally fast and later in a meditative pace, was to become a motif in Astad's performances ... [that would] entrance many generations of audiences' (Coorlawala 2021: 82). Uttara highlighted two distinctive facets of Astad's character: his passion for dance and his genuine love for people. She admired his unwavering dedication to dance, acknowledging the challenges he faced as a trailblazing male contemporary dancer in India, despite his global acclaim.

Among Astad's many international friends was Phainie Xydis, from Athens, Greece, who met Astad in 1977 when he performed Kathakali at Athens' Odeon of Herodes Atticus. Astad had studied Kathakali with Guru E. Krishna Panicker; however, he presented a dance drama that usually has several dancers on stage as a solo—a testament to his confidence. Phainie was entranced by Astad's dance and they became friends. Astad initiated her to Indian cuisine. Phainie visited India often and enjoyed meeting Astad, both indulging their sweet tooth by devouring their favourite kulfi or falooda. Phainie remembers wistfully that during their final get-together in Juhu, Mumbai, in April 2020, they both relished many scoops of ice cream. Phainie cherished Astad's friendship enormously. She regarded him as a devoted and generous friend, as one who 'Devoured life like a scoop of kulfi. Fearless, bigger than life! I carry your heart with me' (int., May 2022).

A major transformation in Astad's thinking about dance was triggered when, during his college days in Bombay, he saw a performance by the Murray Louis American Dance Company. 'The attention to physicality' impressed and fascinated Astad, as he remarked in an autobiographical piece, 'Creating Endless Possibilities' (Deboo 2003). Simultaneously, he was inspired by what he described as the 'decentralization of the body' in this sensory experience. What the body could achieve captured his imagination; its physicality spoke to him. In his early choreography, he boldly decided to draw attention to his male body in unitards and leotards. He needed to remain extremely fit since such a costume glaringly shows one's smallest physical blemish.

Astad's yearning to dance and to learn different dance styles led to his travels. He could hardly wait to complete his college degree for he wanted to break free. A school friend from Jamshedpur had just returned after hitch-hiking across Europe and Astad took his cue. He wanted to travel outside India and learn from his observations of different dance styles. Admirably, he continued his dance education on his own, trying different styles to discover what suited his body and discarding what did not. Along the way, he also developed his acumen for a vast store of music from various parts of the world. Astad's spirit was rooted firmly in Indian soil throughout his creative journey even as his body traversed the globe.

On 23 May 1969, 21-year-old Astad left Bombay port, 'board[ing] the dingy deck class of a cargo ship to Iran [. . .] with goats, cows and vegetabes as his co-travellers' (Bharadvaj 2017: 54). Such a unique first voyage is now a legendary part of his life story and dance career.

CHAPTER 3

Astad the Ardent Traveller

Astad's intrepid energy to travel, to survive with elan, to learn dance styles and to perform in various countries were unique characteristics that drove this fearless young man. No other Indian dancer in the 1970s could claim such a commitment to educating themselves in dance beyond the safety of their homes and their familiar dance styles.

Astad's adventures began on a ship that set sail from Bombay harbour in 1969. He had 300 US dollars in his pocket. At the first port, Korramshahr in Iran, he spent his first night in a gurudwara, or Sikh temple. He had an introduction from a Jamshedpur friend to Meher Pouya, a singer with his own TV show. This led, by chance, to Astad's first TV appearance and his first pay cheque of 50 US dollars (Deboo 2003, Bharadvaj 2017).

Astad then hitch-hiked across Europe, open to opportunities to dance and to learn. His modes of transport varied greatly. Once he was on the road in a coal truck and another time in a Mercedes. He stayed at low-cost youth hostels. He gave dance performances that enabled him to make contacts. Even though he did not like some of the people he met, a visit often meant a free meal. He held on to his strong desire to learn by observing dance even as he faced challenges when he landed in new places with no idea where he would sleep or what he would eat. When in London, Astad got an unexpected opportunity: he was invited by Arabella Churchill, the granddaughter of Winston Churchill, to perform at a fundraiser. There, as luck would have it, he met the rock band

Pink Floyd and, at Arabella's suggestion, danced to their music. He stayed in London for some time, awaiting his visa to the United States.

From the time that Astad first left India, he wished to get to the US to study with Martha Graham since her deeply emotional movement style fascinated him. But a visa eluded him. In any case, when he could learn this style at the London School of Contemporary Dance, he did not feel comfortable with it; his own style followed a different dance history rooted in his training in classical Kathak and later Kathakali. His dance connected intuitively and incorporated Indian aesthetics of mudras and rasas. His spirit resonated with the Indian concept of the Navarasas (nine primary emotions) that featured prominently in his later choreography.[1]

Astad narrates colourful, even audacious tricks of survival on little money during precarious times: dancing for the Turkish police; selling a unit of his blood for 17 dollars in Greece; getting arrested in Munich for sleeping in a park; and getting away with a free meal in an Italian restaurant. He even washed dishes, saying that he had read about famous actors washing dishes at some point in their career so he thought that he must do the same too.

Astad ventured from Europe to Japan for the World Exposition 1970 which was held in Osaka. He was so deeply entranced by this land and by the dance forms of Kabuki and Butoh that he stayed for a year learning Kabuki at the Kabuki-Za School. His dancing spirit was mesmerized by Kabuki's slow and stylized movements, guttural sounds and moveable sets. He survived by teaching English to Japanese children and doing odd jobs. When his visa expired, he took a boat to South Korea, stayed there for fifteen days, performed on Korean TV and then returned to Japan.

---

1 Astad structured his choreography entitled *ContraPosition* with dancers of Chennai's Clarke School for the Deaf in 2005 on the navarasas. Rasas feature in several of Astad's works discussed in Parts III and IV of this book.

Next, Southeast Asia beckoned. There, Astad's imagination resonated with the movements, music, costumes and staging of these regions' traditional dance styles influenced not only by their particular cultural fabric but also by echoes of Indian epics. Astad had a frightening experience in Manila where he got held at knifepoint while staying at the underground club owned by first lady Imelda Marcos's niece. But undeterred, he continued his further travels to South Korea, Laos and Vietnam. He taught and performed in Taiwan and Hong Kong. In Thailand, he performed for the then Queen Mother and was invited to the court of the great-grandson of King Chulalongkorn.

Upon his return in 1972 after a three-year absence, Astad felt as if he had traversed multiple lifetimes during his time away. On the personal front, Astad, always loyal to his family, came home to attend his sister Kamal's wedding. On the professional front, he followed the sound advice of prominent dance scholar, the late Sunil Kothari, to study Kathakali, a classical dance style from the South Indian state of Kerala. Astad trained for the next two years with Guru E. Krishna Panicker. Kathakali is a dance-drama performed mostly by male dancers who embody characters, even female ones, from the Indian epics. Above all, it is a rigorous style that involves jumps and striking body stances along with balancing heavy crowns—painted in different colours to indicate royalty, gods or demons in a story—on the dancer's head. Astad took to Kathakali's strenuous training of the body, with deep focus on the eyes, eyebrows, cheeks and facial expression. The vitality of Astad's was harmonized by his mastery of two classical Indian dance forms: Kathak, which he learned from his childhood, with its intricate footwork, chakkars and naturalistic facial expressions to convey narratives and emotions; then Kathakali, which he took up at age 25, which used highly stylized expressions to tell stories with theatrical flair. After studying Kathakali, he could not find support in India to study other dance forms—or to perform. So, he left the country again in 1974 as his dream of going to the US finally came true.

Astad landed in New York City in 1974 and began studying the Jose Limon technique of modern dance. Astad found a profound connection with Limon's style, which elevated the status of the male body in dance. Limon's ability to imbue dance with dramatic expressions drawn from literature and religion resonated with Astad. Among Limon's extensive body of work, Astad particularly admired *The Moor's Pavane*, one of his most renowned pieces. This passionate rendition was based on Shakespeare's *Othello* and depicted the Moor's consuming jealousy leading to the tragic killing of his innocent wife, Desdemona.

From New York City, Astad went to the state of Connecticut, where he was mentored by Alison Becker Chase who had founded the Pilobolus Dance Company in 1971. Astad was inspired by Pilobolus's emphasis on exaggerating, even contorting the human form, a very different approach from the centring of beauty in Indian classical dance. Astad experimented with distorting his body in his early solo choreography, inspired partly by Chase's imprint on modern dance. He was also inspired by Pilobolus's educational wing that taught the company's creative methods to groups, as is evident from Astad's collaborations with groups later in his life. On the West Coast, Astad studied Afro-jazz dance in San Francisco.

In 1976, Astad travelled to South America and spent 10 months there. He felt a deep affinity with Brazilian music and dance, just like he had with Japanese Kabuki and Limon's style. He visited Buenos Aires, Santiago de Chile, Lima, Bogota, Caracas and Lima, observing the richness of these countries' indigenous cultures and dances. When he returned to India in 1977, he decided to continue three years of intense Kathakali training in the Guruvayur pedagogical system with Panicker. Critics had now begun to respond to Astad's ability to captivate audiences with his choreography and the riveting pace of his work. Indeed, by 1977, Astad was in demand at international dance festivals; ironically, he was better known in many parts of the world than in India.

Before returning to India, Astad stopped in Tehran—not because as a Parsee he was interested in the place where Zoroastrianism originated; rather, because it was the city where he had begun his travels and had performed in 1969. He was featured in the Iranian daily *Kayhan International* as a 30-year-old Zoroastrian: 'A jet set artist, a one-man troupe . . . He was the only Indian artist at the opening of the festival season of the Sydney Opera House in 1973' (Nagarajan 1977). Astad's private performance at the Indian ambassador's residence in Tehran was praised as breathtaking. He also performed on national Iranian television.

In an interview with *Kayhan International*, Astad remarked that the biggest hurdle for him as a professional dancer in India was his gender. He noted that many people in India were surprised that a man—and that too a Zoroastrian—had taken up dancing; they even thought that something was wrong with him. Astad believed that in India, male dancers had not been exposed sufficiently to styles such as modern dance, hence they could not realize their potential.

Astad's bold spirit guided his travels which were like 'pilgrimages to discover his outer and inner strengths' (Bharadvaj 2017: 54). Astad was a seeker learning from different cultures and dance forms. His travels and observations equipped him with knowledge and experience that inspired his signature hybrid dance style, rooted in Indian classical dance but flourishing with Southeast Asian, Japanese and Euro-American modern and contemporary influences. Astad absorbed what suited his body, creating a dance vocabulary uniquely his own.

Sunil Shanbag assessed what Astad gained from his travels in which he watched a wide range of dances being performed in theatres, courtyards, temples and ceremonial spaces: 'Dancing to buy his way forward meant dancing anywhere—in someone's home, in a TV studio, in a cafe, hardly ever on a formal stage. Astad realized that his art can happen anywhere' (2010: 15). He continues: 'The seventies were a heady time in the West. Rules are being broken in art and contemporary dance is vibrant with new energy. Astad fits in easily and his eclectic form is attractive' (2010: 15). Conventional notions of dance, space and spectator–performer relationships were being contested at the time. Boundaries were being extended and broken. Site-specific work was becoming prominent. From this experimental climate in the West, Astad returned to India where he disrupted the conventional dance and theatre scene. He drew attention to the body with his skin-fitting costumes along with his creative use of stage space, unusual props, lighting and visual design as seen in his early solo choreography of the late 1970s and 80s that I explore in the next chapter.

PART II

Milestones in a Dancer's Life

FIGURES 5–6. Astad in
different poses.
*Photographs by
Navroze Contractor.*

CHAPTER 4

Early Solo Choreography: New Themes and Forms, 1970s and 1980s

In India of the late 1970s and 80s, the dance scene was dominated by female performers of classical dance, with audiences favouring traditional movement, Carnatic music, silk sarees and familiar staging. In stark contrast, Astad's choreography was original and provocative. While he sometimes used narrative to connect with Indian audiences, he tackled contemporary social issues, pushing viewers to engage with present realities. A risk-taker, Astad led audiences out of their comfort zones, challenging the norms of entertainment and beauty in classical dance. His innovative approach extended to movement, music and visual design, influenced by his exposure to modern dance and global styles during his travels.

Witnessing Astad perform solos in his early career was a mind-blowing experience for his initially small though loyal audience since he transformed not only movement and music from Indian classical traditions but also lighting, visual design, soundscape, props and the use of stage space. Astad's choreography showcased what he had witnessed and emulated from performances abroad. His preferred costume—the leotard or unitard—was a completely new phenomenon, indeed bold for an Indian dancer and Indian viewers.

Astad's contributions to dance in India during the 1970s and 80s—recognized only later—are comparable to what Rukmini Devi Arundale brought back to India from her travels abroad, such as lighting design and modern stagecraft. Devi, as founder of Kalakshetra, India's premier Bharatanatyam institution, introduced these new aspects into her dance-drama productions. What Arundale did for classical Indian dance, Astad did for contemporary Indian dance—both on the proscenium and in his site-specific works.

Astad presented his early solo choreographies by compiling an evening of short pieces that included narrative to hook Indian audiences, followed by avant-garde works, at times abstract, with titles such as *Confluences*, or *Vicissitudes*. Even in his early choreography, one could see traces of Astad's signature style that includes abstract movement infused with emotion.

I discuss Astad's solos that focused on contemporary realities—not on the past through epic stories as commonly depicted in classical Indian dance—such as *Space Odyssey* (*Zontus*) which was about astronauts and space travel. For my exploration of Astad's early solos, I rely on the dance maker's comments in interviews, on newspaper and magazine reviews, along with key discussions—in interviews I conducted in July 2021—by two of Astad's close friends and collaborators: Ratan Batliboi, an architect, and Sunil Shanbag, an actor, theatre director and documentary filmmaker. They were as excited as Astad about his adventurous concepts for dance and deeply supportive of his creative journey. Along with Ratan, Astad encountered other young students of architecture—Suresh Bavnani, Fali Unwalla—who proposed that he could work with objects (Deboo 2020). Ratan built metal a huge triangle, a rectangle and a cube with metal that Astad danced with in *Basics*. Astad discovered that his choreography with such objects brought him closer to abstract movement that he gravitated towards in his signature dance style.

Astad's friends assisted in the technical aspects of his early dance productions—Ratan was the technical director; both Ratan and Sunil managed lights and stage design; Sam Kerawalla, another friend, was a lighting designer. Astad loved to share ideas and collaborate. Ratan and his wife Banoo travelled with Astad across the world, seeing dance performances and festivals and being inspired by what they witnessed. They got along well, sharing creative ideas and methods.

Sunil, whom Astad considered his 'think tank', had a long and close artistic alliance with him since 1978. A protégé of Indian theatre personality Satyadev Dubey, Sunil supported Astad's creative vision since the beginning of his dance explorations. He first met Astad in November 1978 at Bombay's Prithvi Theatre, where he used to hang out at the cafe and see whatever was being performed. One evening, he got an unexpected opportunity to run the sound for Astad's show since the scheduled person had cancelled and Sunil knew the lighting technician. Sunil had no clue then about Astad, his show or his music, which at the time was played on a reel-to-reel spool tape recorder. In the light cabin of the Prithvi, Astad came by to thank Sunil for running the sound.

When Sunil turned on the machine, he did not know what kind of sound to expect. He realized quickly that this was not music the way he understood it. And that was the first time he was exposed to the whole idea of soundscape. This was just the beginning for Sunil; he acknowledged learning a lot about contemporary music from Astad, who always used the most cutting-edge composers for his dance.

In the light-and-sound booth of the Prithvi, Sunil turned on the sound and recalled that it was going fine. Then, at one point, there was a long pause when his lighting friend panicked, asking, 'What's happening?' Sunil responded that there was a pause and that the tape was running. His friend said, 'Off, off, off . . .' and he put the lights off. And he turned the tape recorder off. The audience clapped, assuming the show was over. But when the claps died down, Astad's voice soared up through the PA system, 'Can I have my lights and music, please? I haven't finished.' 'The lights and sound came on again and I can't remember the rest of the performance,' remarked Sunil, 'because I was so embarrassed.' He regretted having blown it, but Astad was very kind; he even said that the audience took that pause to be a trick! Sunil recalled that his friend who did the lighting got drunk and started crying and it was 'one of those messy evenings'. 'From that day onward, I've been Astad's friend,' Sunil added. 'We met the correct way, because we met in performance and then, of course, it's been a very, very long association' (int., July 2021).

Sunil reflected further in a beautifully lyrical passage on this initial encounter with Astad's dance, music and ability to transform the stage space: 'What emanated from the loudspeaker were sounds, not music, and what the dancer was doing on stage was not dance as I knew it. And most frighteningly, the intimacy of the performance space had been ripped open like a tin can and harsh lighting exposed bare walls, a scarred ceiling, narrow catwalk and giant wings' (Shanbag 2010: 14).

Sunil was stunned since he could hardly recognize this theatre space; even the passage of time appeared to vary—it seemed to race or slow down to a crawl. Sunil found that watching Astad was also an unfamiliar experience since he came across at times as arrogant and at others as so compassionate that he could inspire tears. His use of space was unusual since 'he seemed to occupy spaces conjured out of thin air, filling them, extending them, drawing them in' (Shanbag 2010: 16). Astad introduced Sunil to modern dance, who recounts that walking home that night, he tried to understand why, despite being disturbed by the performance, he 'felt a deep sense of liberation' (Shanbag 2010: 16). That feeling of freedom pervaded the theatre after Astad performed as the rules of performance and performance space were 'being rewritten'.

In the 1970s, the technical aspects of theatre, such as lighting, were done by freelancers who were not particularly invested in a show. Sunil's own work as a filmmaker made him more adept than others at lighting design. Sunil decided to travel with Astad as his lighting designer. He directed a film in Taiwan on Astad's work called *The Sword and the Spear* (2009), with camera and sound professionals whom Sunil knew; they did not get paid much, but they liked the idea of working with Astad.

Space Odyssey (Zontus) (1978–79)

Astad's first solo work, *Space Odyssey (Zontus)*, was about an astronaut going into space, at that time a topical subject which interested Astad, especially because NASA had a 1978 class of astronauts with people of colour. Uttara Coorlawala, who knew Astad since the late 1960s, remembered that *Space Odyssey* was Astad's first solo performance which she found quite unusual and effective (int., August 2021). I believe that Astad, in portraying an astronaut in a black-and-white outfit and moving jerkily like a robot, was commenting on modern life—a reflection on how individuals can become automatons, mindlessly repeating daily routines.

Astad based his self-described science-fiction fantasy on the soundtrack of Steven Spielberg's 1977 film, *Close Encounters of the Third Kind*. Reviewer C. Y. Gopinath (1979) described the dancer-astronaut character of Zontus as having discovered a dark plot by Planet Delta's aliens to turn human beings into robots. This danger was countered by rebellion as Zontus came to rescue humanity. Although such a saviour echoes, I believe, Hindu gods Krishna or Vishnu saving mankind from demons or disasters, in *Space Odyssey*, rooted in the present, only human power is exerted to avert calamity. Wearing leather restraints adorned with metal, encircling his knees, chest and head, Zontus moved stiffly and, as the lights intensified and upbeat music filled the air, he liberated the humans. Astad links the astronaut's abstract movement with emotion—a hallmark of his signature style.

In *Space Odyssey*, as in his other works of the 1970s and 80s, Astad was pushing boundaries of what was regarded as 'dance' in India. Although he was not recognized in this period as a pioneer of contemporary Indian dance, he was staking out new ground. The question posed in critiques of his early works—'But is it dance?'—was based on reviewers' familiarity being limited to classical Indian dance, rather than contemporary themes explored through dance or unconventional costumes like an astronaut suit in *Space Odyssey*. Furthermore, audiences expected dance to tell stories and clearly convey some meaning. A set of abstract movements without overt meaning was not considered dance even though there was already an audience for abstract painting in India. However, it was not only Astad who had to face the question 'But is it dance?'; dancers around the world who veered from received movement vocabularies of ballet and modern dance also met with such challenges.[1] The dynamic interplay between movement and theatre, along with the promotion of dance as a distinct discipline and the embrace of multidisciplinary formats incorporating dance and visual art, gained greater acceptance in India after the 1990s. This shift was catalysed by the internet bringing global trends in dance, music, theatre and visual art into people's lives and homes.

In his early work, Astad embraced different opportunities to perform in Bombay—on stage or in a jazz and rock show as he did with Uttara Coorlawalla or at the Cellar discotheque in Bombay's Oberoi Sheraton Hotel when he acted as John Travolta in a version of *Saturday Night Fever* (*India Today* 1978 [2015]). Astad was forthright in his public media profile about facing what he described as a natural disadvantage for simply being a male dancer whom Indian viewers did not find appealing. Therefore, he had to 'try very hard to hold their attention'. He skilfully deflected—sometimes light-heartedly jesting about—the frequent inquiries about marriage directed at him as a 31-year-old in a society where family and friends' marital statuses are often a focal point.

1978: Meeting George Michell

Astad's personal life as a gay man in 1970s India was a discreet one. However, with friends like George Michell, an art historian and archaeologist, also a gay man, Astad could be open and free about his sexuality.

---

1 In South Africa, a dancer such as Steven Cohen faced the same question about his work in the 1980s, as do contemporary conceptual choreographers such as Jay Pather, Mamela Nyamza, Neliswe Xaba, among others.

When I interviewed George, he noted that Astad was comfortable with his sexuality, though he was circumspect, as was George in India during that time. Astad met George and his partner John when they visited India from the UK for research in 1978. They became close to Astad, who trusted them and confided his personal relationships with them. George appreciated Astad as a very loyal friend who kept in touch.

George bonded with Astad on a personal level where they could unwind and discuss their private lives. Astad's personal life did not overpower his own life, nor did George's, nor that of many of their gay acquaintances in Bombay and beyond. George remarked that Astad was always happy to meet gay people who were comfortable with their sexuality; but in general, he loved to connect with people from different walks of life. George also appreciated Astad's openness and breadth of interest in a variety of arts—theatre, movies, western classical music—not only dance. He also valued Astad's curiosity and his adventurous spirit.

As art historians and archaeologists, George and John took tour groups to historic sites in India. They became friends with Astad's sister Gulshan because she was also a tour guide; they enjoyed sharing their experiences. George's friendship with Astad spanned many decades. They 'shared this sort of slightly common trajectory of trying to do our work in our own way' (int., July 2021).

Unlike classical dancers who inherit music, costumes and themes determined by tradition, Astad had to begin in the 1980s with a blank arena in which he would determine movement, music, costume, lights, props and stage set in order to depict a concept. It is also significant to note that Astad was working at that time all by himself, as the solo modern Indian dancer without a community of dancers. Despite such isolation, Astad was 'extremely prolific in the 1980s', noted Ratan Batliboi (int., July 2021).

Astad's avant-garde solo choreography of the 1980s was characterized by three innovations. First, he pushed the boundaries of representation into what we would describe today as 'performance art', a form in which an artist challenges the audience with in-your-face depictions that can take spectators to the edge of discomfort, even shock—as Astad did when he inflicted pain on his body on stage in *Ritual, Broken Pane, Asylum*. As an artist, Astad drew attention to social problems such as drug addiction, rather than merely entertain his Indian audiences who expected familiar epic stories from the past instead of engaging with serious current topics. Although Astad conveyed messages through his art, he never compromised the integrity of his art to align with a political agenda. A second innovation in Astad's work of the 1980s was that he used speech and drama in playing different characters as in Shanbag's play, *Mangalore Street*. Third, Astad and Ratan worked closely on what Sunil described as design-driven choreographies in *Basics*, *Search*, and *Chrysalis* for which Ratan designed huge props: geometric metal forms in *Basics*, stretched fabric for the stage set in *Search*, and a large black box with apertures for *Chrysalis*. Astad's creativity interacted with these designed objects, often subverting viewers' expectations.

Astad's Performance Art in *Ritual* (1980)

Astad's proclivity to endure pain on stage was showcased in *Ritual* in which he had Ratan, his stage manager, drop him from the top of the stage onto the proscenium floor, in the middle of a circle of 40 lit candles. Astad then picked up the candles and began dancing with them, allowing hot wax to drip on his bare hands. The trick was to keep the candles lit; hence, he moved gracefully and gently, pacing his movements, not flinching when hot wax fell on his chest. I believe that Astad tuned into a ritualistic dimension of purification, even sacrifice. He was then pulled up and suspended in mid-air—an act that evoked the precarious position of his dance career at that time. He played provocatively with breaking the fourth wall. He confronted spectators boldly, urging them to empathize with his pain—pain that stemmed not just from the hot wax, but also from the lack of acceptance for his work since he broke from the goals of beauty and entertainment in classical Indian dance. He had instead focused on torment and suffering on stage, which disturbed audiences. Astad showed his scarred palms to the writer from the *Sunday Standard*, asserting that the undertones of masochism in *Ritual* demanded such display of pain. *Ritual* came across as a trial by fire, testing Astad's resilience in days when he was trying to build an audience for his dance.

Broken Pane (1982)

As in *Ritual*, Astad's high threshold for displaying agony is portrayed starkly in *Broken Pane*, a daring work about the dangers of drug addiction. Astad inserted a real syringe into his arm and then banged his head against the stage floor in a drug-induced frenzy. His body traversed a narrow space between two rungs of a ladder even as the syringe remained in his arm. 'Such blunt literalism made audiences wince,' comments Ramaa Bharadvaj, 'but Astad insisted "it would not have had that impact had it not been so literal".' (2017: 55). Astad wanted to shake up his spectators by inflicting torment on his body, showing it as vulnerable and wracked with the terrible cost of drug addiction.

The roots for *Broken Pane* were sown when Astad was travelling in Vancouver, Canada and danced for methadone addicts who were undergoing treatment with occupational therapy and psychoanalysis. Astad described this experience to reviewer C. Y. Gopinath: he danced half-hour sessions thrice a week and each time simulated situations that might find an echo in the addicts' lives. The first day, nothing happened—no one reacted. But the second day, he enacted a tense family scene featuring an alcoholic father and a mother who was a prostitute. Astad states that 'something snapped in his audience and the session ended cathartically, with the addicts and [him] breaking down and weeping' (Gopinath 1979). Astad achieved his choreographic intentions in *Broken Pane* by evoking spectators' sympathy, even horror at the gut level. He used theatrical elements such as mime through dance to depict drug addiction in a realistic rather than stylized manner.

In *Broken Pane*, Astad displayed raw, bloody emotion on stage in order 'to get visceral responses', as he notes himself, 'through the repetition of explicitly, violently disjunctive moments' (Deboo 2003: 121–22). Such stark representations of the violent realities of life were demanding for any audience to witness and definitely for Indian audiences used to a wholly different dance experience suffused with beauty, in which emotions are contained through a traditional language of gestures. Astad's depiction, I contend, resonated instead with Western approaches to theatre, such as that of twentieth-century drama theorist Antonin Artaud (1896–1948), a French actor, dramatist and essayist recognized for his ground-breaking idea of the 'theatre of cruelty' (Artaud 1958: 159). Artaud, like many Europeans, was deeply disillusioned with the physical and psychic devastation of the First World War and the growth of fascism in the 1920s and 1930s. Artaud wanted to forge a new path in theatre away from entertainment and towards realistic depictions of pain in order to ignite spectators' nerves and guts through non-verbal means of gesture, movement, shocking images, harsh lighting and jarring sound. Some of Astad's early choreography is similar in shaking up Indian audiences and throwing them outside well-known epic stories of the past and into the messy hardships of present-day society.

Asylum, an Unusual Solo

Asylum was as demanding to perform as to watch. The title itself makes me speculate about Astad's intentions. Was he playing on the different meanings of the word 'asylum'? It evokes the notion of a refugee seeking asylum in a new country away from the political, social or sexual violence in his/her homeland. 'Asylum' also conveys a location for those facing mental health challenges, considered 'mad' since they may not fit into societal norms of behaviour. Did such 'deviance' also include gay sexuality as was true until recently? At the time, psychologists who abided by *The Diagnostic and Treatment Manual* (originally published in 1983; 5th edition in 2021) considered homosexuality a mental illness. Homosexuals received harsh treatment in Western and Indian history under colonial rule and in contemporary times.[2] Did Astad feel like a refugee in his own home as a gay man and as a dancer whose efforts at modernizing Indian dance were mostly unwelcome, when Indian gurus shunned him and when audiences thought that his work looked too Western? He himself points out the irony that when performing abroad, his work did not look Indian enough to Western audiences. He was caught between traditional and modern dance. Even when his close friends thought that with so many rejections in India, he should live abroad, he always refused and asserted that India was his home and that he was Indian. Perhaps in his despairing moments, he might have considered seeking asylum elsewhere rather than remain in his native country.

In *Asylum*, Astad lies down on the stage floor at an incline; then, in an unusual gesture, he holds his foot up, caressing his big toe, kissing and hugging it. This action is interpreted by Uttara Coorlawala as

---

2 The British Parliament passed the Buggery Act of 1533, which made homosexual acts punishable by execution. This law continued until 1861 when homosexuals were persecuted and even punished with the death penalty (British Library 2022). Even after independence from British colonial rule, India inherited Section 377 of the British Penal Code as part of the Indian Penal Code which criminalized homosexual acts, prosecuting offenders with long-term imprisonment. Hence, at the time Astad began his dance career in the 1970s, it was natural to be discreet about one's sexuality. However, today the scene in India is very different. For instance, Mandeep Raikhy of New Delhi's Gati Dance Forum created a well-received and widely reviewed work entitled *Queen-Size* in 2009 which featured two male homosexual characters. Raikhy was responding partly to Section 377, which was finally struck down by Supreme Court of India in 2018; he was also invoking his late partner Nishit Saran's article 'Why My Bedroom Habits Are Your Business', published in the *Indian Express* in 2000. For a timeline of the struggle against Section 377, see Maria Thomas (2018).

depicting motherly love—Astad loving his big toe as if it were a baby. Another possible interpretation, I believe, could be Astad conveying gay sexuality, making love, featuring his foot, though in his characteristically discreet way. In a conversation with reviewer Anuradha Vellat, Astad confirms both interpretations: 'That part of the foot is his child, his lover.' Vellat interprets this act as that of 'a madman who fell in love with the edge of his foot'. Of course, Astad had studied Kathakali, a dance form in which 'the edge of the foot plays a crucial role', adds Vellat (2020).

Uttara shared a curious and instructive response to *Asylum* when she showed a recording of it at the Dance Critics Association Conference in New York City in the early 1990s. She selected *Asylum* as an example of 'Indian new dance'. She was dismayed that the organizers kept stopping the video saying that there was something wrong with it. Later, when she heard the sound, it was fine; however, 'the soundtrack was not Indian music, it was "noise".' The listeners assumed that such sound indicated a technical problem with the recording since such 'noise' could not be used for Indian dance, however new! Uttara reflected that 'people had their own preconceived ideas of what Indian dance would be, and therefore, would never think that this [soundtrack] would be okay' (int., August 2021). This story exemplifies that even knowledgeable audiences such as those at the Dance Critics Association Conference laboured under stereotypes about music for Indian dance. Certainly, *Asylum* did not have the expected 'look or sound' of Indian dance, notions that are problematically ingrained in the muscle memory of viewers in India and abroad.

Among Astad's friends, Vidhya Singh had seen *Asylum* when she and her husband took their young son Viraj to see Uncle Astad perform. She recalled that in the middle of the performance when Astad sat on the stage in the dark auditorium caressing his foot, 'a little baby voice suddenly called out, "Why is Astad Uncle touching his foot?"' It was young Viraj. The audience burst out laughing. The interruption did not deflect Astad from his concentration; he just looked up, smiled and carried on, noted Vidhya, but 'he never let Viraj forget this, ever!'

Enter Astad the Actor: *Mangalore Street* (1984)

Astad loved not only to dance but also to act. He did so in Sunil Shanbag's play *Mangalore Street*, in which 'Deboo deployed speech for the very first time in his work' (Vellat 2020). Astad wanted to break the proscenium theatre's fourth wall, thus challenging the boundaries of theatrical representation. So he decided to bring on stage different modes of transport such as a Vespa motorbike, a scooter, then a bicycle. Astad wanted to act as all the characters in the play who came from South Bombay's modest locality near the port. He used different costumes and wigs to portray Joglekar—a simple, dry, uninteresting clerk who turned into a colourful character after hours—along with a chai-wallah and a sex worker. Each character was distinguished by a particular voice modulation. When Astad spoke Hindi with a Parsee accent, says Sunil, some of his friends were offended. Astad also sang from whichever Hindi film was popular at the time, such as 'Main hoon Don' [I am the don] from the film *Don* (1978).

Astad combined the freedom of contemporary dance with theatre using Sunil's written dialogue in *Mangalore Street*. Astad had observed dance and theatre working together in 1981 when Pina Bausch had invited him to Germany. Now, in 1984, Astad acted and danced in Shanbag's play. That same year, at the East–West Dance Encounter, a milestone event in Bombay, Astad was among the invited dancers.

The East–West Dance Encounter (1984)

This gathering was masterminded by Dr George Lechner of the Goethe-Institut / Max Mueller Bhavan and hosted by Bombay's National Centre for the Performing Arts (NCPA). Astad performed *Mangalore Street* as a solo. Fellow invitee Uttara Coorlawala was astounded by this event because, at that time, there were no organizations dedicated to recognizing or promoting Indian modern dance. She felt that except for Astad, she was working in a vacuum.

Uttara recalled that Astad began his performance of *Mangalore Street* on a bicycle in a white unitard: 'I remember, because he asked me if I had one [a unitard].' She did not, nor would she ever wear one! She was astonished that he would come on stage pretty much naked except for that. But she said that Astad's entrance on the bicycle was 'shattering'. He proceeded to make fun of the way women are projected in Indian movies. 'It was sort of very gay in one way,' noted Uttara, 'and now, in hindsight, very Astad in another way. But at that time, one really didn't know what to make of it, in 1984' (int., August 2021). Astad demonstrated his boldness by revealing his male body in a unitard to the assembled dancers, many of whom were well known Indian classical dancers. It was, I believe, an in-your-face show of Astad's commitment to modern dance, his freedom with his own form and his audacious attitude.

Uttara's essay entitled 'East–West Dance Encounter (1984)', published online in *The Routledge Encyclopedia of Modernism* (2016), assessed that in this week-long gathering of dancers, critics and discussions, even though Indian traditional dance dominated, space was made for innovation and experimentation. Uttara appreciated that 'modernist aesthetics, including expressionism and minimalism, alongside postmodern initiatives like parody' were included. She continued: 'The gatekeeping notion of authenticity—which had hitherto meant a demand for unchanged tradition—was recast as a demand for individual artistic integrity. This watershed event officially opened the door for new choreographies not only in modernist and post-traditional choreography, but also within classical forms' (2016).

George Lechner and Jamshed J. Bhabha recognized artistic attempts at innovations and even tentative changes within traditional forms. Those working from within tradition were dancers such as Mrinalini

Sarabhai and Chandralekha, and those working to combine Eastern and Western influences included Kumudini Lakhia, Ritha Devi, Uttara and Astad. However, very few dancers 'ventured forth into the realm of dialogue between eastern and western dance forms'. Lechner and Bhabha stated clearly that this dance encounter

> will not declaim—either extolling or condemning—pre-conceived opinions on East–West synthesis but try to create a forum for a meeting of minds and exchange of information, where the respective artistic basic concepts, dance styles and work modes as pertaining to India and the West will be analysed in depth. Dance, like music, is replete with examples of how influences from other cultures were and still are artistically recreated and assimilated in many different ways. (1984: 7)

Chitra Sundaram, a Bharatanatyam dancer who later ventured into contemporary dance and who had known Astad since 1971, was included 'accidentally' in the East–West Dance Encounter since a senior dancer had backed out. She had seen Astad and Uttara perform in the 1980s when there was a kind of buzz about 'modern' dance. This included Chandralekha's choreography with Kalaripayattu, a martial arts style from Kerala, and before that, Uday Shankar's 'creative dance', which relied on Indian classical dance's 'symmetry' and 'linearity'. Chitra recognized that Astad was unique and engaging in his movement style and musical choices; plus, she found him 'playful and funny, with naughtiness and mischief', as she recalled Astad's black-and-white striped outfit that evoked Marcel Marceau, the mime artist, though without a white face (int., August 2021). Chitra was struck by Astad's 'emotional sincerity' in exploring himself, his dance and its place in India and beyond. She recognized him as a serious artist, 'a bhakta, who belonged to India; he had an Indian spirit'. As a dancer herself, Chitra delineated an important concept: Astad's work 'gives form to an emotion. Astad could flesh it out, paint it out and make it vivid for us to enjoy though not always comfort us with it'. Astad could masterfully 'give form to an emotion', whether he depicted motherly love or gay sexuality in *Asylum*, or endured the burning candle's hot wax for purification or sacrifice in *Ritual*, or spilled blood or banged his head on the stage floor in a drug-induced frenzy in *Broken Pane* (int., August 2021).

Astad's participation in the East–West Dance Encounter brought an invitation from Mrinalini Sarabhai, a renowned Bharatanatyam dancer, to come to Ahmedabad and perform with her daughter, Mallika (Bana 1984: 87). Bana remarks that 'both Mrinalini and Astad will be choreographing the items which will have an Indian base.' Astad was always willing to collaborate with Indian dancers, though he had few opportunities such as this one.[3] In the same *Society* piece, Astad lamented 'regionalism among dancers and bureaucratic patronage and favouritism [that] blemish the field of art' (Bana 1984: 87).

Astad's identity as a Parsee dancer, though supported fully by his parents and family, was not endorsed by the community. When Bana asked if 'being a Parsi made any difference to his profession', Astad replied, 'They think it effeminate for a man to dance. Music is fine, painting is fine, but dance, hell, no!' (Bana 1984: 87). He noted that his older relatives often suggested, even in the 1980s, that he give up dancing and start working in a bank. Like other communities in India, the Parsee community would prefer Astad to have a traditional job and be married with children, rather than pursuing a career as a dancer. But of course, Astad followed on his own path in his inventive dance works, though he was not alone in being a gay Parsee. Anita Ratnam remarked that Astad never spoke about being gay, nor did he wish to be part of any kind of group identity. 'We all in the artistic world just sort of knew. We were aware, but it never had an impact on our relationship with

---

3 Although many Indian classical dancers knew Astad's work, they were not open to collaborating with him. It was only a year before his death in 2019 that Astad was invited to collaborate on a work entitled *Inai* (*The Connection*) with Bharatanatyam dancer Hema Rajagopalan based in Chicago.

Astad, nor our access to and relationship with his art.' Ratnam added that 'maybe he never actually wanted to be tied down or allow one person to control or dictate *to* him' in any relationship—gay or straight—because 'his art was too important for him' (int., August 2021). Dance took precedence in Astad's personal as in his professional life.

Aahavan with Arpana Theatre Group (1987)

In 1987 Astad became an important part of Sunil Shanbag's Arpana Theatre Group, which had been founded two years earlier. Although the actors at Aparna were not trained dancers, Astad worked with 15 of them. He was very tough, recalled Sunil, demanding rigour and discipline, a useful experience for theatre actors. Their collaborative work was a synergy of dance and theatre, culminating in a show entitled *Aahavan* (The Challenge). Sunil recalled it as a wonderful experience though, unfortunately, there was only one performance. *Aahavan* was performed in the open air at the Elephanta Dance Festival in Bombay, where Astad demonstrated his creativity in dancing outdoors amid the historic Elephanta Caves, situated on an eponymous island 10 kilometres from the Bombay harbour.

Sunil's Arpana actors had previously worked with sarod player Brij Narayan, and in 1988 an opportunity arose for Astad to collaborate with Brij. A meeting was arranged at Brij's house. Astad described this first meeting with the sarod maestro. He had requested a recording of Brij's music ('Creating Endless Possibilities') and responded to it with a dance right there in that small room crammed with furniture. He used every available inch as he whirled, transforming it into a performance space. He picked up a rolled-up dhurrie and used it as a prop. The sarod maestro got up and embraced Astad saying, 'This is the room where I teach my students. I use it every day. But today it is as though I am seeing it for the first time.' Astad and Brij collaborated on a successful dance-and-music jugalbandi that opened Astad's 90-minute programme entitled

En Counterpoint. 'If Hussain can paint to Bhimsen Joshi,' asks reviewer Veena Gokhale, 'why can't Deboo dance to Brij Narayan?' (1988)[4]

Design-Driven Solos of the 1980s

Astad's design-driven solos used unique props created by Ratan Batliboi. Ratan and Astad would listen to music, discuss themes and how to structure them. At times, Ratan would think of a prop and Astad would create a dance; sometimes, it would be the other way round (Batliboi, int., July 2021).

Basics

The title *Basics* indicated the use of basic geometric forms in three dimensions that Ratan made from aluminium. They were huge—the rectangle was the size of a cupboard and the triangle was six feet tall. Astad danced with each piece, interacting with it independently not as a prop but as if it were animate. For instance, he would enter the space of the triangle, then emerge out of it. He manipulated each shape from the outside as well as explored the performance space within it. The in-between spaces inside and around the huge props also witnessed Astad dancing. Each prop had its own presence on stage. Even as Astad danced with one shape, the other two retained their quiet presence, 'defining their own spaces', noted Ratan, and challenging Astad 'to trespass into their space or breach the spatial relationships they ha[d] set up' (Batliboi 2010: 57).

Astad was strong enough to lift the huge rectangle and swing it around. Astad brought the same energy to these geometric metal shapes

---

4 I am grateful to Sunil Shanbag for a copy of this article. Along with the jugalbandi that opened the programme at the Prithvi Theatre, Gokhale comments that Astad included three other works in *En Counterpoint*: '*Duel* influenced by Kathakali, set to Mussorgsky's music depicting good and evil, *Vicissitudes*, set to Mahler where Deboo tried to trace the link between man and nature and *Asylum*, which uses mime to portray the fantasies of a madman' (1988: n.p.).

as he did to the puppets made by Dadi Pudumjee in *Friends* and *Thanatomorphia* (see Chapter 5) and later with the Salaam Baalak youth in *Interpreting Tagore* (see Chapter 9).

Endless

Endless demonstrated Astad's masterful interpretation of any stage space in which he performed taking into account the height, depth and flatness of a three-dimensional proscenium stage. He also danced on a stage with different levels. His vivid imagination could pick up any object lying around—a stool, chair or a rolled-up carpet—and use it as a prop. In *Endless*, some 20 chairs were arranged symmetrically on one side of the stage; Astad weaved through them, while the other side of the stage was free of objects. Ratan contended that such ordinary props as chairs worked since Astad could use the space around and between them imaginatively (Batliboi 2010: 57).

Ratan's expertise in understanding space as an architect and Astad's movement and space acumen resulted in their amazing creative collaborations during their association for nearly 30 years. Astad could delineate space, even translate any traditional space to create new possibilities. Astad's work *Confluences* demonstrated such a 'translation' with his interpretation of space. Ten tension cords were tied, five to each of Astad's hands with their opposite ends affixed at different heights upstage and downstage. When Astad moved, these strong lines moved with him as he defined the visual geometry of the entire stage space. He brought the space around him alive as he danced.

Search

Ratan created a unique, even intriguing stage set for *Search* by stretching 50 to 80 metres of translucent fabric across each side of the stage and from the floor to the top. This was different from the use of tension cords in *Confluences*; the fabric, stretched with invisible nylon ropes, gave character to the space by appearing to float in it (Batliboi 2010:

53). Ratan noted that this was one of his most beautiful stage sets, and he regretted that there are no photographs of it; unfortunately, it was quite difficult to find a photographer in those days before smartphones with cameras (int., July 2021).

Astad performed *Search* differently for each show, as the set was assembled anew each time, and he would see it only 15 minutes before the performance, even though the music remained consistent. He improvised as he danced through the space, his alternating slow or fast movements creating a dramatic effect along with the lighting that caught him from different angles. The piece was literally a search—first, for Astad's signature movement style that he was framing and re-framing through experimenting with his solos in the 70s and 80s; and second, for Indian spectators with open hearts and minds who would appreciate his unusual works. I contend that *Search*, which played with fabric, was a precursor to Astad's passionate adoption of his long angarkha costume. The ample and rich fabric of this costume became a partner with the dancer as he held it, twirled with it and made it glide and move with him. The dancer and the costume fit hand in glove.

Insomnia

Insomnia was another design-inspired work that portrayed the troubling sleeplessness that many endure. Ratan created a 'bed', which was not really a bed but a frame with two pipes at each end on which Astad supported his head, neck and ankles. He held his body taut, balanced between the pipes. 'That was the skill', remarked Ratan, 'that only Astad had' (int., July 2021).

Insomnia was part of *Quintet*, a five-part show performed at NCPA's Tata Theatre in 1987 when Astad's intense choreography was praised for depicting the state of a person in between sleeping, dreaming and waking. Prominent dance critic Leela Venkataraman (2019) asks incisive questions about Astad's ability to withstand physical pain: 'Mind and body are both tortured in *Insomnia* (1982) and in *Asylum* (1979).

Why this self-flagellation? Is it a constant challenge he wants the body to overcome or something more compulsive?'

Chrysalis

For *Chrysalis*, Ratan created a giant black box, 10 feet high, 12–15 feet wide, and 2½ feet deep with apertures, which echoed his huge props for *Basics*. The box was large enough for Astad to stand inside it and for Ratan, too, who opened and closed the slots. The box had platforms inside at different levels and pipes from which Astad could hang.

The two meanings of chrysalis play out in this work—one refers to the protective covering of what transforms into a butterfly and the other indicates a transitional stage such as puberty that takes human beings from childhood to adolescence. One stage transforms into the next, such as the chrysalis-covering absorbed though not visible in the beautiful butterfly. Yet, the chrysalis stage is significant in the cycle of a butterfly. Humans too have visible and invisible bodily changes in adolescence.

In *Chrysalis*, an iconic solo with startling choreography, Astad was interested in what could be seen and what remained unseen. Astad played with deconstructing the body, a fascination he had cultivated ever since he first saw modern dance in Mumbai in 1969 at a performance by the Murray Louis Dance Company from the United States. As the slots of the box opened, Astad would perform with one arm, then with a foot and so on. With different body parts emerging or remaining hidden inside the box, he would disrupt spectators' expectations by hanging upside down on pipes inside the box and thrusting out his head from a bottom slot and his foot from a top aperture. He also moved his arms in and out of the slots. This magical spectacle of the human body fascinated viewers.

Chrysalis was a unique display of the dancer's body emerging in parts from a confined space. The choreography prompted spectators to contemplate the possibilities of movement within such constraints and showcased how Astad could fluidly manoeuvre and dance through the gaps in the box. The challenge with such a dance piece was that the choreography had to be fixed since the lighting designer needed to know which aperture would open when and accordingly focus the spot-light on it. The complexity of visual impact was enhanced by the spare lighting, which emphasized that Astad's black box 'was a frame within the black box of the theatre space!' (Batliboi, int., July 2021).

Astad remarked:

Chrysalis which was done for the Bach centenary for which I had Pablo Casal's Concerto No. 1 on the cello. [In this] abstract work' [. . .] I wanted to show each part of the body moving individually. [. . .] It was very surrealistic for the viewers. Different parts of the body got exposed, just the waist to the knees, just the two arms, just the eyebrows, just the neck, part of the upper torso and eventually the entire body but no neck. Then the entire body coming out. (Deboo 1995: 39)

Astad had packed the box hoping to perform this work again, but it was extremely difficult to carry abroad.

When I complimented Ratan on creating this remarkable prop for *Chrysalis*, he was quite humble in his response. He observed that their collaboration was so seamless that he couldn't distinguish whether the idea and its execution were his or Astad's, nor who ultimately named it. 'Sunil would sort of wordsmith it,' noted Ratan, 'to make it sound like it was a dance piece. And we'd have our code names for it. It was quite exciting.' He recalled fondly that they seized on many creative opportunities; at times, it was the availability of a prop in a theatre that might create a world premiere. Astad named Ratan his technical direc-tor 'because he had to give me a title [. . .]. But I was his Man Friday, would iron his clothes, if necessary, feed him or whatever had to be done. It was a lovely situation' (int., July 2021).

This lifelong friend Ratan, whom Astad affectionately called Rato and who addressed Astad at times as Asti or, from Astad's Japanese

FIGURE 7. (TOP) Group photo with family after Astad and Gulshan's Navjote ceremony. *Courtesy Deboo family*.

FIGURE 8. (BOTTOM) Astad with his parents, sisters Gulshan and Kamal, with Kamal's husband Jimmy and their two sons, Xerxes and Danesh. *Courtesy Deboo family*.

FIGURE 9. (LEFT) Astad and Gulshan after their Navjote ceremony. *Courtesy Deboo family.*

FIGURE 10. (TOP RIGHT) Astad carrying his sisters Kamal (older) and Gulshan (younger). *Courtesy Deboo family.*

FIGURE 11. (BOTTOM RIGHT) Astad with his friend Bharti Patel. From Patel's book, *My Kahaani*; photographer unknown.

FIGURE 12. (FACING PAGE) Astad with his mother Rhoda showing the toran she made. *Courtesy Parzor Foundation.*

FIGURE 13. (LEFT) Astad with dancer Uttara Asha Coorlawala. *Courtesy Coorlawala's personal collection*.

FIGURE 14. (RIGHT) Astad and Uttara dancing. *Courtesy Coorlawala's personal collection*.

FIGURES 15–16. (FACING PAGE) Astad in *Basics*. *Photographs by Farrokh Chothia*.

FIGURE 17. (ABOVE) Astad in *Chewing Gum. Photographs by Farrokh Chothia.*

FIGURES 18–23. (FACING PAGE) Astad in *Circle of Feeling* (depicting the Navarasas). *Photographs by Farrokh Chothia.*

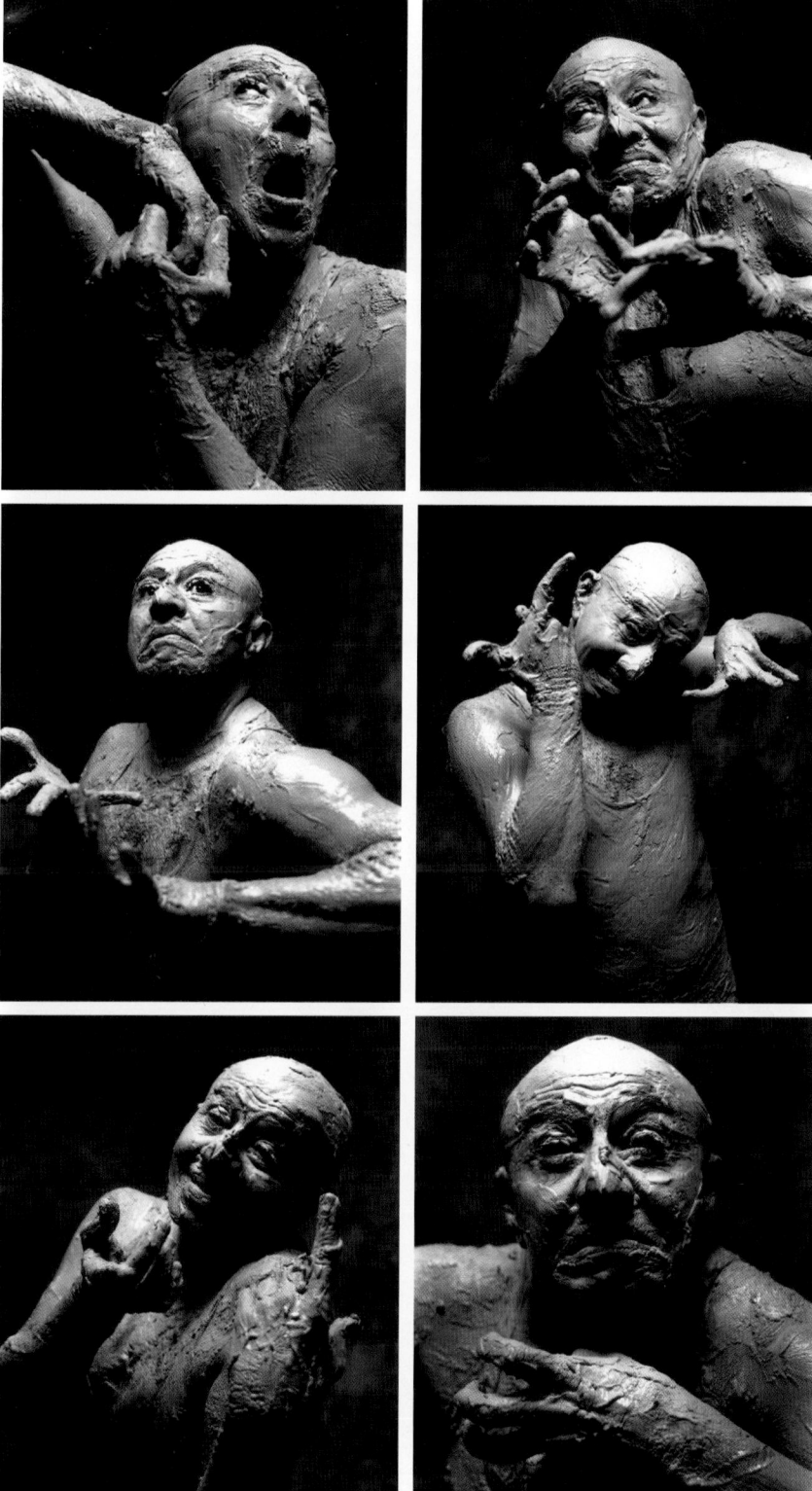

FIGURE 24. (FACING PAGE) Astad in classical Indian dance costume. *Courtesy Deboo family.*

FIGURE 25. (ABOVE LEFT) Astad in classical Kathakali costume. *Courtesy Deboo family.*

FIGURE 26. (ABOVE RIGHT) Astad putting on Kathakali dance make-up. *Courtesy Deboo family.*

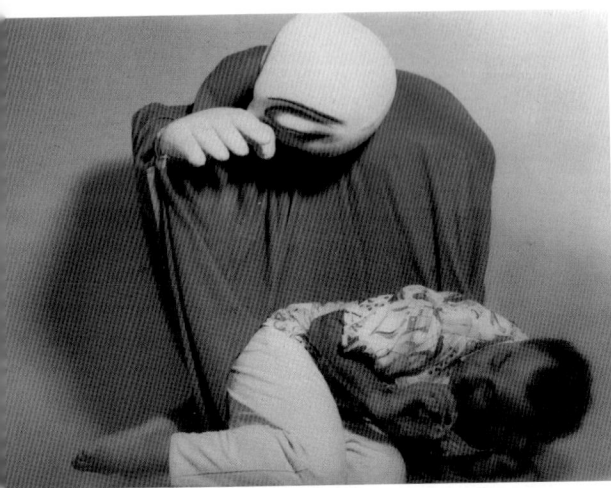

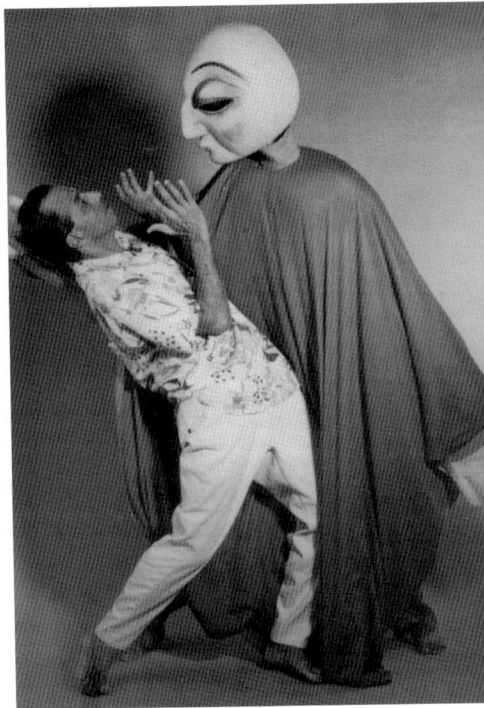

FIGURES 27–29. Astad and Dadi Pudumjee (with mask) in *Friends. Courtesy Deboo family.*

connections, as Babusan, utilized his architectural skills to create (quite literally!) out-of-the-box props and sets for Astad. Ratan and his wife Banoo travelled with Astad across the world, with Rato providing Asti tech support with lights, set design, stage machinery and fostering his creative endeavours. Ratan leaves us this beautiful portrait of Astad: 'the most kind-hearted, generous guy and there's no doubt about that. He'd just give willingly. I mean, he gave of himself. It was just beautiful' (int., July 2021).

In concluding this section of Astad's early solo choreography, I discuss a unique opportunity that Astad had in 2014 to revisit his experimental 1970s and 1980s solos with Rani Nair, a dancer-choreographer based in Sweden. They were introduced by Banashri Bose Harrison, the former Indian ambassador to Sweden, who saw 'Future Memory' by Nair in 2014 and was eager to support a collaboration between the two artists working in different dance forms, aiming to highlight the cross-fertilization of cultures. Their first collaboration took place in Delhi in 2015. After that, *An Evening with Astad* was developed through residencies in Lund, Malmo, Pondicherry, Linz and Mumbai.[5]

While creating *An Evening with Astad*, Rani took on the role of archivist and biographer focusing on 'cataloguing Deboo's choreography and stories and finding new ways to share those with an audience' (Nair 2024). Astad remarked that his early work was never recorded given funding constraints, but 'now Rani turns the clock back and [. . .] it's amazing to see how much the body remembers' (Nair 2024). In *An Evening with Astad*, through 'a relational duet form', with Astad and herself, Rani aimed to provide 'a new point of access to this formidable artist'. She achieved an 'intergenerational chronicle of contemporary

---

5 Rani Nair kindly shared this with me, along with her work, *An Evening with Astad*, which 'deals with ideas of dance history and archive between two continents—a biographical dance form that retells histories that have not yet been written' (int., June 2021).

Indian dance, one that travels backward [to Astad's early choreography] and into the future' (Nair 2024). As dramaturg Kate Elswit notes: 'These artists were born 27 years apart, but both are invested in contemporary manifestations of Indian Dance . . . *An Evening with Astad* extends the possibility of using dance to retell histories that have not yet been written' (shared by Nair, int., June 2021).

Through Rani, Astad looked back at the early years of his creations that were made in isolation. He hardly ever got to perform these works a second time because there were no opportunities and audiences, too, were small. Seldom would other dancers see a work in progress and give feedback. Astad deeply valued Rani's chronicling of his early work because it gave him the chance to question why he created a particular work, his motivation and his process. Astad regarded Rani's archival/biographical recreation as 'dance history', adding that 'it's very very important for me . . . through this, a record of material can be made available for the younger generation if they choose to inquire' (shared by Nair, int., June 2021).

During the 1970s and 1980s, Astad's dance works remained marginal in India. A rare commentary in 1987 that praised Astad came from Krishna Chaitanya, in his essay 'Indian Dance: Naïve Longings for Winds of Change'. Chaitanya acknowledged Astad as the pioneer of modern dance in India, adding that 'as in the West, his modernism too absorbs elements from tradition in a new synthesis' (1987: 13). He regarded Astad's international commissions as significant recognition from abroad and hoped that 'classicists in India take notice of this achievement and begin to incorporate the expressive modalities of modern dance. That need not at all be a betrayal of tradition, it can be one of many possible lines of modulating tradition in tune with changing time and sensibilities' (1987: 13). Nonetheless, Astad found himself caught between the traditions of Indian classical dance, which hewed closely to its established forms, and modern dance, which emphasized bodily expression and the freedom to explore contemporary issues.

FIGURES 30–31. (ABOVE AND LEFT) Astad and Rani Nair in *An Evening with Astad. Courtesy Rani Nair.*

FIGURE 32. (OVERLEAF) Astad in one of his iconic angarkhas. *Photograph by Ritam Banerjee.*

Astad's early solo choreography of the 1970s and 80s was distinctive with creative uses of stage space, unusual props, lighting, and global soundscapes. The year 1990 marked a significant turning point in Astad's dance career with Dhrupad music and puppetry.

CHAPTER 5

The 1990s: Dhrupad, Puppetry and Dance

A major turning point in Astad's career came in 1990 with an invitation to dance at the Khajuraho Dance Festival in the Madhya Pradesh state in central India. This was the first time that he was asked to participate in an Indian dance festival. Sunil Shanbag recalled that Astad was very excited by Satyadev Dube's invitation because he was waiting for—indeed, craving—some recognition and validation from the Indian dance establishment (int., July 2021).

Although Astad had been active, even prolific with his professional career since the 1970s, his work remained marginal in India's mainstream classical dance scene. Although Astad always identified as an Indian artist, it was only after his training in Kathakali that there came a distinct change in his presentation (Shanbag, int., July 2021). This was reflected in the stark, strong movements and facial expressions that emphasized the eyes and eyebrows, characteristic of Kathakali's theatrical style. Kathakali also opened, for the first time, a comfortable space for Astad as an Indian dancer. Although he felt at home in the West, where many of his significant influences came from, he deeply yearned for recognition as an Indian dancer, rooted in the land of his birth and its rich heritage. I agree with Sunil's estimation that Kathakali was the first step that shifted something internally for Astad as someone who could display his dance skills as a modern Indian dancer.

This internal shift manifested externally in Astad's choice of costume: it changed from skin-fitting leotards or unitards to his signature angarkha—a long, flowing ankle-length robe made of ample fabric, with a more recognizable 'Indian' feel and affect. He did go back and forth between the leotard and the angarkha—especially since only the full-length flowing costume would look dramatic on stage with the spinning that soon became a distinct motif of Astad's style (Shanbag, int., July 2021).

At Khajuraho, Astad was thrilled to dance to the performance of dhrupad—a major vocal style of Indian classical music—by the Gundecha Brothers. Astad had been very moved when he had heard them for the first time in Bhopal. When he introduced himself to them, suggesting the possibility of working together, he found the singers simultaneously interested and apprehensive (Deboo 2003: 126). Astad was clear from the beginning that he did not want them to experiment but to sing in the traditional dhrupad style. These musicians had not seen Astad's type of dance and movement; however, they agreed to a trial work session. Then, when the opportunity to work together came up at the Khajuraho Dance Festival, Astad was ecstatic.

One of the criteria for participating in this festival was that dancers had to either create a dance about the Khajuraho temples, a group of exquisite tenth-century structures which form the backdrop of the performances, or set their work to a poem written by a poet from Madhya Pradesh, where these temples are located. Astad decided to use Gajanan Madhav Muktibodh's *Lakdi ka Ravan*, a well-known dramatic poem in Hindi. Sunil described it as an anti-fascist poem that he helped Astad to condense (Deboo 1995). Astad portrayed Ravana (usually evil and conniving, a contrast to Rama, from the epic *Ramayana*) as a politician and had an actor recite each verse of the poem as the Gundecha Brothers sang ragas that embodied the different emotions depicted in the poem. Astad relied on his stage designers Ratan and Banoo Batliboi to put up curtains like the ones used in Kathakali performances. Banoo created two black panels featuring blank faces that depicted crowds of people, while Astad danced between them.

Sunil recalls Astad's piece as effectively theatrical with his dramatic entry like a minister accompanied by bodyguards and commandos. In his autobiographical piece, 'Creating Endless Possibilities', Astad noted that he entered the stage in 'a *lal batti wallah* official car [with red flashing lights used by VIPs]'. His backstage team was converted into Black Cat commandos with AK-47 guns. He strutted like a government official vainly oozing self-importance, 'even as he methodically started disrobing an assortment of garments, which symbolized the tiers in our society' (Deboo 2003: 126). Astad also performed a solo entitled *Aahavan* (literal translation, 'Challenge', also 'An Invocation'), dedicated to the space in which he danced. It was an abstract work on Raga Bhimpalas that evoked the emotion of love tinged with sadness, sung by the Gundecha Brothers (Deboo 1995).

The Gundecha Brothers' dhrupad sound that entered Astad's consciousness after this 1990 collaboration returned in future works. Indeed, music played a key role in Astad's dance career. 'With me, music has been everything,' he says. 'The centre of attraction, sometimes supplementary, sometimes silence' (Deboo 2003). Astad, a lifelong learner, wanted to discover how collaborating with musicians could impact his work and what he could gain from the synergy of a sarod or a saxophone with his movement. Astad had a gift for connecting with musicians as he danced. His body moved fluidly to different sounds, his angarkha swirling in chakkars, while his mind synchronized with the musical notes and subtle in-between tones—the *gamaka*s—which his fingers followed in perfect rhythmic and movement response.

Astad has collaborated widely with singers and instrument players in India as well as in Europe, USA, Japan and South Korea. 'I have found it easy, for their medium speaks to me,' remarked Astad in a 2020 interview, 'whether saxophone or flute or piano, both Indian as well as Japanese, the Korean Kayegam, the Japanese Koto, the Rudra Veena, dhrupad singers Amelia Cuni, Uday Bhavalkar, the Gundecha Brothers, Carnatic musicians, percussionists like the pungcholum drummers of

Manipur, and painters like Jayashree Chakraborty, Sunil Gawande with his art installation on lights, dancers Thomas Mettler, Padmini Chettur' (Deboo 2020: 168).

Astad performed *Aahavan* again to Gundecha Brothers' dhrupad sound when he opened the evening performance of the 14th Festival of Asian Arts in Hong Kong in 1992. He wore a turquoise leotard that looked striking against a backdrop of stretched white fabric. Astad received a positive review for his dance to classical dhrupad; particularly noteworthy was his deeply expressive face from his Kathakali training. Astad once again presented *Aahavan* at the Purush Festival in Bhopal in 1994. He recalls: 'There the Kuchipudi performer Venapati saw my work and really liked it. He really marveled at the control and even the imagination' (Deboo 1995: 44).

At a lecture demonstration in Chennai in 1995, when Astad participated with the gatekeepers of Indian classical dance, he received a very good response. During the question–answer session, one of the dancers in the audience asked Astad how he would dance *Poothana Moksham* (Putana's salvation), a popular story in the Kathakali tradition, in his own style. The Kathakali story, rooted in an account from the Ramayana, goes like this: The demoness Putana is on a mission to kill infant Lord Krishna to avert the prophecy that her brother, the evil King Kamsa, will be killed by Krishna when he grows up. Putana, disguised as a beautiful maiden, offers her poison-coated breasts to the infant Krishna to suckle, hoping to kill him instantly. But Krishna holds onto the demoness, who realizes that her life is being sucked away along with her milk, the poison having had no effect on the infant god. Putana dies instead of killing Krishna. This Chennai audience was unaware of Astad's early choreography in *Asylum* in which he had imagined his big toe to be a child and a lover. In interpreting the story of *Poothana Moksham*, Astad embodied Krishna as his toe, impressing his audience of traditional dancers with his intellectual acumen in connecting his avant-garde piece to his knowledge of the myth.

Puppetry and Dance

In 1989, Dadi Pudumjee and Astad created a work entitled *Friends*. Astad had met Dadi in 1980 at the Sri Ram Centre for Performing Arts in New Delhi, where Dadi had founded the Sutradhar Puppet Theatre and served as artistic director until 1986 before founding his own company, the Ishara Puppet People Trust. A renowned puppeteer with national and international awards, Dadi was elected president of UNIMA (Union Internationale de la Marionette) in 2008, the first non-European to hold this position in which he served until 2016. Throughout his career, he has created different puppets following the themes he wanted to depict, ranging from simple rod figures to larger-than-life ones that entertain children and adults. Dadi believes that puppetry should be used not as an end in itself but rather as a means of communication.

Both Astad and Dadi faced the limited and stereotypical expectation that their work, when presented outside India, would look 'Indian', that is, 'traditional'. Dadi had presented a contemporary show in 1984 in Dresden, Germany, that astonished the audience since they could not imagine that such work could come from India.

Astad's collaboration with Dadi in *Friends* premiered in Delhi. It was presented by Indian Council of Cultural Relations (ICCR), one of the major funding institutions of the Indian government—'Astad's first ever official sponsor', remarks Shanta Gokhale (1990). Gokhale recognizes in conversation with Dadi and Astad, 'how difficult it is for an innovative performer to find a place in the mainstream culture of the country'. This dance piece featured Astad and a larger-than-life puppet made with thermocol, papier mache and cloth that Dadi manipulated while Astad danced. *Friends* depicted a common occurrence in friendship when personal politics intervenes and one friend dominates the other, leading to tension. This was enacted between the human being played by Astad and the puppet until the latter suddenly found its power, throwing the person to the ground. The puppet has the upper hand in this interaction, which causes a rift between the two who try to reconcile but cannot. *Friends* was set to music by Ryuchi Sakamoto, the Japanese composer who scored for the film *The Last Emperor* (1987), David Byrne and Cong Su. Dadi, Astad, Ratan and Banoo Batliboi, along with others, travelled widely with *Friends*, including a performance at Café de la Danse in Paris (Pudumjee 2020).

'Dance crept into my work because of Astad,' remarked Dadi (int., 2021). Astad, always open to collaborating with a variety of artists, was the first dancer who suggested linking puppetry with dancing to Dadi. That resulted in *Friends*, their first portrayal of these two arts together at Mumbai's Tata Theatre on 12 October 1989. Dadi manipulated a giant puppet that had a calm, Buddha-like face while his body was covered by a red robe. Astad was in a floral short-sleeved shirt. Apparently, both artists selected the theme of friendship since they had known each other for nine years.

Astad danced in *Friends* along with his selected solos: *Broken Pane*, *Skin-Deep*, a satirical piece done in total silence about the importance of clothes in defining a man, in this case, a politician; *Confluence*, with music by Hari Prasad Chaurasia and Zakir Hussain; and *Passage of Life* with music by Philip Glass that presented a journey from birth, through frustration and rejection but ending with hope (Gokhale 1990).

Astad's work with Dadi continued in *Thanatomorphia: The Many Faces of Death*. The title, Astad's invention, evoked Thanatos, the Greek god of death, with 'morphia' conveying death's many aspects. One part of the piece explored death from within Hindu mythology, evoking Yama, the god of death; in another part, death was welcomed by an old man. Although Astad admitted to being apprehensive about the dark, even morose theme of death, he also said he wanted to find 'new insights' by exploring death as a lover, even a liberator 'through little vignettes. The puppets performed alongside [him]' (Deboo 2018). *Thanatomorphia* was structured in five parts. Part 1 showed death as ever-present in life via shadow and light; in Part 2, death was 'the seductive dancer' who surreptitiously enticed pleasure seekers into a fatal embrace; Part 3 portrayed death as the passionate lover though the relationship was doomed since the love is obsessive and courageous though the lover is death; in Part 4, death the liberator was welcomed by the ageing body, crumbling long past its prime; finally, in Part 5, death was a celebration.

Astad's 'Choreographer's Note' (courtesy of Pudumjee) for the performance at Mumbai's NCPA, poses questions: 'Why death? . . . Is it a preoccupation with the morbid? Is it a search sparked off by the death of two close friends in the space of one year? Or is it the fulfilment of deep-rooted fantasies where my imagined death is always elaborate and sad?' The last line presages Astad's own death 30 years later. Today, we remember Astad by celebrating his life, his passion and his commitment to his art and to his many friends and collaborators.

Astad danced and acted in *Thanatomorphia* with four others, including the 2013 Sangeet Natak Akademi Award winner Puran Bhatt. Dadi designed the masks and puppets; Sam Kerawalla, the lighting; Ratan Batliboi, the stage; and Banoo Batliboi was the programme designer. Astad's talent in selecting eclectic soundscapes for his choreography was evident in *Thanatomorphia* for which he amalgamated the sounds of 'Vedic mantras and Pakistani qawwali' as noted by reviewer Srimati Lal (1990), along with 'Pink Floyd's *Momentary Lapse of Reason*, German New Wave, Zakir Hussain and Moroccan folk.' *Thanatomorphia* was performed in the US, UK, Canada and Singapore.[1]

International Invitations

Astad was unique among Indian dancers to receive prestigious international invitations before he gained wide recognition in his own country. In 1980, when he was eagerly crafting his style, he took up renowned

---

1 In 2020, Dadi remarked: 'I found a lot of dance inspiration for my works, and he [Astad] used puppetry in many ways, most recently in a piece on Goddess Kali called "Your Grace" (part of *Interpreting Tagore*) in 2012, which was with the younger puppeteers from Delhi, among others' (Pudumjee 2020).

German dance choreographer Pina Bausch's invitation to visit Germany. Bausch's legendary style was intense and emotional, evoking visceral reponses. Could such characteristics become part of Astad's own style? However, the connection with Bausch was not harmonious—she wanted Astad to allow her to use Kathakali gestures in her work but he refused. Hence, she did not allow Astad to choreograph independently; she asked him to stay and observe but not be part of her company. This experience further solidified Astad's resolve to create his particular style. Unlike classical dancers who use set themes and music, Astad had no ready-made blueprint to follow; he had to decide on a concept, then find the appropriate music, props, staging and lighting.

In 1982, Astad was invited to dance at the Pan Asian Music Festival in Seoul for which he received the sponsorship of the Indian Council for Cultural Relations. During this seven-week sojourn, he attended international dance festivals in Jakarta and Tokyo where he worked with Sankai Juku, Japan's well-known dance company.

In 1984–85, Astad's keen interest in Asian musical forms inspired a two-month tour of the Far East and Southeast Asia. He improvised his dance on one track of music by the Samul Nori group in Seoul. His interest in Korean classical percussion instruments resurfaced years later in 2015 when he collaborated with Korean and Indian musicians in *Same Same but Different* (which I will discuss in Part IV of this volume).

In 1986, French designer Pierre Cardin invited Astad to choreograph for famous Bolshoi ballerina Maya Plisetskaya. Astad and Maya performed at the Espace Cardin in Paris between 24 February and 2 March. Astad choreographed a piece called *The Queen of the Underworld* and also danced his own piece entitled *Fusion*. Astad's international reputation was furthered by his performances at Aix en Provence in France and at the Royal Opera House in Sydney, Australia, in addition to programmes in the US, Japan and Thailand.

One remarkable feature of Astad's career was that he got to perform for royal families around the world. In Japan, he danced for Crown

Prince Akihito and Princess Michiko; in Thailand, he danced for the Queen Mother and was invited to the court of the great-grandson of King Chulalongkorn. On 17 February 2017, Astad was one of the Indian dancers, alongside Aditi Mangaldas, selected to meet Queen Elizabeth at Buckingham Palace at the launch of the India–UK Year of Culture. When Astad was introduced, the Queen said, 'You are a dancer? I hear you are a pioneer.' Astad noted that the Queen 'sort of started showing little hand gestures—and said, "See this is how I move." So that was very cute!' (Deboo 2017b).

Although Astad had received impressive commissions and by 1984 had performed in 50 cities across five continents, earning more recognition abroad than at home, Indian audiences remained largely ungenerous and resistant to engaging with his unique creativity, even when they were impressed. Only foreign institutions in India like Goethe-Institut / Max Mueller Bhavan and the British Council supported Astad's dance. Astad was frustrated by the fact innovations in modern painting and writing were accepted by Indian institutions but not those in dance. Modern dance, with its openness in exploring contemporary topics and its freedom with the human body, continued to be alien in India. This modernity in dance clashed with the classical Indian dance traditions, which focused on epic stories from the past and featured traditional silk saree costumes that modestly covered the body.

An invitation in 1982–83 to the International Contemporary Dance Festival, celebrating 50 years of the American Dance Festival (ADF) at Duke University in the US, brought Astad closer to what had inspired him in the Murray Louis Modern Dance Company's performance in Mumbai in the late 1960s: its emphasis on physicality and the body.[2]

---

2 ADF, which began in 1934, led a revolution against classical ballet's formality, constraining costumes, pointe shoes and well-worn stories, and had a worldwide impact. Although a revolt against an incredible ballerina such as Anna Pavlova was difficult, modern dancers resisted her portrayal of animals (dying swan, dragonfly). 'We are going to dance as man and woman,' declared Charlie Weidman,

Astad and Bharat Sharma were the solo male invitees from India, along with Kolkata's Uday Shankar Indian Cultural Centre dance company. Astad reached out to an Ohio-based friend from his Jamshedpur days, Rohini Desai Mulchandani, to join him for the two-day event with contemporary dancers from across the globe. At this event, Astad danced in a leotard and was praised for his facial expressions and mudras.

Rohini recalled a gathering in 1984 of Astad's Jamshedpur friends now living in New York State, Ohio and Connecticut, who had all agreed to attend Astad's solo performance at Yale University. They all gathered at Anup Mody's house in Easton, Connecticut and travelled as a group. Anup was Astad's Loyola classmate and the two had kept in touch. Unfortunately, by the time I interviewed Rohini, Anup had passed away. Rohni supported Astad's work as 'an occasional donor' and had sponsored one of his students from Kolkata's Deaf Action Players who had come to Gallaudet University in Washington DC. 'This began a new chapter in our friendship,' remarked Rohini (int., June 2021). Astad was the master dance teacher who spent six weeks at Gallaudet one summer, training both American and Indian students.

In concluding this chapter, I allude to Astad's 2020 interview a few months before his passing where he discussed the development and challenges facing contemporary Indian dance: 'As more and more young dancer-choreographers began exploring th[is] genre and experienced what was being offered overseas, they unmoored themselves from the past and chose to choreograph in the present. Audience reception also improved. We see a lot of this kind of work now' (Deboo 2020: 160). However, he regarded these positive developments as 'a mixed blessing', since 'traditions for contemporary dance training' that could have been developed over the past two decades were 'entirely missing' (Deboo 2020: 160). Astad believed that without rigorous training, dancers

---

an ADF pioneer who envisioned that modern dance would give freedom to artists and encourage them to take risks (Polichetti 1985: n.p.).

attempting contemporary forms relied on spectacle instead of innovating their movement vocabulary or use of space. He viewed such dance as more of a pastiche than a truly realized work in the contemporary style.

Astad critiqued Indian cultural institutions that even by 2020 had neither established artistic standards nor displayed nuanced appreciation of what artists and audiences should value in contemporary Indian dance. Although funding for contemporary work had improved, funders were hasty in supporting young dancers while neglecting older, more experienced ones. According to Astad, cultural institutions perpetuated a damaging generation gap.

Astad ends this reflective interview with these telling words about truth and art: 'Increasingly, I have found that dance is not just dance but an elemental expression of truth and individuality that brings various performing disciplines together in a magical cohesion of talent that produces art of a very high level.' Although eager to succeed, Astad says that 'even failures are nothing but pit stops on the journey to the ultimate goal of creativity. This is to be true to yourself and your art' (Deboo 2020: 167).

From such dedication, Astad evolved his signature style from a *fusion* of dance styles which he had witnessed, studied and imbibed, as seen in his early avant-garde choreography that engaged with current social issues and that used unusual props, to a *hybrid* dance language by the 1990s and into the 2000s. Here, distinct dance styles were not fused but individually recognizable. His style synergized abstract movement with emotions based in rasas, rooting his pioneering contemporary dance firmly in Indian soil. He did receive recognition in India, though it came slowly and late in his career. Few dancers and critics in India could tune into his hybrid and distinctive signature style.

CHAPTER 6

Astad's Signature Style in Contemporary Indian Dance

'A maverick maestro with a distinctive contemporary dance style that sprouted in Indian soil.'—Ramaa Bharadvaj (int., August 2021)

Astad's signature style is original and distinctive, a synergistic hybrid of Indian traditional and Western modern dance along with diverse movement styles observed and imbibed during his travels in Europe, Japan, Southeast Asia, South America and the US. He evolved his style over many years, arriving at his own language rooted in the Indian classical styles of Kathak and Kathakali imprinted on his body. Astad loved modern and contemporary dance's focus on the body and on physicality. However, as a pioneer of contemporary Indian dance, he transformed modern dance by grounding abstract movement in Indian rasa aesthetics expressed through his face, eyes, eyebrows, body stance and lyrical use of arms and fingers in evocative mudras—whether he extended his hands in a gesture of profound bhakti or turned his face away sharply to indicate displeasure. Even in his early choreography, we glimpse echoes of his style that retains the rigour of modern dance that he makes his own and makes it Indian.

Astad honed his style to be minimalist, meditative and meaning-fully slow, taking his time to unfold a piece. 'It did not begin that way,' he tells Ramaa Bharadvaj (2017: 56). When he was searching for his own dance idiom, he experimented with different styles and his dance was 'fast-paced—here, there and everywhere.' His singular dance form stands out for his ability to internalize and then communicate emotions elicited by a particular work, whether it is spiritual as in *Eternal Embrace* with Japanese flautist Yukio Tsuji or the thrill of percussion played by Indian and Korean drummers in *Same Same but Different*. Astad's social conscience inspired him to impart his confluence of movement and music in his choreography to the deaf, to Manipuri dancers and to street youth (more in Part III). He passed on his legacy of intense concentration, body rigour, balancing poses and synchronized group patterns to these bodies.

Indeed, to witness Astad dance his signature style is to marvel at how he retains grace with physical prowess in gravity-defying balancing poses and backbends. His style exudes strength and focus. He is in control; each gesture, even as it appears to flow spontaneously, is crafted carefully to draw in spectators. His dance is never remote since he appeals always to his audience's heart and spirit with profound empathy. As spectators stay with Astad's movement and music, he gives them an experience. They may not be able to articulate what that precisely is, but they are moved to think and feel deeply with this artist. Astad believed that his 'dance need not always have a meaning. It could be interpreted as just a flow of movement, a pattern, a minimalist abstraction. I've used fabrics as a way of reaching out; I've explored geometry . . . I don't do things just for effect' (quoted in Lal 1990).

Astad was an innovator. To execute his style successfully, he undertook bold transformations of the performance space (proscenium and site-specific), selected eclectic soundscapes from global music for his choreography, and incorporated stunning visual design with striking lighting and overall presentation. 'For me,' remarked Astad, 'contemporary dance has been the deepest expression of joy and commitment to the finer things of life. I have never lost sight of this truth about myself' (Deboo 2020: 167).

Astad's dance training, based on classical Indian dance styles Kathak and Kathakali, provided a foundation for his signature style.

However, Astad did not wish to be a professional dancer in these Indian classical styles. Nonetheless, his Kathak guru Prahlad Das was shocked when Astad gave up his Kathak ghagra and ghungroo after studying under him for eight years and turned to modern dance. However, his Kathakali guru, E. K. Pannicker, at age 64, accepted Astad's taste for both Kathakali and modern dance. This unusual guru attended his disciple's performances and in fact also danced duets with him at the Mookambika Temple in Karnataka as well as in Ahmedabad, Gujarat. Indeed, Pannicker's traditional training had brought Astad integrally into this Indian dance style after his travels abroad.

Although Astad's feet traversed the world searching for his own style, he always identified as an Indian dancer with roots firmly planted in the land of his birth. 'I haven't worked in different forms of dance,' he explains, clarifying that he studied primarily Kathak and Kathakali, and when overseas, he 'took classes to see what would complement my body. In that way, I became aware of my body in its totality' (Deboo 2016a). Whatever he picked up from the colourful palette of dances he watched and tried had to suit his body and his choreographic intent in a particular work. He was most drawn to Japanese dance forms, both classical and folk, and to Brazilian music and dance that resonated with his Indian spirit. Indeed, Astad's natural gravitation to Indian aesthetics, motifs and culture gives his choreography an Indian feel and appeal. His work remains remarkable for his creation of 'a genuinely new language in codified India,' as evaluated by Ramu Ramanathan (2008). In Bharadvaj's words: 'Astad's unique technique is distinguishable by its internalization and tranquil shaping of space. He describes it as being "deeply emotional, minimal and meditative with physicality of strength, concentration and controlled extensions"' (2017: 56).

Astad's approach to working with different styles was never a matter of simply adding on, but rather discovering connections between his own technique and other styles. As he did so, he transferred the new bodily awareness and choreographic insights of his style to differently trained artists. At the Ananya Seminar in New Delhi in 2014, the day after his performance of *Rhythm Divine* with Manipuri dancers, he explained how he made Manipuri martial arts movements—strong and physical—flow into his own dance style that shares those characteristics.

Astad's Singular Choice of Music and Soundscape

Astad's contribution to contemporary Indian dance is as significant as his eclectic and wide-ranging musical choices for his choreography, whether it is the deep sonorous sound of Dhrupad, or the high pitch of a stirring opera singer, or the lilting notes of a piano or cello or the tugging-at-the-heart saxophone strains. Astad had a vast collection of global music that he would share with other dancers.[1] He collaborated with master musicians, vocalists and instrumentalists in India and abroad. His spirit resonated with Indian classical, Japanese folk and Brazilian soundscapes. He tuned into the Korean kayegam, the Japanese koto and the Indian rudraveena. Among singers, he loved Amelia Cuni's Dhrupad singing, the Gundecha Brothers, Carnatic musicians and Pung Cholum rhythms of Manipur. Astad's body could flow to different sounds and his mind could tune into musical notes that his fingers could follow in perfect rhythmic response.

Astad's musical gift was noted by dancers whom I interviewed, such as Anita Ratnam, who believed that Astad does not get credit for his musical sense, his ability to both work with and against the music. She said that when Astad used music in his unique way, he involved his whole body—face, shoulder, back, fingers, wrists. Astad's rhythm came

---

1 Astad was generous in sharing music, as Uttara Coorlawalla recalls. Once she told Astad that she was 'having a hard time with music' and asked him for 'recommendations'. 'So, the next time he came to New York, he came with a bunch of CDs and handed them to me. And you know, they are very useful to me because they still are some of the best examples I have of Indian music with rhythm.' Uttara said that once she admired a beautiful photograph of his, and 'he sent me the photographer, and said, go take pictures. He was very generous' (int., August 2021).

from his musical knowledge. 'Not all his musical scores had rhythm'; he'd create 'a bed of sound, over which he'd overlay his kind of dance musicality as another bed'. Astad also made exciting musical choices that accompanied his 'rhythmic knowledge, his knowledge of silences' through which he 'could bring everything [movement, music, silence] into him, including us the audience' (Ratnam, int., August 2021).

Astad's Unique Chakkars

A prominent detail of Astad's style is his chakkars. These are markedly different from spins executed by Kathak or ballet dancers, in which a dancer relies on spotting while turning in a straight posture. Astad's skilled execution of what appears to be familiar Kathak chakkars is instead his creation—a distinctive way he covers space, bending gracefully at his waist, moving backwards while still spinning, his arms circling his body in undulating motion. Indian classical and contemporary dancers whom I interviewed discussed Astad's style of spinning along with his ability to balance stillness with it. He achieved more than most dancers can, as Anita Ratnam remarked, with stillness.

Kathak dancer Aditi Mangaldas said, 'Kathak chakkars are done on the heel', when the dancer is centred. She continued, 'Astad changed the axis of his feet with his shifting spine as he turned with both feet without spotting (to retain balance)—he would also twist and keep turning which is very difficult.' So, in accomplishing this Astad-spinning, he had invented an original way of turning—not keeping his body stiff and centred as in Kathak, but allowing his spine to bend, gazing fondly towards spectators watching dumbfounded and breathless with anxiety and awe as he continued to spin. Aditi described further how Astad's feet moved and in which direction during his chakkars: 'Suddenly, oh my God, he's bending backwards and moving—or, oh my God, he's in one place, just twirling' (int. with Ratnam, August 2021).

From the first time Aditi saw Astad perform, at the East–West Dance Encounter at India International Centre, Delhi, she was 'mesmerized' by him and by the energy in his body. In the 1990s Aditi, younger than Astad, used to call him 'Astad-ji' as a mark of respect. 'He tapped my head,' she recalled, 'and said "No, you call me Astad."' Astad connected with Aditi as a friend and fellow artist without any age barrier.

Once, Aditi invited Astad to conduct a workshop with her troupe. She was apprehensive since she had heard about Astad's temper, but she found him generous-hearted and encouraging towards her young dancers. At the workshop, Astad made the Kathak dancers bend from the waist, instructing them to 'let [their] torso be parallel to the ground'. He knew that the dancers could spin, but 'he placed them out of their comfort zone to bend their spine and to spin'. If a dancer could not do this, he was always ready to help.[2] Aditi admired how Astad had absorbed different styles and 'had the courage to stand up and say, "This is my dance."' (int. with Ratnam, July 2021).

Astad could spin 'with complete abandon', and as he gradually honed his style, his spinning changed, as noted by dancer Uttara Coorlawala, who had first auditioned Astad in 1967 in Bombay for her dance piece, *The Joyous Cosmology*: 'In the beginning, it was kind of wild, and he was all over the place . . . turning and turning.' Uttara found this appealing. However, 50 years later, in 2017, when Uttara saw Astad perform, 'he was spinning with a lot of structure. So, within the spinning, the arms would come to a completion of a phrase, and then start a new phrase. And it would slow down or change levels slightly, not a lot, because he

---

2 Aditi remembered Astad calling her to convince her to visit the Queen of England after her initial refusal: 'Why did he bother? . . . Only a very generous person would do that.' As generous as Astad was to Aditi's students so he was with Anita's young dancers in 'a contemporary neoclassical work' at Mumbai's National Centre For Performing Arts. Astad attended the show even though he was on his way to a foreign country. 'He posed with the dancers. He congratulated everybody, then he took me aside. He said, "I like your solo. I think you can work on it a little more, but it works. It's the direction—I think you've got the direction"' (int. with Ratnam, July 2021).

was spinning. Very much phrased with the music as he's very musically conscious and aware' (int., August 2021).

An Astad 'Experience'

Choreographically, Astad remains a fascinating subject. He wanted his performances to be experiences for his audience. 'He was going to ask us to be prepared to acknowledge a reveal. I've not seen any other soloist do so much with so little. Astad had found that [choreographic] intention even before all of us who now use the word [experience]' (Ratnam, int., August 2021).

Anita discussed Astad's 'choreographic motive'—he knew exactly what he was doing, even while improvising or 'creating in the moment'. Astad surprised his viewers constantly, 'even those of us who are in the craft. And I think he almost wanted to surprise himself.' He so internalized the music that he could follow it in both rehearsed and improvised movements; the music 'was in every pore of him. It [music] moved from his toes to his incredibly fancy haircut' (int., August 2021). Dancers recognized something enviable in Astad—in how he 'lived his dance with complete involvement and conviction' (Ratnam, int. 2021).

Uttara believed that Astad's early work was 'unstructured, if I may say so. Then, when I saw him at the end, the structure was very clearly there. And very impressive and made his work a lot deeper and richer', since structure enables an audience to relate to the performer (int., August 2021). Uttara's piece in *Seminar*, written after Astad passed on, spoke of how his work became 'more finely structured with more nuanced details and elegance'. Throughout Astad's journey even with collaborators, Uttara found that he 'always managed to stay true to his own personal style which he had evolved with elements of Kathakali, Butoh and other contemporary forms' (Coorlawala 2021: 82–83).

Astad's Sisyphean Search

Before being recognized as a pioneer of contemporary Indian dance, Astad had faced a long and arduous journey akin to Sisyphus in the Greek myth. Because Astad was ahead of his time, he struggled for validation, for funding and for an audience. Government recognition came late in his life—in 2007, at age 60, the Padma Shri, one of India's highest civilian honours. And even after that, the scramble for fund-raising continued.

The venues and sponsors for Astad's dance in India were mostly foreign cultural institutions. 'It took me two years,' he told Vichitra Sharma of *Contour* magazine back in 1980, 'to get a sponsor in Delhi'. The same article notes that 'To add to the woes, Delhi TV gave him clear-cut instructions: "I hope you will be decently dressed in the studio" (hinting at his skinfitting leotards)' (Sharma 1980). His audience did not include Indian classical dancers who resisted recognizing Astad as a serious dancer. This lack of attention from the Indian dance community led him to depression; however, he never lost his commitment to dance. He continued to work in isolation as the only male modern dancer in India who created work from a blank slate.

Astad struggled also when presenting his dance in the West since Indian dance only meant the classical and not his innovative modern Indian dance. His search for an audience in India that could appreciate modern dance continued in the 1980s.

Anita Ratnam pointed out that Astad was recognized in many parts of the world before he was in India:

When you're invited to perform for the royal families . . . to choreograph on the famous Maya Plisetskaya, you know you're something special. Before India even acknowledged its amazingly brilliant son, the world had already seen what Astad Deboo could do, the magic that he could create, deeply introspective, a go-to favourite for international collaborators, his signature, his presence, his artistry, his thought, his poetics were everywhere. (int., August 2021)

Since Astad had missed recognition from Indian classical dancers, especially in his early career when he was forging his path, I interviewed prominent Indian classical Bharatanatyam dancers, Alarmel Valli and Malavika Sarukkai, in August 2021. Although they respected Astad and his courage and dedication to his art, these artists had not openly supported his art, his innovations in movement, space, nor his humanitarian work with marginalized communities.

Malavika, who spoke warmly and thoughtfully about Astad as 'an inventive artist', regretted that the Indian dance community did not embrace this artist 'as they should have when Astad was alive. I felt everything came pouring out when he passed away.' (int., August 2021; same for subsequent quotes).[3] Why was this adulation not showered on Astad when he needed it during his life? Malavika saw such holding back of appreciation as a shortcoming of the dance fraternity; she admitted that such recognition would have been enormously significant for Astad. She added that 'it was a kind of personal learning' for her to express openly her appreciation for any artist who moves her and not to keep her feelings 'masked'. Further, she wanted other dancers and herself to have the 'strength to be vulnerable', by sharing in words not only their intellectual assessments but, even more importantly, their emotional responses to dance. She asked herself if she could 'personally be more generous in [her] own interactions with people'. Malavika admired Astad's total dedication to dance. She was taken with Astad's 'visual design' in performance, the way his body caught light, as well as his relationship with fabric that she described as 'his partner'. She too regarded Astad's performances as 'experiences'.

Malavika was deeply touched by one experience of Astad's friendship and generosity towards her. She was to perform at the Alchemy

---

3 I am grateful to Yasmine Stafford, a Mumbai-based dancer who was good friends with Malavika Sarukkai, for kindly putting me in touch with her.

Festival in London in 2010 when her lighting designer from India could not join her because he did not get a visa. The performance was sold out and she was very stressed. When Astad learned about the situation, he told her not to worry. He watched the rehearsal, sitting on the floor with a notebook, jotting down the lighting cues. Although Southbank Theatre had its own technical crew, Astad 'was the only person', recalled Malavika, 'who would even know something about my dance and could follow it'. Before the performance, Astad came backstage and said, 'Malavika, don't worry about anything, just go out there and dance. Even if the lights don't really follow you, don't hassle about it, don't even think about it.' That meant a lot to Malavika. Coming from a fellow artist who understood the nerve-wracking experience of performing to a packed house, Astad's encouragement held a lot of weight. She knew he would do his best with the lights, guiding her through the entire performance.

Malavika echoed Astad when she shared that she does not have many mentees, since

> most people don't have the mental, emotional, spiritual stamina to train hard. And I'm saying, why should dance be easy? Why? It isn't; if you just make it easy, you're missing all the adventure [and] the difficult routes. It will be a wonderful learning experience; we come through it with some value in our life, something which is added to our life because dance is that, right?

When Astad was in the hospital, he called Malavika and told her about his illness. He also said that 'he really respected my work. He needn't have said it, but he did. And that was terribly moving for me that an artist chose to express himself to another artist when he knew he was seriously ill.'

Alarmel Valli spoke generously as Astad's friend who knew the difficulties that he faced 'as a true pioneer' (int., August 2021; same for subsequent quotes).[4] Astad danced because he felt compelled to, noted

---

4 I am grateful to Ramaa Bharadvaj for putting me in touch with Alarmel Valli.

Valli, not to impress others. 'To be a pioneer in any field, when you're walking a path that is not trodden, less trodden, least trodden, there is always a problem.' Valli noted that in the 1970s and 80s, 'people were purists', who could not accept Astad's artistry presented in his original and inventive ways.

I have had chats with Astad that it hurt him [. . .]. He deserved recognition because of his artistry, his vast creative expression and the depth of his expression. But I think people's minds were much more closed in those days [. . .]. For Astad there was a sadness, something poignant and forlorn because he did not receive recognition until rather late in life.

Valli endorsed Astad's intense need to belong to his homeland as an Indian dancer; she recognized that although he was 'global in the best sense, his strength came from being rooted in our ethos, tradition and culture [along with being] an intrepid, feisty explorer'. She regarded Astad as a courageous traveller 'both physical and metaphysical in the best sense of the term. How else would you describe the enormous range of his artistic expression, the sheer diversity?' He grew many different roots and connected with many geographies and dance influences, 'yet his work had grown organically, it never seemed to have elements added on at one stage or another'.

Valli recognized Astad was 'an original who did not fit into any definition even of the contemporary'. She regarded him as a visionary, ahead of his time. Anyone who is a true artist or 'a true seeker appreciated Astad for what he was and his work'. For Valli, as for Astad, 'poetry, music and dance go hand in hand'. Astad could internalize the music, hence he could respond not only to 'the notes but to the pauses between the notes', making his body sing and the music dance.

Valli gave credit to Astad who had 'paved the way, made the path easy for others'. The generation of contemporary Indian dancers that followed Astad recognizes his pioneering influence. They credit him for building the path for male solo dancers in the 1970s and 1980s, a journey that had been particularly challenging before his time. His artistic experimentation and innovation not only propelled his own art but also established a model for them to emulate.

Astad's Legacy for the Next Generation of Contemporary Indian Dancers

Vikram Iyengar, a dancer of both Kathak and contemporary Indian dance paid a beautiful tribute to Astad (int. with Ratnam, July 2021; same for subsequent quotes). Vikram believes that Astad felt strongly about easing future Indian contemporary dancers' pursuit of their visions, to be bold and to experiment as they wished, to make sure that they would not face setbacks as Astad had. Astad took time and trouble to make phone calls and keep in touch with younger dancers. When he visited Kolkata, he would just call Vikram 'for no reason at all', Vikram shared, just for a short chat even if they could not meet—'He just kept an eye out for you, in a protective kind of way.' For Vikram, 'that kind of generosity is very difficult to come by.'

Astad was able to create a 'stillness' that enticed his audience. Vikram experienced this when he first saw Astad perform a triptych at the Interface Festival in Kolkata in 2004. Vikram was confused and frustrated, even wondered if this could be called dance—but he could not look away. Astad exuded a riveting energy that Vikram believes 'is something inborn. Astad had it even off-stage.' He appreciated how long and deep Astad had thought of any choreography so that even the smallest action on stage had a certain weight of intention. Vikram aspired to such detailed work in his own process and dance form.

Vikram regards Astad 'as a beacon and an icon [who has shown] that it's fine for men to dance'. When Anita asked about Astad's pedagogy, Vikram said that Astad's creation of his syncretic form 'is unrepeatable in a sense and perhaps even unteachable'. Some dances like Astad's 'should be unrepeatable', he contended. Now that Astad had passed away, he had taken his dance with him, so some people will never see him perform. After all, that is both the beauty and evanescence of dance—it vanishes with the dancer.

Another male dancer, Deepak Kurki Shivaswamy, echoed other dancers in noting Astad's talent in giving spectators an 'experience', even though they might not really get what he presented. Deepak's advice was to 'shut that brain, just watch' (int. with Ratnam, July 2021; same for subsequent quotes). He admired how Astad approached him or other collaborators 'as an artist. He never walked in as an "institution".' Deepak had observed how down-to-earth Astad was when talking to artists from different backgrounds. Astad could as easily engage with kids in school, creating 'a human connection'. That was Astad's 'magical' quality as man and artist.

Deepak, like Vikram, was moved by Astad's generosity in looking out for the younger generation of dancers. Astad would simply call Deepak to come by and help with the sound, although he did not quite need Deepak since he had technicians for that. But Astad wanted Deepak as an artist to be in the same space with him and even paid him for his time. It was meaningful for Deepak to observe an artist like Astad go through the process of dealing with dancers, with music, light, costume and the theatre. It was revealing to see how Astad configured the end of his performances when Deepak saw Astad boldly 'demand(ing) from the audience: "This is time-based, this is dance and I'm here to be with you."'

'There is no pedagogy of Astad's,' said Deepak, quoting the senior dancer: '"I danced everywhere, I took decisions."' Astad would try a dance move, and if it did not suit his body, he would move on. Deepak noted that such a pedagogy is not based on one dance form—'It was almost like, find your dance.' He found different traces of styles such as Kathakali or jazz in Astad's work, 'but you never see the form. You just see the dance, the performance. That's something that we tend to forget. It's about performance.'

Deepak had observed Astad's enticing performative energy when he captivated an ordinary person from Ranga Shankara watching Astad twirl and counting all the circles. That person was mesmerized by just one movement without any concern about the dance form. 'It is just a layman enjoying dance,' said Deepak, 'and that's the pedagogy, at the end of the day.' He admired the fact that Astad 'never stopped dancing'. Dancers were definitely not essential during the pandemic and they would wonder what they were doing. Astad used to call and inquire warmly if Deepak had any financial or artistic problems. 'Whatever happens, just dance,' Astad told him, 'because that's why we started dancing.'

Astad for 'always [met] people at a human level', Deepak pointed out. Astad was always democratic with whomever he met, never treating people differently. He gave his full presence even if he had a few minutes. Deepak noted philosophically that such an ability to treat all people in the same way is not something that one learns in school. 'You learn this from a person's life'—these are Astad's gifts bestowed on the younger generation of dancers. Like Vikram, Deepak agreed with Anita's assessment that for their generation of male dancers, Astad was somebody who truly walked his talk, encouraging contemporary Indian dancers to believe in themselves and their art. Astad's qualities as a human being and as an artist that guided his life and his dance provided a model for dancers coming after him.

PART III

Pioneering Choreography with Marginalized Communities

FIGURES 33–34. Astad with Manipuri dancers. *Photograph by Farrokh Chothia.*

CHAPTER 7

Deaf Actors and Dancers in Kolkata, Washington DC and Chennai

The Action Players, Kolkata

While performing in Kolkata in 1988, Astad asked Zarine Chowdhury, a theatre director who worked with the Action Players, a company of deaf actors, if he could conduct a workshop with them. Empathetic to their disability, Astad was curious about teaching dance to deaf actors and if it would enable them to discover how body movements and expression of emotions could be enlivening, even liberating. But since they could not hear music or sounds from nature, how would they learn to dance?

The workshop that Astad conducted was an eye-opener; he both taught and learnt. Initially, he could not connect with the deaf actors, but after using techniques of improvisation, mirroring and counting rhythmic beats, he succeeded (Deboo 2018). From the beginning, Astad appreciated that these actors were hard-working and eager to learn and he was gratified that the director let him conduct the workshop for three weeks, culminating in a modest performance.

Astad began his process of teaching deaf people by recognizing the importance of counting as a group; counting enabled them to follow the music's rhythm despite not hearing it. This initial work with the Action Players led to Astad choreographing several shows for this company, and organizing exchanges between them and students at Gallaudet University in Washington, DC, which had been founded in 1864 as a school 'for deaf and blind children'. Subsequently, Astad shared his techniques for training and performing with deaf groups in various locations in India and beyond.

In 1993, Astad choreographed *Dancing Dolphins* with the Action Players using a dance language that he had developed over nearly two decades. He evoked a mood of prayer set to the alaap in Dhrupad-style singing by the Gundecha Brothers.[1] *Dancing Dolphins* was presented again in 1995, entertaining the audience with well-executed mime sequences depicting characters such as a barber, a washerman and a cobbler. The programme also included adaptations of three poems from Vikram Seth's *Beastly Tales from Here and There* (1991). The second part included Astad's solo in abstract dance. Astad, as a tough taskmaster, made the actors work hard and he was proud of their performance. He considered himself as a catalyst in drawing out the actors' performance.

The Action Players performed *Dancing Dolphins* with Astad in New Delhi in 1995, having been flown there from Kolkata courtesy of Indian Airlines. Reviews of this show were equally positive. Ashish Mohan Khokar, writing in the *Times of India*, complimented Astad's use of mime as it brought artistry to the actors' joyful rendition of characters like Miss World that delighted the audience. Seth's *Beastly Tales* were depicted in dance— the world of media and advertising were conveyed in *The Frog* and *The Nightingale*, performing arts were showcased in *The Crocodile* and *The Monkey* and the corporate world in *The Hare* and *The Tortoise*. Khokar admired how Astad could make the actors look professional. Further, 'only an art like [Astad's] could make the dolphins dance to his frequency' (Khokar 1995).

The Action Players performed *A Tapestry of Movement*, using theatre and dance at the University of Poona campus, as well as in Jamshedpur and in Mumbai at NCPA's Experimental Theatre and Prithvi Theatre. Writing in the *Daily*, a reviewer commented that

---

1 An alaap is the introductory section of a Dhrupad performance, featuring slow, improvised intonations of recurring syllables without words. The duration can extend up to an hour, depending on the artist's skill.

Astaad [sic], Zarine and their team of actors and technicians are so down to earth about their work and their lives. [. . .] The second half of the show is a tapestry of movement, woven together to some exotic music (which has always been the hallmark of Astaad's productions and performances). [. . .] The shows have been possible thanks to the generosity of Indian Airlines, Oberoi Hotel, Dodsal India and others. (SS 1995)

In these performances, Astad demonstrated his hallmark selection of eclectic music—Gregorian chants and other fusion sounds.

Chowdhury, director of the Action Players, explained that not all hearing-impaired people knew the same language, hence, when they performed in other cities, they needed translators to understand each other. The Action Players, she explained, used American sign language, whereas India's diversity in languages has managed to create 'dialects' in sign language depending on the mother tongue of the hearing impaired.

Because of his success in working with deaf actors in Kolkata, Astad had an opportunity to work in 1992 at Gallaudet University, a world leader in educating the deaf. He was introduced (through his cousin's brother-in-law) to the artistic director of the Performing Arts Department of the Model Secondary School for the Deaf (MSSD) at Gallaudet. Astad ended up working with high-school students for nearly six years on different projects; altogether, he remained connected to Gallaudet until 2002. One year, Astad brought Gallaudet students on a tour to India. Gallaudet then invited 15 Action Players to the US for a month-long camp where they found many more facilities for the deaf than were available in India. In 2002, Gallaudet hosted a festival for the deaf with participants from 70 countries and Astad was selected to represent India with his deaf students.

I discovered Astad's rich activities at Gallaudet during the 1990s through Mary Ann Whitten, who knew Astad during that time. Astad had worked with Tim McCarty, a faculty member of Gallaudet's MSSD in the late 1990s, recalled Mary Ann, and at least once they had organized a joint performance with students from MSSD and India.[2] Tim McAfee, director of the Performing Arts Department at Gallaudet, also invited Astad to conduct a workshop to be followed by a performance. This led to Astad serving as an artist-in-residence who choreographed dance for the deaf students for their upcoming concert.

Astad had evolved a teaching process with a strict counting regimen whereby he could choreograph synchronized movements and mirroring techniques that required quick responses. The counting followed an eight-beat cycle, progressing from slow to medium to fast tempos, similar to how the basic Indian-classical-dance *adavus* are taught in three speeds. Deaf students mastered this approach, performing with a level of synchronization that astonished audiences who could hear the music, even though the dancers could not.

Gallaudet's Young Scholars Program held summer camps for 15- to-18-year-old deaf students from across the United States, which focused on a particular country each year. In 1996, India was selected and Astad was asked to curate events for the American students, exposing them to Indian dance with the help of local Indian artists living in Washington DC. The programme also included documentaries on India, a visit to a Hindu temple, a fashion show and 'theatre [training]

---

2 I owe this connection to Gulshan Deboo. Mary Ann and her husband Ben, both US diplomats, worked for what was then the US Information Service in India between 1984 and 1988, when they met Astad, became good friends and kept in touch. Astad often visited them at their other postings and in San Francisco after they retired. Astad was known for always remembering his friends' birthdays, so Mary Ann was puzzled when she did not hear from him in January 2021 on her birthday. She had sent an email to Gulshan on 11 April 2021, on hearing about Astad's passing, noting that 'it is painful to lose such a dear, longtime friend'.

After Tim McCarty left Gallaudet, he began his own company, Quest Arts for Everyone, which produced QuestFest, a visual theatre festival for the deaf for several years. In 2010, QuestFest organized an international gathering that performed at Gallaudet.

with Mike Lamaitola [who] took some stories from the Panchatantra.' (Bhaskar 2002). The month-long 'India experience' culminated in a theatre performance of Panchatantra stories and a dance that Astad had choreographed.

This Young Scholars Program entered its second stage when the curator of the first phase organized a visit to her or his country for the American students. In 1998, Astad set up a three-week tour of six cities in India, prioritizing opportunities for the students to experience high-quality performances. He then returned to Gallaudet to choreograph a work with American students along with one of his best actor/dancers from the Action Players. In the Program's third and final phase, in 1999, Astad and the Kolkata group returned to Gallaudet and spent a month with 20 Americans in the summer programme.

The International Deaf Way II Arts Festival and Symposium, held in July 2002 at Gallaudet, included deaf companies from Cuba, Germany, Israel, China, Japan and India. Astad was selected to represent India (from 80 countries, with 200 applicants) with the Action Players and with R. Karthika, who had trained in Bharatanatyam at Chennai's Clarke School for the Deaf. The organizers wanted Astad to include a deaf Indian classical dancer.[3] Astad choreographed a piece called *First Step* for Karthika because this was the initial move of trust and communication for her to dance outside India and for an international audience. Astad's choreography used Karthika's training in Bharatanatyam but he transformed her movements into his signature style that was danced to music by the Brazilian composer and performer Egberto Gismonti. Astad also had Karthika mirror him, so the choreography changed with each performance. Karthika was a quick learner. Dr Leelavati, principal of the Clarke School, remarked that even Astad was surprised by how effortlessly she adapted her Bharatanatyam movements to his style of

---

3 Later in 2005, Astad worked with the Clarke School for the Deaf in Chennai. At this point, he only choreographed for R. Karthika who attended that school.

dancing (Mahesh 2002). Sixteen-year-old Karthika communicated to reviewer Mahesh, 'When I dance, I forget myself.' Karthika's 20-minute performance, displaying her talent and confidence, included *First Step* with Astad and two solo items, *Pushpanjali* and *Thillana*, which were rendered by the voices of prominent Bharatanatyam dancers Anita Ratnam and Ramaa Bharadvaj.

Raising funds for Deaf Way II was a lengthy and difficult process; the festival paid for some airfares and Astad raised additional funds from the Tata Group of companies, HSBC, HDFC, the Jamshed and Shireen Guzdar Trust, Air Freight, Eveready Industries and *Ananda-bazar Patrika*. Astad was heartened that many Indian dancers helped through the outreach of the web magazine *Narthaki*. Musicians provided recording services for Karthika without charge.

At Deaf Way II, the Action Players danced *Circle of Feelings* choreographed by Astad. He described this 40-minute work as creating an awareness of space for the performers along with mirroring and improvisation where they followed Astad's lead. Astad used the rasas in the first part of *Circle of Feelings*, beginning with bhakti rasa, then exploring the rasas of joy, despair, anger and frustration in a 22-minute piece. The second part featured robotic movements reflecting our mechanized modern lives. The final part expressed joy; it was accompanied by the Japanese percussion group, Kodo. Astad used the Indian artists' familiarity with abhinaya in choreographing *Circle of Feelings*. 'I made them work extremely hard', said Astad to reviewer Someshwar in *India Abroad*, which described Astad as 'India's most famous contemporary dance artist'—'I had absolutely no pity. After all, the challenge before them is enormous; they had to dance to music that they cannot hear but the audience can' (Someshwar 2002).

Astad also organized performances for the deaf actors/dancers from India at the Smithsonian Institute's Meyer Auditorium and in Arlington, Jacksonville, Florida, through an old school friend Dr Anand Kuruvilla. He did not want their experience to be limited only to Deaf

Way II. These deaf artists were doing something different—like Astad in his early work. Astad was motivated by memories of his own struggles to get recognition and performance sponsors. By 2002, he was happy to use his name and influence to benefit these artists.

While in Washington DC, Astad reconnected with a Bombay friend, Satya Achayya, who had moved to DC in 1990. Satya remembered Astad in 1972 'with long hair, quite the hippie', when he had just returned from his travels abroad. Now, in DC, Astad visited her often while he was teaching at Gallaudet University. She told me that Astad always had time for his friends and that every moment with him 'was special'. Satya's own story was remarkable—as a single woman, self-described as 'a migrant', who had moved from Bangalore to Bombay to work at the US Consulate. Satya ended up as a paying guest in Shapur Baug where she 'masqueraded as a Zoroastrian!' since this residential colony was only for the Parsees. Satya cherished her time with the Deboos, savouring their dhansak lunches and noting Astad's mother's constant weaving of kustis. She was deeply touched by the abundant love and affection in their household. In 2020, Astad called Satya with news of his cancer diagnosis. Satya fondly remembered Astad as 'a very special human being. Too bad he left us when we badly need such people' (int., July 2021).

In 2002, the same year as the Deaf Way II Festival, Astad established the Astad Deboo Dance Foundation (ADDF) to support artistic work by deaf and other marginal groups in Indian society. Educational institutions' funding priorities favour reading, writing and arithmetic skills, usually leaving art at the bottom. Physically challenged students and those hindered by caste and class hierarchies are doubly disempowered when creative arts are not taught. Astad wished to use his professional renown to bring significant attention to these groups' artistic abilities. Journalist Carol Andrade noted ADDF's goals which were to establish dance as a discipline in schools and colleges with support for training and dance productions; to offer creative opportunities to people with disabilities; and to create an archive of materials for future generations. 'Eventually, with funding, the foundation hopes to create a centre where such activities can continue over the long term' (Andrade 2017). The latter, a laudatory goal, was not realized in Astad's lifetime. Nonetheless, Astad's work with the Action Players and with Gallaudet did have a cascading effect, leading to Astad sharing his skills with the Hong Kong Deaf Theatre Company, the Sena Y Verbo Deaf Theatre Group in Mexico, and then again in India with the Clarke School for the Deaf.

Clarke School for the Deaf, Chennai

Astad's journey in working with the deaf continued in Chennai with R. Karthika and other young women trained in Bharatanatyam. I was fortunate to be in Chennai in 2005 on a Fulbright Research Award to work on my book *Contemporary Indian Dance: New Creative Choreography in India and the Diaspora* (2011). Astad was a key figure in that study, although in my scholarly life up to this time, I had not followed his career. When I approached him, he was characteristically generous with his time and resources.

Astad invited me to rehearsals where I observed his collaborative spirit that honoured and respected these deaf students' Bharatanatyam training before he adapted and reinvented from his own style. Since these students were proficient in the classical style, Astad went beyond his usual technique of counting in eights when choreographing for deaf actors/dancers, to counting in four-, seven- and nine-beat cycles. He was a demanding teacher, not easily satisfied, drawing out his students' abilities in movement and expression and teaching his dance idiom with slow movement and balancing poses. For this group, Astad choreographed a piece called *ContraPosition*, dancing with them and deploying the Navarasas from the *Natyasastra* as a linking mechanism.

During breaks between rehearsals, Astad shared in an interview with me that his extensive travels, both within India and abroad, enriched his art by exposing him to diverse audiences, whose reactions provided valuable insights. What was most important was that '[he] is still working and will continue to work' (int., October 2005). When I asked him if he could imagine settling down with a dance company, Astad replied that, after 40 years of constant travel and never spending a full year in one country, he could not see himself doing so at this stage of his life. He admitted that travel had become a way of life for him, and nothing was 'exciting' enough to ground him in one place. He constantly needed a change of environment, of food, music, people, though not change in his work: 'My work is with me all the time.' Perhaps, working with the deaf involved its own kind of mental travel with new challenges that Astad faced in teaching his style to them.

I witnessed several rehearsals of Astad's moving choreography for *ContraPosition* and saw its performance in Mumbai. *ContraPosition* opened with joyful *nritya*, in which dancers in green sequined tops and loose pants created formations in lines and circles using Bharatanatyam mudras, neck and arm movements that Astad then disrupted with modern dance physicality such as a taut palm or a rigidly held fist. Astad's solo, performed in a loose salwar with a sequined brownish-gold sleeveless top, showcased clear, minimalist lines that highlighted his keen focus and precise control in executing emotion-infused abstract movements. Poignantly, the performers' hearing aids were visible behind their ears, not quite like earrings though evoking a type of aharya.

In *ContraPosition*, Astad relied on the dancers' familiarity with abhinaya, part of their Bharatanatyam training. He individualized each of the eight dancers as they portrayed the Navarasas. Shringara rasa, which depicts love—romantic, maternal or between friends—was portrayed physically and erotically through an evocatively lyrical duet. Astad, as Lord Krishna, and Karthika, as Radha, Krishna's chief consort, embodied this rasa with sculpturesque poses and longing looks. The other female dancers displayed dejection and rejection, as if representing the gopis trying to attract Krishna. If Radha was upset with Krishna's flirtation with the gopis, he cajoled and won her back. Karthika's Bharatanatyam expertise meant she could be both rooted and inventive.

The performance then depicted bhayanaka rasa, the sentiment of fear, with the dancers cowering and covering their eyes. Next, bibhatsya rasa, representing disgust, was powerfully rendered by Astad in a solo under a bright red spotlight. Drawing on his Kathakali training, Astad's protruding eyes, contorted and wide-open mouth and expansive stance, balanced on the sides of his feet, conveyed a striking sense of other-worldliness. As in Anita Ratnan's contemporary Indian dance work entitled *7 Graces*, in which she portrays disgust vividly, so does Astad in *ContraPosition*—an intensity rarely seen in classical Indian dance during the portrayal of this emotion. But it can be cathartic for audiences to see disgust represented openly and forcefully since this emotion is rife in our violence-prone world. In *ContraPosition*, disgust gave way to the emotions of sorrow, grief and sadness, karuna rasa, which Astad expressed in Kathakali style through his quivering mouth as the other dancers offered solace to the grief-stricken figure.

The dancers' costumes then changed to long, bright red skirts trimmed in black with glittery sequin tops as they moved in a joyful sequence. Astad entered in an ankle-length, glowing purple costume with white churidar, executing chakkars as he joined the dancers, weaving in and out of their formations. In a characteristic Astad movement, the dancers made a tight fist which they alternately held close to their bodies and then thrust out, evoking feelings of valour and heroism—vira rasa. In the finale, the dancers adopted the gesture of *adaab* typical of Astad's choreography as they acknowledged and thanked the audience in all corners of the theatre. I was touched by these deaf dancers exuding confidence in their movement and facial expression. Amit Heri's original music composition moved evocatively from melodious (for love) to jagged, disjointed sounds (for fear and jealousy). Astad led the dancers in an improvised modern dance sequence wherein they placed their taut palms in front of the face. In this move as in others, the dancers rose to the challenge of embodying Astad's signature style.

Astad told me that although teaching these dancers how to convey rasa with abstract movement was difficult, 'We've been able to dissolve the bridge from a very Indian movement to an Astad Deboo gesture'. (De 2004). Dance proved to be a powerful tool of self-assurance that the women would carry over from the stage into their daily lives.

Reviews across India were ecstatic about *ContraPosition*, admiring the achievement of these deaf dancers who enabled spectators to 'hear' the sounds of silence even as they expressed emotions powerfully. At times, as reviewer Baptista (2005) commented, Astad silenced the music without telling the dancers, which made the audience 'experience and empathize with the soundless world experienced by the dancers. The dancers continued to dance without music since their skill and talent enabled them to be in rhythmic unison.' It was a very successful show not only for the accomplished deaf dancers' performance but also for stunning visual effects and striking costumes in bold colours by designer Aruna Rai. Lighting and stage design by Sunil Shanbag and Ratan Batliboi respectively illuminated the emotions of love, valour and fear that the dance showcased.

The year 2004 marked 16 years, since 1988, of Astad's work with deaf people through dance and drama. The women dancers gained a lot from this show. Reviewer Sharavati Choksi recognized that their intense practice of 'five hours a day for three months' paid off a thousand-fold since they found that working with Astad 'opened a door for [them], which [they] never knew existed' (Choksi 2004). Astad achieved more than dance and performance skills for these dancers; indeed, they gained self-esteem as artists and as human beings.

Astad as performer and tour manager put his heart and soul into arranging 75 performances of *ContraPosition* from 2004 to 2007—across India, in Bangalore, New Delhi, Mumbai, and abroad in Malaysia,

Singapore, Granada, Barcelona and Antwerp. The dancers confidently showcased their art to diverse audiences, embracing the thrill of learning something new each day and pursuing their passion without hesitation. Reviewer Sejal Mehta (2005) found them 'extremely endearing . . . It's their spirit that takes you by surprise'.

ContraPosition was selected as the opening show at the 20th Summer Deaflympics in Melbourne, held between 5 and 16 January 2005, for which Astad created a special five-minute celebratory dance. With the dancers, he had wished to stage *Kabuliwalah*—a short story by Rabindranath Tagore about an unconventional friendship and affection between a young Bengali girl and an Afghan moneylender—but he did not have enough time. In 2007, the group from Clarke School danced for India's president A. P. J. Abdul Kalam at Rashtrapati Bhavan, New Delhi, when Astad received the Padma Shri at age 60.

During the 2000s, when Astad was choreographing for groups, he was involved with other creative activities—a solo dance in March 2004 for the Jahan-e-Khusrau festival, where along with artists like Shubha Mudgal, a prominent North Indian classical vocalist, Astad captured the mystical element of Sufi style. In September 2004, two video films were showcased at the Max Mueller Bhavan, Mumbai. One of these films featured a dance workshop led by Astad Deboo, highlighting his June 2004 work with German deaf students, where movement served as a foundation for building trust.

Astad's gifts to deaf groups transcend dance skills; it includes opportunities that he created for them to perform and receive warm accolades as they shared the stage with their mentor, teacher and choreographer. This is in the same vein as Astad's work with Manipuri dancers, which I will now discuss.

CHAPTER 8

Dancers from Manipur in India's Northeast

'*Rhythm Divine* believes dance is a system of ideas. Dance is not a method. Together with music, dance can enrich the moral, the material and the intellectual. Together, they can make a newer beginning.'—Astad Deboo, Choreographer's Note, *Rhythm Divine I*

During the 1990s, Astad was keen to involve performers of different Indian dance styles in his artistic work. But most of them were not forthcoming; the few who were interested were afraid of incurring their classical gurus' displeasure. 'One day [in 1998] a window opened,' Astad said in a long text emailed to me in 2017 titled 'Personal Piece', in which he reflects on his long association with Manipuri artists since 1998. Initially, he was invited to choreograph a performance for Zee TV's first television award night. Accompanying this invitation was a budget to travel and explore ideas. So, Astad left for Manipur, a state in the north-eastern corner of India, whose dance and arts remain marginal to other classical Indian dance styles showcased in major cities.

When Astad visited Imphal, the capital city of Manipur, in 1998, he did not know that his connection with artists of this region would extend for over 16 years. Initially, Astad wanted to investigate if Manipuri Thang-Ta (sword and spear) martial art practitioners could become part of his choreographic landscape. With them he created an innovative choreography called *Celebration*. After that, Astad worked with Pung Cholom drummers, who dance with their drums in Astad's choreography in *Rhythm Divine I*, which premiered in 2005 at NCPA in Mumbai, and in *Rhythm Divine II: The River Runs Deep*, premiering in 2014 in New Delhi.

During his initial visit to Imphal, Astad was moved by a paradoxical combination of the geographical beauty of this region and the rampant violence it was subject to. Manipur has an ongoing history of insurgency against the Indian state whose military presence to fight separatist sympathizers is deeply resented by local people.[1] This history and Astad's

---

1 The history of Manipur is not widely known across India or abroad. Originally called Kangleipak, the region was renamed Manipur, meaning 'Abode of Jewels', in 1714 when King Pamheiba adopted Hinduism as the state religion. It has remarkable natural beauty, with an oval-shaped valley surrounded by nine hills, evoking a precious gem. Manipuris constitute three main ethnic groups—the majority Meiteis, and the Nagas and Kuki-Chins. The Meiteis are not classified as tribal, though they (like other minority groups such as the Sidis, Indians of African origin) are demanding 'Scheduled Tribe' status that would ensure them certain governmental benefits. Aspects of this history of strife and turmoil feature in Astad's choreography.

Manipur has had a history of ethnic violence and insurgency. A separatist movement seeking independence from India was fuelled by grievances over the region's underdevelopment and the exploitation of its natural resources by the Indian government. Violence escalated in the late 1970s with social unrest and attacks on police and government buildings. In response, the Manipur state government appealed to the central government in New Delhi for support. This led to widespread resentment due to the increased powers granted to these forces under the Armed Forces (Special Powers) Act (AFSPA) of 1958. The act authorized indiscriminate arrests and the use of deadly force against individuals deemed terrorists.

Between 1980 and 2004, Manipur was labelled as 'a disturbed area', which allowed Indian security forces and army to exert violence, torture and enforced disappearances. Among the numerous civilian protests against military violence, one stands out: a 500-week hunger strike by Irom Sharmila Chanu (b.1972), who demanded the abolition of AFSPA and an end to the use of deadly force against suspected terrorists. In 2016, Chanu ended her hunger strike after 16 years.

But ethnic disturbance continues to plague Manipur. In 2023, violence broke out between the Meiteis of the Imphal Valley and the Kuki tribal community in

first impressions of this region seeped into his consciousness. He saw ordinary people overwhelmed by hunger and lack of housing. 'And yet,' Astad remarked, 'their lives are heroic. Even today, when I recall the scene, my heart splinters into a thousand pieces; and then there is a smile. Cause that's life. And somehow it percolates into our dance. That's art' (pers. email, 2017).

Astad met Guru Seityaban Singh, head of Shree Shree Govindji Nat Sankirtan in Imphal, with whom Manipuri dancers trained. Astad knew that these artists were protective, even possessive of their art; hence he sought the guru's permission to work with them. At their first meeting in 1998, Guru Seityaban recognized Astad's sincerity and dedication as a serious artist—after all, as the 1995 winner of the Sangeet Natak Akademi's Creative Artist Award, Astad would not act as a superficial passer-by interested in appropriating Manipuri artistic traditions. Astad believed that both for the artists and for himself, 'it was a unique experience of weaving their martial art forms into my movements, blended [. . .] into a new vocabulary' (pers. email, 2017). Astad always ensured that their traditional practice was represented with respect and acknowledgement of their discipline wherever they performed.

Astad choreographed a 15-minute work called *War* with Manipuri martial artists with the blessing of their mentor, Guru Devabrata Singh. *War* was so successful that Astad was inspired to explore possibilities of working further with these artists. He was impressed with the martial artists' remarkable agility and dynamism along with their willingness to try Astad's movement vocabulary. Astad created *Celebration* with four Manipuri Thang-Ta martial artists who performed to the music of Louis

---

the surrounding hills. The violence, sparked by a dispute over the continuing Meitei demand for Scheduled Tribe status, led to at least 221 deaths, the displacement of more than 60,000 people, and the widespread destruction of homes and religious structures.

For my discussion of exclusions that nations regularly impose on marginal groups, see Ketu H. Katrak (2021).

Banks and Sivamani—a *tour de force* that seamlessly connected Astad's abstract, meditative, introspective modern dance with Manipuri martial arts. Astad opened the work with his hands outstretched, as if making an offering. In one interaction Astad stamped his feet to draw the drummer into an accelerating rhythm, persuading him to join the dance.

Astad's musical and rhythmic finesse synchronized his dance style with warrior-like techniques of martial arts, thrilling the audience with energetic acrobatic movements that featured swords and spears as stage props. The martial artists' movements appeared to be both graceful as dancers and martial like warriors. They used the floor and leaped high in the air creating a thrilling spectacle with their movement and expression.

Astad was interested in the drummers' training as dancers and acrobats, 'something which I wanted to incorporate in my work and wanted to see if it was possible' (Deboo 2017a). Initially, Astad worked with martial artists by observing phrases of movement in Thang-Ta. Interviewer Sangeeta Barooah Pisharoty asked Astad what attracted him to the war dance form—was it the use of clear-cut steps and definite turns similar to Astad's style? Astad responded: 'We need our feet to move. So, in Thang-Ta, even when they will pick up their leg and take it forward, it is a distinct move, while it may not be the case in most Indian dances' (Deboo 2017a).

Astad was a master collaborator open to generous give-and-take with the highly trained Manipuri dancers. He discussed the collaborative process with them; it involved explanations, demonstrations and listening. This could lead to arguments or, at times, silence. The process was long and arduous; hours of work often yielded only a few seconds of choreography. Astad wanted them to work hard with complete dedication. 'The form demands it,' he said forthrightly. And then, in his typical perfectionist way, he added: 'I keep saying, if it doesn't kill you, then you're no good. I mean you have to go at it full time. You can't afford to dip in and out' (pers. email, 2017).

After working with Thang-Ta artists, Astad explored the beautiful art of Pung Cholom, where drummers leap high and spin mid-air while playing their drums and dancing, to create *Rhythm Divine I* (2005). That same year, Astad was invited by the Government of India's Ministry of Culture to create a 25-minute work for the Frankfurt Book Fair where India was the country of honour. Prominent artists such as Chandralekha and Gundecha Brothers were presenting their work. Astad managed to get Guru Seityaban Singh to collaborate with him to showcase Manipuri drum dancers in *Rhythm Divine I*. This was so well received that both Astad and Singh, described by Astad as 'a young dynamic guru with a fine mind', wanted to collaborate further. In 2007, excerpts from *Rhythm Divine I* and *Celebration* were presented at the Festival of India in Belgium and Spain. It was in Spain that Astad received news that he was to receive the Padma Shri award from the Government of India. Indeed, Astad's dedication and effort had successfully brought Manipuri artists from the margins into mainstream performing arts centres in India and abroad, leading to their artistic exposure and financial benefit. It was also an affirmation for Astad that contemporary concepts could 'cohabit' with traditional drumming from Manipur.

In 2008, the Government of India commissioned Astad to create a work for the coronation of the king of Bhutan, Jigme Khesar Namgyal Wangchuk, which was scheduled for 6 November that year. Guru Seityaban Singh played a key role in helping Astad work with 30 Manipuri drummers. The performance in a huge stadium with a large audience was not appropriate for Astad's choreography that, according to Sanjiv Shah, aimed to elicit 'the inner spirit of the viewer', rather than entertaining the audience with a spectacle (2010: 34). Nonetheless, Astad triumphed; his eclectic music and slow movements resonated with both royalty and commoners, who were entranced by the profound experience he created with the Manipuri dancers.

I experienced *Rhythm Divine I* at Delhi's open-air venue of Purana Quila in 2005. The programme opened with a moving body on centre stage wrapped by a large, amorphous plastic sheet—like a foetus inside a womb—surrounded by kneeling bodies. Astad's body emerged from the plastic as he greeted the audience with a low and challenging back-bend paying homage to spectators and to divine powers. The soulful sound of an operatic soprano intoned the profound feeling reflected in Astad's body. (Astad had told me in interviews that he found the operatic voice very inspiring for his movements.) In the performance's first two segments, a pervasive sense of devotion turned everything into an offering to a higher realm, drawing on the reverence and spirituality inherent in the Pung Cholom tradition. The programme notes asked: 'Is this choreography or is it philosophy?' Indeed, Astad's movement evoked philosophical questions about survival in strife-ridden Manipur.

As *Rhythm Divine I* continued, Manipuri dancers in white dhotis entered with *khartals* (brass cymbals) attached to red cloth; they carried them silently in their hands. Astad opened his arms as the dancers covered their eyes with one hand, as if to block out the difficult reality of Manipur. Next, eight white-turbaned dancers entered with red sashes around their necks that would be used to tie their drums. They jumped and made half-circles in the air without the drums. Their body language evoked the drums in a deeply engaging circle of artistry.

At Purana Quila that night, a packed audience sat under the stars, watching Astad's perceptive choreography moving from slow and devotional to martial arts movements. In one section, the dancers played the *khartals* etched beautifully by the stage lights against the outdoor night sky. Astad's entrances into and exits from the group seemed at times both imperceptible and concerted. He interacted energetically with the drum dancers, imitating their movements, then leading them with his movements in a buoyant *sawal–jawab* (question–answer) sequence such as in Kathak between the dancer and the tabla player. This led to Astad's chakkars with breathtaking speed and aplomb. The ecstatic whirling seemed to call on the divine like a Sufi devotee—though Astad has stated in interviews that he does not go into a trance. Ritual gongs punctuated the choreography and then turned to silence before piercing gunshots reminded the audience of ongoing violence in Manipur. Despite this shocking rupture, the overall effect of *Rhythm Divine I* was ritualistic and meditative.

Astad used *bol cholom* (drum syllables) loudly recited with dance steps typically performed with actual drums. But here, in a creative twist, he chose to reference the drums with hand gestures and clapping, with dancers rhythmically beating their palms on the stage floor rather than wearing the drums with a sash around their necks. The performers mimed playing the 'invisible' drums with gestures, holding viewers in suspense until the last segment, when the actual drums appeared. The vivacious dancers then played the booming drums, jumping high in the air, spinning and landing, thrilling the spectators in the process.

In his 'Choreographer's Note' for *Rhythm Divine I*, Astad noted that this work created a new form that effectively expressed the theme of violence in Manipur. For this he credits Guru Seityaban, the forward-looking guru who suggested alternatives in the creative process that discovered, even invented, new ways to present traditional dance in a contemporary manner. Thematically, Astad wanted to create a disturbing work that reflected the troubled lives of Manipuri people: 'I don't design soothing dance pieces. I don't like them. I like art to have some raw, vital, earthy quality' (pers. email, 2017).

When the Pung Cholom drum dancers had first entered his life, Astad had found them, as he states in his 'Choreographer's Notes' to *Rhythm Divine II: The River Runs Deep* (2014), 'steeped in their own cultural traditions, performing with their instruments in a comforting cycle of familiar security. I wanted them to change.' Despite this desire for 'change', Astad remained deeply respectful of their traditions that he sensitively brought into his dance style. He innovated from within the traditional frame of Manipuri dance, such as taking away the drums and encouraging the dancers to work with imaginary ones. He made them realize that the sound of drums was contained in their very bodies. This aesthetic rationale was persuasive even for Manipuri traditional gurus who uncritically accepted this change.

Astad's note for *Rhythm Divine II* analysed the choreographic arc that incorporated the region's political strife. The show began on a gentle note reflecting ordinary life; then gradually, insecurity, fear and anxiety began to take over to represent how people lived with military presence. The crescendo built powerfully 'with the drums coming into play, the tempo now frantic'. Later, in his 'Personal Piece' emailed to me, Astad characterized *Rhythm Divine II* as 'a reflection of the frustrations of being within a militarized state, the rebel within and the power to overcome' (pers. email, 2017).

Rhythm Divine II is a tautly choreographed, 70-minute work (at times 80 minutes) featuring Astad and ten dancers. The piece opened in low light, with Astad centre stage in his characteristic, flowing, full-length angarkha touching the floor; he was flanked on both sides and front by bare-chested, dhoti-clad Manipuri dancers, green scarves tied at their waists. As the ones in front began their slow movements, turning from side to side as if vigilant to signs of danger, the ones next to Astad in the foreground moved forward and kneeled. The movements were punctuated only by the sound of a gong from time to time.

Astad began to move his arms to the front in his characteristic gesture of offering, as gunfire-like sounds in the background invaded the spectators' consciousness. The dancers in low plié were crouched and ready for attack; they dropped to full plié and hugged the floor as ominous sounds continued. They were in two rows facing Astad in the middle; the play of light and shadow added to the mysterious, disturbing soundscape. The dancers formed a circle facing forward, then moved into a forward fold around Astad who echoed with a low forward fold. Two dancers were in front with their arms crossed over their chests like sentries protecting the group. Then they clasped hands and faced forward, making a tight circle around Astad in the middle. With hands still clasped, they widened the circle, balancing on one foot, inching forward. Suddenly they were not visible as the spotlight caught Astad in one of his gravity-defying backbends. He turned, then rose very slowly as he moved into a low forward fold with arms touching his feet. The spotlight picked up the eerie shadows of his body, his arms like a bird in flight.

As the stage went black, the silence was broken by eight dancers entering with arms held up as if ready for attack, speaking loudly in Manipuri. Then they recited dance syllables, clapped their hands and twirled without the drums. Next, two dancers entered with round dhol drums hanging from a sash around their necks; the other eight re-entered with drums in the same manner. They began to beat the drums, jump up high and turn rapidly in the air. These awe-inspiring traditional movements in a contemporary setting always drew thunderous applause.

Astad integrated his own vocabulary of controlled gestures with the drum dancers' body movements—from leaps in the air to pirouettes on the ground—to create a piece that was both minimalist and layered. His style showcased an economy of movement along with subtle connotations stitched into the interstices of the dancers' physicality—such as hands crossed over the chest to convey guards on watch, or low crouching postures and stealthy movements to denote anticipation of oncoming danger.

Astad presented his choreography in Imphal for the first time on 15 January 2015, at the Sangeet Natak Akademi festival. A local reviewer, Chitra Ahanthem, was curious about how Manipuris would respond. She knew that even in the hands of collaborators, traditional Manipuri elements usually stayed intact, since any variation was unwelcome in Manipur, 'which has no dearth of people or organisations ever ready to take affront at whatever they feel should remain sacrosanct' (Ahanthem 2015). Purists did not accept innovation or even the slightest dilution of their customary styles. Astad had certainly not crossed such strict boundaries; however, he had carefully taken elements of Manipuri style and synergized them with his own. Astad's interventions were most appreciated by 'the younger generation who are caught in the push and pull of the state's politics and who are stifled by impositions that must not be questioned' (Athanthem 2015). Astad's 'great respect for Manipuri aesthetics' brought a welcome gust of fresh air. The traditionalists recognized that, 'inspired and challenged by Pung aesthetics', Astad considered himself 'lucky [in his own words] to be able to take the essence of Manipuri aesthetics to the world stage' (Athanthem 2015).

Astad's able ally in this choreographic transformation was the highly respected Guru Seityaban, a broad-minded teacher who also accepted the fact that the avenues for the practice of Pung were shrinking. As one of the Manipuri artists noted, when they lacked opportunities to perform, they worked on construction sites to make ends meet. This art form was mostly confined 'to courtyards on occasions like deaths and marriages—that made him [Guru Seityaban] say yes when Deboo approached him. For both, the challenges were the same and yet different' (Athanthem 2015). The same—because the challenge for them both was to retain the sanctity of the traditional practice. The difference—Astad's infusion of new life into their dance traditions by blending them with his signature style. Astad had indeed changed the lives of the Pung dancers by showcasing their art and allowing them to perform across India and abroad as respected and well-paid professional artists.

Rhythm Divine II traversed the Indian subcontinent from Delhi to Pondicherry and Kolkata to Mumbai, Jamshedpur, Bengaluru and Chennai; internationally, it was presented in European cities and in South Africa—Johannesburg, Cape Town and Pretoria. In 2018, Astad took the show to Santiago, Chile, and Sao Paulo, Brazil.

An amazing opportunity came up when the Manipuri dancers were invited with Astad as a 14-member troupe to dance at Opéra Bastille in Paris on 3 October 2016, as part of Namaste France, a 75-day festival showcasing Indian culture. *Mid-Day* proudly reported on 23 September 2016 that 'there's no stopping Astad Deboo who turns 70 next year. [. . .] Deboo is known for his masterful technique of blending folk, traditional and contemporary styles with theatre' (Uchil 2016). Astad could barely contain his excitement, saying that this was

the first time ever that a contemporary dance troupe from India has been invited to represent the country on such a large stage. It is a dream to be performing at the Opéra Bastille which is one of the most prestigious opera houses in the world. [. . .] Earlier, big venues such as these would invite only classical dancers, not contemporary [ones]. But now, the atmosphere is right internationally. After years of dancing professionally, this feels good. My persistence has paid off. I've found success. (Uchil 2016)

Since the invitation arrived only six weeks earlier, Astad and his artists did not have time to choreograph a new work; they would perform *Rhythm Divine II* with Astad who would return to France after 20 years. After Paris, the troupe performed in Lisbon, Portugal, at the Fundação Oriente, and then in Belgrade, before returning to India.

Astad touched individual lives among the Manipuri artists, as one of them, Chakpram Narendra Singh, told me:

If Astad-ji had not come into my life, I would have never reached the stage [to perform]. Only after I met Astad-ji, his advice and guidance enabled me to understand how to take care of family. When I met Astad-ji, I was in Class 8; Astad-ji encouraged me to continue my studies and today I am completing my Master's in dance and music from Manipur University where I will continue to do my PhD. (int., August 2021)

Although Astad moved on to other projects, he kept in touch with Manipuri artists, often giving financial assistance—be it for festivals or weddings. Indeed, during India's strict Covid-19 lockdown, when support for artists was non-existent, Astad financially helped many Manipuri artists and their families. Around the first anniversary of Astad's passing in December 2021, his sisters travelled to Imphal and experienced a deeply moving and reverent tribute by the dancers to Astad's memory.

In closing this chapter, I'd like to recount Bharatanatyam dancer and rasika par excellence, Ramaa Bharadvaj's 'first experience of seeing Astad on stage in 2016', when he danced with the Manipuri dancers at the Kalakshetra auditorium in Chennai (int., August 2021). Ramaa described this 'as a mystic[al] experience', one that 'first strips you, and finally when you give up resisting, only then it embraces you. Astad's performance was like that for me.' For spectators of the Manipuri dancers and Astad, the experience was entirely unfamiliar, unlike watching a Bharatanatyam performance where a well-known story and characters are portrayed through traditional mudras. Astad did not offer such predictable fare; rather, he kept open-hearted viewers engaged with emotion and thought as they followed his every move and those of his dancers.

Ramaa's further description of how she encountered *Rhythm Divine* provides an exceptional description of how a spectator can enter any of Astad's choreographic works: 'The first thing that happened was the stripping of any superficial satisfaction of having "understood" the work. Astad does this by pulling the viewer away from the intellectual obsession of wanting to know the meaning of every gesture.' Ramaa admits that her mind 'rebelled, screamed silently, wandered, turned itself off, attempted to sneak into crevices in the dance in search of "meaning" and when nothing worked, it finally gave up!' Once this occurred,

> layers of interpretations began to organically unfold within and I realized that instead of me trying to enter the dance, the dance had entered me. I was no longer a passive (even lackadaisical) receiver but had become an involved co-creator. For the next

hour, I experienced an astounding state of acute awareness as if time had come to a standstill. Having lived in the US, I have seen some exceptional modern dance companies and soloists. But I have never felt anything like that, either before Astad or after Astad. (Bharadvaj, int., July 2021)

CHAPTER 9

Street Youth of Salaam Baalak Trust, New Delhi

'The key for me was a new generation of dancers who enlarged
the circle of people who danced the dance—so as to include all
races and economic classes.'—Astad Deboo, Programme Notes,
Breaking Boundaries

As an artist with a social conscience, Astad empathized with people on
the margins of Indian society. Such was his motivation in working with
the deaf and Manipuri dancers for over 16 years. Similarly, Astad
believed that dance would bring light and hope into the difficult realities
of youth who had survived on the streets; he wanted to inspire these
youth, even transform their lives. In 2007, the New Delhi–based not-
for-profit non-governmental organization (NGO) Salaam Baalak Trust
approached Astad to work with them. Founded in 1988, this NGO sup-
ports shelters for street children in Delhi and Bombay, funded initially
by profits from Mira Nair's successful film, *Salaam Bombay* (1988). It
protects street children and provides them nutritious meals, education
and performing arts skills such as dance and puppetry. According to
their website, the children respond

> to the arts in miraculous ways—giving up drugs, making
> friends, discussing their lives, [. . .] finding themselves. [. . .]
> Many of the children have become successful choreographers,
> photographers, puppeteers, actors; their capacity to earn
> money and respect in society as artists is great. Also, they get

immense exposure to art; they travel the world and learn so much about art and life. (Salaam Baalak Trust 2024)

With his aesthetic and social vision, Astad brought his high-calibre dance to this group for whom he choreographed three performances: *Breaking Boundaries*, *Interpreting Tagore* and *Unbroken Unbowed*.

Breaking Boundaries (2009)

Shamshul Mohamed, Astad's star student from Salaam Baalak, shared his first encounter with Astad's style of dance in 2007: 'I thought, "What is this? Dance?" I could not understand it, I had not seen [this before]. My limbs hurt. Sit on a bench and lean back, freeze your legs. My reaction was "This is not dance." As practice continued, the body began to be painless.' From this initial puzzlement, Shamshul imbibed Astad's style and revered him not only as a great dancer, a legend, 'but as a mentor who gave step-by-step guidance, very necessary for an artist, how to earn a living, how to stay in this dance world even if not getting platforms, how to be disciplined' (int., August 2021).

I was fortunate to be in New Delhi in 2008 when Astad was working with street youth. I observed several rehearsals in Salaam Baalak's modest shelter space in Delhi's crowded Paharganj area. Astad was a fierce taskmaster who did not hesitate to shout at and scold the youth to inculcate discipline and focus in them. He was single-mindedly involved in teaching his style replete with challenging, slow, synchronized movements, backbends and balancing poses. After much sweat and even some tears that did not deter this maestro's resolve, he achieved the results he desired.

After rehearsal, Astad showed a totally different side of his personality—he was incredibly loving, jovial and friendly with the young dancers for whom he had bought movie tickets to the latest Bollywood extravaganza for that evening! And he would treat them all to dinner before the film. Astad made a telling comment to prominent dance critic Leela Venkataraman (2009) on his choreography in *Breaking Boundaries*: 'Shaping these kids into dancers was an incredibly demanding and ultimately rewarding task since they were only exposed to Bollywood film style free dancing.' But Astad was struck by 'their hunger and thirst to do something in life.' Venkataraman, who lauded *Breaking Boundaries*, found it heartening that an artist like Astad, rather than pursue his career, was involved 'with the plight of the less fortunate' (2009).

Almost all the Salaam Baalak youth who worked with Astad were runaways from home, escaping the violence and poverty-related challenges 'often beyond the capacity of children to withstand' (*Deccan Herald* 2009). Venkataraman's article on *Breaking Boundaries* includes testimony from a youth named Anil Kumar, who left home in Rae Bareli, Uttar Pradesh, at age six to escape his drunken father's regular beatings. Anil said: 'When Sir [Deboo] started our workshop six months ago, we found the whole thing very strange, but now we realize how we can use our bodies to perform very unique and difficult manoeuvres' (2009).

The youth relished the huge success of their show *Breaking Boundaries*, which Astad choreographed. The performance, divided into five segments, required synchronized movements. Astad had taught the youth his style of slowly unfolding a work with total focus. Through this, he built not only body awareness in them but also their self-confidence and a strong spirit of group unity, much like he had done with deaf performers. It was remarkable how successfully the youth imbibed Astad's slow, meditative, emotionally expressive movement style while exploring the stage space.

For both *Breaking Boundaries* and *Rhythm Divine*, Astad taught dancers to move in unison and use space to draw imaginary lines— V formations, groups of three and four creating circles and symmetrical mandalas. He demanded almost punishing balancing poses, the use of benches as props and dancing to complex rhythms, through which the youth also discovered their physical strength. Of course, Astad's work with Salaam Baalak's youth who were exposed only to Bollywood dance was very different from his collaboration with Manipuri artists who were well trained in their traditional dance styles. In October 2009 I watched both shows—*Breaking Boundaries* at NCPA in Mumbai and *Rhythm Divine* at Purana Quila in Delhi. I felt that both groups of dancers had internalized Astad's style which they executed with virtuosity and feeling.

In the performance brochure, 'Exploring Space', Astad states that *Breaking Boundaries* is about 'body and space . . . I had to deprogram the Bollywood moves, the *jhatkas* and *matkas* [fast movements] and inculcate the *rasas* and the *mudras*.' He trained the youth for nearly six months, instilling an astounding level of concentration, even meditative stillness, in a group of inexperienced dancers ranging in age from 15 to 21. This was a testament to Astad's teaching which reached for the highest standards. Further, as a caring human being, he inspired and encouraged the youth to excel and to think of themselves as artists. Astad took them seriously and his tough love paid off. Like with the deaf dancers, Astad's training provided the Salaam Baalak youth an avenue to self-esteem and also fostered a sense of shared purpose and community. The youth presented their art with genuine professionalism.

Breaking Boundaries also showcased his careful selection of a moving soundscape. He used a different sound for each segment— piano (Phillip Tan), North Indian flute (Hariprasad Chaurasia), and classical Carnatic vocals (U. Srinivasan). The show opened in half-light and half-shadow, evocatively lit by Milind Shrivastava. Amid a breathless sense of expectation, 13 dancers bent forward, almost crouching as the light moved over them. The stillness of Astad's style was full and intense; it resonated from his dancers' total concentration. The audience's vision was guided by the lighting as much as the movement. The dancers lifted their bodies very slowly with minimal gestures, with their heads rising last, as if emerging from foetal positions. The gradual unfolding revealed strong, upright bodies, symbolizing the many struggles they had endured in their young lives. Astad mentioned to me that when he initially taught them this choreography, the puzzled young dancers asked if standing still also constituted dance!

After the opening, cartwheeling bodies traversed the stage diagonally, followed by a circle of six dancers. Even as they moved in unison, each dancer's individuality was on display. They assumed difficult, often weight-bearing poses in pairs or threes, building on trust. In one such move, three male dancers clasped hands and descended into deep backbends; then, using the strength of their grip, they pulled themselves back up. In another, two dancers stood back to back, as one lifted the other onto his back, then gently lowered him to the ground, while the dancer in front took a wide, stable stance.

Some of the choreographer Chandralekha's legacy in body movement and energy, a lot of which has become part of Indian dancers' collective subconscious, echoed in segments of *Breaking Boundaries*—as bodies came together in pairs or in threes, with faces almost touching, the energy fields and shared breath created a special resonance. Movements unfolded as if the passage of time itself filled the spaces in between bodies. The techniques of prolonging movements, practising slowness and layered significations that Chandralekha boldly executed in her work are also an integral part of Astad's legacy and style.

As the dancers' bodies spun in Kathak-style chakkars, they deliberately broke the classical symmetry by clasping their hands in front of their faces, and then transitioning into the Virabhadrasana yoga pose with hands raised above their heads. Much like in yoga, counter-poses balanced both sides of the body, dispelling negative energies. Balance was sought between nritya (dance) and abhinaya (acting). Astad envisioned gestures shifting in style and intensity, from softly outstretched palms, as if making an offering, to bold and sharp movements, as in martial arts. A single gesture, repeated like a choreographic mantra, saw the palm of one hand held taut, slicing through the air in diagonal sweeps as the body bent low.

The final segment, touching yet unsentimental, evoked bhakti rasa, the sense of devotion that the dancers felt—towards their own artistry and one another, towards their teacher Astad and the audience. Having endured caste and class prejudices, these youth used *Breaking Boundaries* to powerfully express their full humanity. With the breaking of boundaries, a profound sense of wholeness, of unity enveloped the audience. Through determination and personal effort, Astad secured shows of *Breaking Boundaries* in major cities across India—Mumbai, Kanpur, Chennai, Kolkata and Bangalore. Some of the dancers stepped out of Delhi for the first time, seeing other parts of India and experiencing different cuisines with Astad.

Breaking Boundaries received critical acclaim. Astad said that he was proud to work with the street youth. Viraj, one of the dancers who had run away from Jamshedpur as a child, said to me, 'This is our family, and this performance has helped us strengthen that bond.' Another group member noted that many came to Salaam Baalak to volunteer their time and share different skills, 'but Astad's teaching is different. It is great.' Dancer Priya shared, 'Initially, [our] bodies would ache like anything after the strenuous movements, but now [we] are used to them.'

Shamshul recalled with immense love and gratitude how Astad taught them to behave in public, talk to people and conduct themselves at dinner, including using forks and knives. Most of them came from underprivileged backgrounds, so the glamour of living in posh hotels while touring the country was new to them. Shamshul spoke to me about 'a most surprising day' for him as a dancer: the premiere of *Breaking Boundaries* in Kamani Auditorium, New Delhi, where he was overjoyed to read on the brochure—'Choreography by Astad Deboo. Assisted by Shamshul.' Astad's gesture of giving due credit meant the world to the young artist in his burgeoning dance career (int., August 2021).

Shamshul narrated an anecdote about Astad's democratic spirit. The Salaam Baalak group was invited to Sikkim to perform with Astad for the King of Bhutan in November 2008. A government official who arrived to receive them told Astad to go in a special car, with the rest of his troupe going in another vehicle to a different hotel. Astad refused to leave without knowing exactly where his troupe would stay. When the official made distinctions between 'senior' and 'junior' artists, Astad literally shouted him down. The official had to bend to Astad's demand to provide a decent hotel for his troupe and to treat them with the same respect that they afforded him. This was also a life lesson for Shamshul. Astad would always remind them that they were not helpless or 'low caste'; wherever they came from, no one could rob them of their dignity and talent (int., August 2021).[1]

Interpreting Tagore (2011)

After several shows of *Breaking Boundaries*, Astad mentioned to the Salaam Baalak youth the possibility of another production with a different theme. They were excited at this prospect and motivated to learn new dance styles. This production would materialize in 2011 as *Interpreting Tagore*. Shamshul worked with puppeteer Dadi Pudumjee and trained in jazz and the classical dance forms Chhau and Kathakali; Anil learned jazz and puppetry with puppeteer Anurupa Roy. This education proved valuable for their participation in *Interpreting Tagore*.

---

1 In 2010, a different creative experience awaited Astad when he was invited by Indian film director Mani Ratnam to choreograph an escape sequence for prominent film star Aishwarya Rai Bachchan for his film *Raavan*. Cinematographer Santosh Sivan, who had worked with Astad on other films—M. F. Husain's *Meenaxi: A Tale of Three Cities* (2004) and Vishal Bharadvaj's *Omkara* (2006)—had suggested his name to Ratnam. Initially, Astad thought that he would be asked to choreograph a song in the film, but Ratnam wanted Astad to portray the escape sequence in a stylized manner. Astad was apprehensive since the escape scene had a waterfall and a cliff with a sharp drop. However, he was impressed with Aishwarya's professionalism, especially since she had to perform the escape scene twice—for the film's Hindi and Tamil versions.

The seeds for *Interpreting Tagore* were laid as far back as 1995 when *The Indian Express* newspaper had planned a festival on Rabindranath Tagore and had called Astad to participate. At that time, he had performed a solo to Tagore's poem to the Mother Goddess, combining abstract movement with rasas, moving seamlessly between Indian mudras and his signature balancing poses. He performed the solo again at the Asian Art Museum in San Francisco on 23 August 1997, when he danced to three Tagore poems set to Astad's eclectic soundscape.[2] According to the programme notes for the performance, the simplicity, accessibility and universality of Tagore's 'unique poetic vision' appealed to Astad. He drew from Kathakali 'for the power and strength it gives to the idea' and from Kathak 'for the sheer exuberance and joy of the chakkars'. Astad's 'Prayer to the Devi' was based on Tagore's poem 'Your Grace', in which he danced to Dmitri Shostakovich's classical music. In the poem 'Walking Tall', Tagore 'exhorts the reader to walk alone but with head held high'; Astad, dancing to the music of Graeme Koehne, drew personal strength from these words, infusing them into his own work. In the final segment, set to Tagore's poem 'Every Fragment of Dust Is Awakened', Astad performed to the music of Yoichiro Yoshikawa, twirling nonstop for a magical two and a half minutes, inspiring awe in the audience.

Interpreting Tagore premiered in 2011 at Mumbai's Tata Theatre with Astad's group choreography based on three Tagore poems— 'Surrender', 'Your Grace' and 'Walking Tall'—and his solo set to a fourth work, 'Awakening'. Astad took three months to get this 80-minute work ready and two weeks to choreograph the 15-minute piece for 'Walking Tall' in which three sets of movements unfolded simultaneously. Subsequent shows of *Interpreting Tagore* took place in 2012 in New Delhi as a fundraiser; in 2013 again in New Delhi, sponsored by the Astad Deboo Dance Foundation; and in 2014 at the Music Academy in Chennai.

---

2 My thanks to Mary Ann Whitten for sharing this programme with me.

The poems in *Interpreting Tagore* were recited by actor Akash Khurana. The soundscape had nine global musicians, including Italian composer Frederico Senesi, who had played percussion for santoor (a dulcimer-like instrument) stalwart Shivkumar Sharma and master flautist Hariprasad Chaurasia. Astad danced to a Dhrupad composition by Italian vocalist Amelia Cuni for his solo 'Awakening'. *Interpreting Tagore* also featured music by Japanese composers, a tabla player from Milan, and Iiro Rantala, a Finnish pianist.

The premiere at the Tata Theatre demonstrated how Astad's choreography used space accented by the rhythm of the poems. He masterfully negotiated the external space of the stage even as he reflected on the inner space of his imagination and art. He whirled no less than 242 times, even though he admitted to doing 310! At the conclusion, Astad's intensity and his homage to a higher presence were deeply moving, amplified by Yoshigawa's music and Gautam Bhattacharya's sensitive lighting. The Tata Theatre was filled to capacity, culminating in a standing ovation and even tears, as Astad unveiled a new work after three years. Astad planned to take this work to Japan and Korea, sponsored by the Indian Ministry of Culture.

Interpreting Tagore used huge puppets on stage to astounding effect. Astad himself handled four ten-foot figures of the goddess Devi for the 'Your Grace' segment. Uttara Coorlawala said (int., August 2021) that Astad skilfully used the size of the gigantic puppets to make himself look much smaller, even vulnerable in comparison. She recognized the psychological impact of the larger-than-life puppets in relation to Astad's human body.

The late Dr Sunil Kothari, a prominent dance critic, reviewed the New Delhi performance of *Interpreting Tagore* in which he complimented Astad's concern for 'the less privileged section [that] has brought cheer to the disabled and street children' (Kothari 2012). Singling out Astad's dance to Tagore's poem 'Your Grace' that 'cast a spell', Kothari provided a lyrical translation into English of the Bengali poem:

Mother, I shall weave a chain of pearls
for thy neck with my tears of sorrow,
the stars have wrought their anklets of light to deck thy feet,
but mine will hang upon thy breast.
Wealth and fame come from thee
and it is for thee to give or to withhold them.
but this sorrow is absolutely mine own,
and when I bring it to thee as my offering,
thou rewardest me with thy grace.

Astad used Mayurbhanj Chhau dance movements for four massive figures dressed in red, wearing masks of Goddess Kali, that walked from among the audience onto the stage. Astad bowed as a devotee to all four goddesses, their large hands seeming to almost caress him as he appeared like a vulnerable child before his mother. 'The mother's love for the child,' commented Kothari (2012), 'epitomizing Grace found a felicitous expression in those five figures: Astad and four Goddesses.' The young dancers, trained by Pudumjee, carried and balanced other puppets that were adorned with flowing red saris.

The show was spectacular with its eclectic music, superb lighting and Astad's choreography that included 'more than four hundred pirouettes' (Kothari 2012). Anil and Shamshul were assistant choreographers and performers; Mohammed Shameem and Anil created the masks and puppets; and Archana Shah was the costume designer. At the end of the New Delhi show, Sanjay Roy, a co-founder of Salaam Baalak Trust, informed the audience that Astad's mother had passed away in Mumbai the previous evening. Still, Astad had insisted on performing, as he said his mother would have liked him to dance, even if it was in her memory. The audience rose for a standing ovation to show respect for her and Astad.

Interpreting Tagore gave 'a new meaning [to] the life of street children who act in it' (Chatterjee 2012). This 'contemporary dance-puppet theatre' was challenging for Astad to explain to the youth: 'I sat with them and explained what each dance and corresponding poetry was all about. They tried to understand the dance. They knew that Tagore was a poet but as the translations were in English, language was a barrier' (Chatterjee 2012). However, as the youth had experienced Astad's style since 2008, they caught the essence of the poems and were able to perform according to Astad's direction.

The troupe leader Shamshul, who was in his early 20s at the time, was singled out as a particularly talented performer. He had come to Delhi from Saharsa, Bihar, in the early 1990s and had trained under Pudumjee 'before "Sir" [Astad] picked me up in 2008' (int., August 2021). Grateful to Astad for teaching him his style of dancing, Shamshul has built a professional career as a dancer and puppeteer. He has also given back to his family in Bihar where he has built them a home with the money he earned from dancing. He worked for four years on the reality television show *Khul Ja Sim Sim*. Shamshul's dancing mate Avinash, a runaway from Purnea, Bihar, trained in theatre at the Indian Technical Institute and under the Theatre in Education scheme of the National School of Drama. In one of the several informal conversations I had with the Salaam Baalak youth in 2008 and 2011, Avinash said, 'I wanted to be an actor (and a professional dancer) but it was difficult. I went to learn Chhau for six months at Gol Market and worked as a free-lance performer.' One of the youngest dancers of the troupe, Salim, had sampled fame as an actor in the Oscar-nominated short film *Little Terrorist* (2004).

A Meaningful Award

On 1 July 2018, Astad received the Yagnaraman Living Legend Lifetime Achievement Award given by Sri Krishna Gana Sabha, one of the fore-most classical music, dance and cultural institutions in Chennai. On receiving this award, Astad made a moving speech about his journey over fifty years and where the Indian dance world was headed. He noted that 'being a professional classical dancer in India is hard', and being a contemporary dancer based upon classical training is even harder. This often made him feel pessimistic about the future. He pointed out the unfortunate, rigid divisions between classical dance and 'its modern, contemporary twin'. I believe that Astad knowingly used the word 'twin' to indicate that his contemporary style is rooted in Indian dance traditions, symbolisms, cultural motifs and overall effect. The boundary between the two has 'sadly crystallized', he noted, 'instead of softening over the years'. Astad thought that the two forms were operating as 'separate disciplines marching forever onward with little hope that they will ever meet. And it is with this in mind that I must point out', he stated emphatically, '[that] what the Sri Krishna Gana Sabha has done today, in giving me this award, is nothing short of absolutely remarkable.'

Astad asserted that despite his time abroad, 'it was in a constant return to [his] roots that the actual development could be shared with audiences'. In other words, he evolved his contemporary Indian dance vocabulary by returning constantly to his native India and to his training in Kathak and Kathakali. Astad believed that with collaboration between classical and contemporary dancers, 'the ultimate victor will be dance itself', though he recognized it as 'an impossibility [to even] imagine a future in which the two kinds of dance . . . could sustain and nurture one another'.

So, what does the future development of contemporary Indian dance look like to Astad, a pioneer of this style? When in a 2018 interview, Emmaly Wiederholt asked this question, Astad's response was cautiously optimistic: 'It's very difficult to find a body proficient in Indian classical dance but also physically athletic from the Western point of technique. When I do work with my street children, I try to imbibe in them my kind of movement and some of them are able to pick it up' (Deboo 2018). Although Astad did not believe that he had 'any protégés', those whom he trained, such as Shamshul, would beg to differ. I agree with Shamshul that Astad has imprinted his legacy, his signature style of contemporary Indian dance on many, including those at Salaam Baalak Trust.

Unbroken Unbowed (2019)

Created and performed in 2019, *Unbroken Unbowed* was Astad's final stage performance at age 72 with Salaam Baalak dancers. The title conveyed Astad's strong spirit and indomitable will to pursue his passion for dance over half a century. Astad found inspiration in Mahatma Gandhi's words. Like Gandhi, Astad was disappointed in some educated people who were not open-minded enough to accept his experimental early work. Astad also used Gandhi's words—on respect, understanding, acceptance and appreciation—that echoed his personal struggles and triumphs. According to Anuradha Vellat (2020), *Unbroken Unbowed* was 'not only a tribute to the Mahatma; it also echoe[d] the master choreographer's own journey.'

The world premiere of the 68-minute work shared a double bill for NCPA's 50th-year celebration in Mumbai on 29 November 2019 with renowned dancer Mallika Sarabhai performing *In Search of the Goddess*. *Unbroken Unbowed* was performed also in Delhi in January 2020 and later in Bhubaneshwar, Odisha.[3] During conversations with host Anita Ratnam on Astad's birthday celebration on Instagram on 13 July 2021, Swapnokalpa Dasgupta, who was the dance curator at NCPA at the time, said that presenting Astad in a double bill with Mallika Sarabhai was daunting because they were both 'great people who had fantastic work'. Astad started the anniversary festivities 'on the right note,' she said, 'so everybody just carried over that light on the first day.' Astad understood that this was a special event for NCPA; he had shared a close connection with NCPA and its personnel over many years, often premiering his shows there.

---

3 For more, including captivating images of the performances in Mumbai and New Delhi, see Joyain S. (2019) and Shveta Arora (2020) respectively.

Dasgupta admired Astad not just as a dancer but as a fine human being. She recalled that when she joined NCPA as curator in 2013, Astad would talk to her in her native language Bengali. He inspired her to undertake more 'inclusive programming'. 'You just can't leave out such potential,' Astad would say, referring to the deaf. 'We were looking forward to a production by him addressing disability arts,' noted Dasgupta. Astad would come to NCPA to see other artists—'he would buy his own ticket. . . . He always had his favourite seat' (int. with Ratnam, July 2021).

A tribute to Gandhi on his 150th birth anniversary, *Unbroken Unbowed* was inspired by Gandhi's quotations, interwoven with move-ments reflecting Astad's five-decade journey as a dancer. In the show's four sections, Gandhi's words were interspersed with Astad's signature musical choices—his favourite Dhrupad singer Amelia Cuni, composi-tions by Italian composer Alio Die, koto player Satsuki Odamura, the Fado (a music genre from Portugal) and a composition specially created for the production by Dom Bufford. Astad, as the lead dancer, moved with five young male dancers to the sonorous voice of Andalusian clas-sical musician Amina Alaoui, accompanied by the sounds of a flamenco guitar.

The choreography, with dancers holding sticks and performing gravity-defying jumps, was evocative, inventive, minimal and technically perfect. 'Being minimal is harder than sort of prancing around', said Astad. 'That's been a gradual dissolve. With a much slower movement, I will take my real time and get you into it. The expression comes but in a very different rhythm' (Khurana 2020a). Dressed in a white khadi tunic, Astad held the stillness in the centre as the other dancers per-formed athletic movements around him. They leapt, crawled, did cart-wheels and headstands while Astad transitioned into his signature chakkars, culminating the performance in a powerful crescendo, marked by his unique presence and the vibrant energy of the ensemble which included Shamshul, Rohit Varma, Narayan Sharma, Govind Godiyal, Pradeep Kumar and Vicky Yadav.

The masks for the show were designed by Shamshul who wanted to create a mask for each section of the performance and one for the figure of Gandhi. But Astad wanted only one mask that combined an abstract design with a Gandhi likeness. Shamshul created several designs, made sketches and Astad approved some of them with modifications. For the final mask, Shamshul used Styrofoam and papier-mâché.

The costume designer for *Unbroken Unbowed* was Sandhya Raman, a graduate of Ahmedabad's National Institute of Design (NID), who was inspired by Astad to use khadi or hand-spun cotton for this production, since Gandhi promoted khadi over British-made clothes during the Independence struggle.[4] In an online conversation with Anita Ratnam on the occasion of Astad's 74th birthday celebration on 13 July 2021, Sandhya said how she considered khadi 'the fabric of the soul' and that Astad's khadi costume 'should be an inspiration and make a statement'. Since Astad was interested in a 'very minimal costume', Sandhya created a silhouette with a 'serene look', in line with Gandhi's personality. She was taken with Astad's sincerity towards his work, his research and his ability to not impose his views. He shared with Sandhya 'what looked good on him, how he used his muscles, the tips of his fingers'. For the ensemble of dancers, Sandhya designed dhotis to be tied in Gandhi's style with torsos staying bare. She added a top at a different point in the choreography 'to show a different mood'. Astad told Sandhya that he wanted to explore the concept of 'looking within' in this work, and Sandhya translated this idea into her costume design, reflecting the layers of emotion he mentioned and creating a pristine effect for the show. 'The second section had a two-layered costume and the third had

---

4 Recall Margaret Bourke-White's iconic 1946 photograph of Gandhi, a pioneer of civil disobedience, seated beside his beloved spinning wheel. He is seen as someone who spun cotton and wore Indian-made clothing rather than British imports.

a three-layered one,' described Sandhya. 'It was the same costume with added layers rather than a costume change' (int. with Ratnam, July 2021).

It was a coincidence that 13 July is both Astad's and Sandhya's birthdays. She missed talking with him and missed his call for her birthday. Sandhya ended her interview with Anita with a kind of life lesson for artists, which she learnt from Astad: to remain dedicated to the kind of work that one wants to do, to believe in oneself, 'and the universe will make space for you. There will be enough work for you—Astad believed in that. He was a rebel in the way he did things on his own terms; that is what made him Astad and made him so special.'

Astad was not alive to celebrate when Sandhya, as secretary of Rasaja Foundation, generously awarded six promising dancers who would take forward Astad's legacy a one-time scholarship of 25,000 rupees each. The dancers honoured were Shamshul, Vicky Alex, Pradeep, Narayan Sharma, Govind Godiyal and Rohit Verma. Rasaja Foundation hosted the production of *Unbroken, Unbound* as a tribute to Mahatma Gandhi.

The time when *Unbroken Unbowed* was performed in New Delhi in January 2020, mass protests were being held around issues of citizenship and nationality and how the minority communities, especially Muslims, in India were adversely affected by proposed new laws. Astad linked Gandhi's words to 'what's happening in the country' (Arora 2020). Around the same time, Astad gave a talk at the Mudra Institute of Communications, Ahmedabad (MICA), Gujarat, where he spoke up about the divisions in Indian society. He later shared how everybody was surprised by this since, as a Parsi, he was not expected to be affected by all the negativity. 'But I was born and brought up in India,' he said, 'I am a Hindustani first . . . . Unfortunately, dancers have never been vocal. In my own way, I try to speak.'

March–May 2020: India's Strict Covid-19 Lockdown

During India's stringent Covid-19 lockdown in March–May 2020, Astad remained active though grounded in his Mumbai flat. He continued choreographing with his dancers in Delhi—this time via video, creating the visually stunning series called *Boundaries*. The title itself harkens back to his initial work with Salaam Baalak youth, *Breaking Boundaries*—borders of movement, of hidebound stereotypes about caste and class, of personal freedom, of confinement and creative fervour. Working with his star student Shamshul, Astad used technology to significant effect in his choreography for *Boundaries 1, Boundaries 1.1* and *Boundaries 1.2*, avidly sharing videos of these with friends on WhatsApp and being impatient, expecting prompt feedback. If they did not immediately respond, he would call them and berate them angrily!

Many artists around the world lost work during the Covid-19 pandemic since performance venues were shuttered. The Government of India offered no support to artists and their families; anecdotally, one heard of disastrous consequences for musicians who accompany classical dancers and theatre technicians who manage light and sound. These artists had no other skills and no alternative means to support their families. During this time, Astad actively raised funds to support artists and their families, often lying awake at night, worrying about their survival without work. My brother and I donated to the Astad Deboo Dance Foundation, which aided artists in Delhi, Chennai, Kolkata and Manipur, as well as a school for the deaf in Worli, Mumbai, where Astad worked with students. Meanwhile, in the US, I, like Astad, contributed to various organizations supporting medical needs in India, Indian musicians and their families, and a Kolkata-based initiative by singers raising funds for theatre technicians, some of whom had tragically died by suicide due to financial despair.

Shamshul told me that during the lockdown, every month 1.5 lakhs rupees (approximately US$1,800) would arrive in his Delhi bank account from the Astad Deboo Dance Foundation, which he was asked to distribute to 15 dancers in Delhi, to Manipuri performers and to artists who had worked with Astad in Chennai and Kolkata. Astad regularly supported some 50–60 dancers until he passed away in December 2020.

'The way Astad-ji taught us dance was very different', says Shamshul in his personal homage in an article published on *Rediff News* on Astad's 74th birth anniversary. 'He was a perfectionist and he was stubborn about every detail. He taught us to take pride in our work. To take responsibility for our colleagues. I have worked with many gurus, but no one like him.' After Astad's passing, Shamshul felt 'very lonely. There is no one to stand by us now. Astad-ji taught us more than dance. He taught us how to be good human beings. He taught us that there was a vast world of dance beyond Bollywood. He taught us generosity' (Rediff News Bureau 2021). Shamshul, now an established choreographer in his own right, has carried on Astad's legacy by contributing to the field of dance for the past 15 years.

In conclusion, I believe that Astad's legacy is indelibly imprinted on the bodies, minds and spirits of the Salaam Baalak dancers. They are a living testament to Astad's contemporary Indian dance style with its unique idiom. His innovative choreography lives on and provides creative models for younger dancers to emulate. Although Astad himself worked in isolation in his early career, keeping faith in himself and his art, he remained a generous mentor to younger artists. Indeed, he wanted to make sure that their path was easier than his had been, and that they could pursue their creative visions with courage. Throughout his career, he welcomed collaborations with celebrated musicians and dancers and this biography now travels into that aspect of Astad's creative journey.

FIGURE 35. Manipuri dancers leaping with model and actress Sushma Reddy (in foreground), as staged by photographer Farrokh Chothia.

PART IV

Collaborations with Artists
in India and Beyond

FIGURE 36. Dancing in an angarkha with crane motifs, designed by Ashdeen Lilaowala. *Photograph by Neelesh Kale; courtesy Deboo family.*

CHAPTER 10

Astad's Transnational Collaborations: South Korea and Japan

Collaboration with Korean Theatre Director Hyoung-Taek Limb in *Hamlet_Avataar* (2015)

Artistic collaborations between Astad and artists from South Korea were both unusual and significant. Typically, such joint creative projects are more common between artists from the global South, such as from India, and those from the global North, such as the US and Canada, despite the power imbalances. Astad's work showed that meaningful cultural connections and collaborations among dancer-choreographers from different global South nations are not only possible but also rewarding, even when facing challenges like limited funding. In such ventures, both participating nations shared common goals: supporting the creativity of their artists; shedding new light on both regions' cultures through theatre, dance or music; and enhancing audiences' knowledge and engagement in the arts. These goals were explored when, in 2015, Astad was invited to work with Korea's prominent theatre personality Hyoung-Taek Limb, the artistic director of Seoul Factory, in a production called *Hamlet_Avataar*. How did this intercultural initiative proceed? And, importantly, did the project unfold on an equal playing field between Astad and Limb?

The individual who was the key facilitator of this alliance was Rathi Jafer, the director of InKo Centre (Indo-Korean Cultural and Information Centre), a Chennai-based non-profit arts and culture initiative supported by industrialist T. Srinivasan (Deboo, int., March 2018).[1] According to Jafer, the InKo Centre's mandate is to strengthen intercultural dialogues between India and South Korea, as well as to underwrite various projects in India such as Korean language courses, writer's workshops and ceramics camps.

The centre provided funding to Astad for a three-month residency in South Korea to develop a project, research its theme and mount experimental performances before the final presentation. Jafer opined that devoting time to research was important since this helped artists 'share and respectfully absorb each other's artistic vocabularies' as well as explore similarities and differences in their styles, techniques and aesthetic approaches. Indian and Korean artists also discovered a 'global dimension while showcasing the local and national characteristics that underpin such exchange' (Jafer, int. with Ratnam, July 2021).

In a telephone conversation with me in 2015, Astad described this intercultural collaboration from its inception: Limb had invited Astad to be part of the residency on the *Hamlet* project since he had admired Astad's performance with Manipuri drum dancers. For Astad, 'it was a joy' to work with Limb. His overall experience was positive, especially considering the knowledge he gained and the ideas he exchanged as a 'co-choreographer'. Since this was a theatre project, it also gave a boost to his penchant for acting.

In *Hamlet_Avataar*, Shakespeare's drama received new life as a Korean interpretation through acting, dancing and music, with the 'avatar' as an underlying concept. It combined different cultural frameworks and included key participants from South Korea and India, including singer Parvathy Baul, one of the few leading female practitioners of Baul music, a Bengali folk musical tradition with elements of mysticism. Limb, as director, described Hamlet as a man 'educated to

---

1 I am grateful to Astad for sharing his collaborative work experiences with me via a phone interview in March 2018, and for putting me in touch with Rathi Jafer.

be a thinker, but who becomes a man of action, motivated by the dark force of revenge' when he finds out that his father was murdered by his uncle. Limb says that Hamlet decides 'to be a clown who can play the fictional truth. He now will live in the shape of his "Avataar" Hamlet'. As in any adaptation, Limb drew on concepts in the play that resonate in modern times, such as '[d]islocation, entropy, obsession, discord, disillusionment, conflict, cracked ego, rampant sense of defeat, lethargy, lies, tricks, drug, sexual abuse, collapse of a family, betrayal' (InKo Centre 2014: 9). Limb's goal was to let his audience imagine and discover their 'real avatar', and not be driven by superficial pursuits of money and power: 'Hamlet_Avataar is an exploration [. . .] seeking sublimation through Indian spiritual culture as well as its music and dance fused with Korean art forms' (InKo Centre 2014: 10).

Jafer praised Astad for bringing his vast experience, his feel for the stage and 'his dance aesthetics' onto the production, all of which energized the young Korean artists involved in the project. He did all this 'with his typical rigour' along with a lot of compassion that enabled him 'to cut through the stuff that didn't work' (int. with Ratnam, July 2021). Astad portrayed Hamlet's father's ghost and the master of the playmakers; singer Parvathy Baul took on the role of Ophelia. Together, they infused their portrayals with innovative energy, blending traditional dance and music styles—Astad's combination of Kathak and contemporary dance and Parvathy's Baul music. They created a synergy of Kathak *bol*s and Baul syllables to accompany the Korean sounds and vocabularies on stage, rendering the performance visually and aurally rich.

Discovering Korean artists and their theatre, music and dance, Parvathy was moved to find similarities between Baul tradition and Pansori, a musical storytelling tradition cherished as both folk and high culture in Korea, featuring a vocalist who performs expressive singing alongside a drummer. Parvathy recognized how contemporary Korean theatre and dance practitioners were working for 'a new language through the universal story of *Hamlet* and the "crazy wisdom" within it. This language relates a lot to the ancient Asian philosophies and practices' (InKo Centre 2014: 11), which explore the opposite forces of good and evil, the meaning of life and death, vengeance and forgiveness. These themes play out in *Hamlet_Avataar* along with the significant role of theatre itself in exploring such human conundrums.

The collaboration succeeded because Indian and Korean artists worked together respectfully. '[T]he work process' enabled the artists to uncover 'each other's individual style, practice, and methodology', said Parvathy. Challenged to find 'a new way to relate as a Baul performer, to bridge the gap between us [Koreans and Indians], sometimes to "let go" to be able to connect', she found that with trust and mutual respect, artists could let go. Since the Koreans found it difficult to pronounce her name, they gave her a new one: 'Pa-sem'—in which 'sem' means 'teacher' (InKo Centre 2014: 11).

Hamlet_Avataar premiered in India at the Hindu Theatre Festival in August 2015. Later, in October 2015, it was presented at the Seoul Performing Arts Festival in Korea where Astad was featured in 12 performances. The next year, in October 2016, it was performed in Bengaluru and Chennai.

Astad believed that the main difference between collaborations within India and the ones with foreign artists, such as in South Korea, is that, apart from good funding, the work process in foreign collaborations is very methodical and professional (phone conv., 2015). He described how in South Korea, everyone was assigned a specific task, whether in production or technology, and the entire team of actors, dancers, musicians and technical designers worked very hard. Even the rehearsals for *Hamlet_Avataar* felt like full performances, thanks to the dedication of all the actors and technicians. Astad was impressed with the theatre company's precision in following set times for rehearsals and their highly professional work ethic. As someone with exacting work ethics, Astad relished being part of such a team. On the other hand, within India, collaborative ventures often suffered from a lack of financial support. Yet, Astad found it credit-worthy that, in spite of the process often being 'harrowing', so much creative work was produced nonetheless.

While in Korea, Astad had heard Yukio Tsuji, a Japanese shakuhachi flute player, and wanted to work with him. They met in New York City and created *Eternal Embrace* which was performed at the Metropolitan Museum of Art. Then, with Tsuji, Astad returned home to perform this piece. Astad's crisscrossing the world brought the creative synergy between East and West to spectators in the US and in India.

Collaboration with Japanese Flautist Yukio Tsuji in *Eternal Embrace* (2015)

Astad had a unique sense of musicality that breathed life into his dance. In 2015, he collaborated with Yukio Tsuji, a Japanese flautist, per-cussionist and multi-instrumentalist. Both artists began their work based on a shared belief that music can elevate the human spirit. As a musician, Yukio aimed to open a pathway for his listeners to experience a higher dimension, one that is different from their daily reality. 'It is very easy for me,' remarked Yukio, 'to do that [reach for a higher realm] through music.' What Yukio described is akin to a rasika's experience in appreciating art. Astad's dance moved Yukio so deeply, he noted, that it took him to a transcendent realm (int., July 2021).

The two artists met for the first time online—Yukio was at La MaMa Theatre in New York and Astad was performing in South Korea. Astad was won over by the sound of Yukio playing the shakuhachi flute and selected him to work with over other artists and percussionists. Astad's collaborative style was always open, generous and receptive; he did not walk in 'with an ego'. Rather, he aimed to learn from his collab-orator's process of putting work together, communication strategies, visual design and stagecraft to find new illuminations for his own work (int., July 2021).

Astad and the New York–based Japanese musician worked well together. They created *Eternal Embrace*, which premiered in 2015 at New York City's Metropolitan Museum's (or the Met's) Department of Islamic Art, and in a new space, Gallery 463, which is devoted to the art of Mughal South Asia. Subsequently, in 2016, *Eternal Embrace* was performed in Indian cities—Mumbai, Delhi, Chennai, Bengaluru and Ahmedabad. And for the first time, Astad made this performance available to audiences through a streaming service called Cennarium. He hoped that people who could not attend his performances in person would now have an opportunity to see and enjoy his work.

Eternal Embrace 'introduced a new art form to the series: dance', says Julia Rooney of the Met in her interview with both artists (Deboo and Tsuji 2015). Rooney's questions and the artists' responses informed Met audiences about their artistic journeys and their goals. When she asked Yukio about how he decided to become a musician, he charmingly narrated his story. Initially, without any education in music, he was a singer. Then, he said, 'I began to play everything—country, western, jazz, folk songs—as a self-taught musician.' Yukio pointed out that he learnt from life experience, from playing music and from 'the La MaMa Experimental Theatre Club [which] was like a school for [him]'. He could experiment in different ways when performing for La MaMa productions.

Rooney asked Astad about his goals as a dancer 'beyond the world of entertainment and the arts'. He said that for the past 20 years, he had been 'a catalyst or artistic director', with the deaf and with street children in India; such information about Astad's work would not be widely known to Met viewers who had come to see *Eternal Embrace*. Astad elaborated that in the 1970s, there was no tradition of contemporary dance in India, but that now the reality was different—indeed, 'every classical dancer wants to be contemporary'. He added that although he did not have a dance school, he 'mentors various groups of individual performers, brings them to a standard and then lets them go in the different directions they want to explore' (Deboo and Tsuji 2015).

Eternal Embrace's music and choreography were inspired by Mughal-era Punjabi and Sufi poet Hazrat Bulleh Shah's (1680–1757) poem, 'Maati', translated as clay, dirt, earth, dust or soil. The poem meditates on the mortal and ephemeral which disappear like dust in this material world:

> Oh, see how the quickened dust doth move.
> The horse be dust, dust the shield
> Dust the rider that rides the steed
> Dust the hunter, dust the game
> The clamour they make is made the same . . .
> Creatures of dust who laugh and play
> And then under the dust they lay
> Bulleh, when you this dusty knot undo
> A great burthen from you will move.[2]

Astad explained that 'the essence of "Maati" is related to mortality, death and suffering'. However, he used these concepts metaphorically:

> *Eternal Embrace* is leading me into another direction of more Sufi-based music. My work has a lot of spirituality and a lot of emotions that are very much a part of my creativity. The fact that I am trained in Indian classical dance makes the rasas very important, but at the same time there is a lot of work I have done that is abstract. (Deboo and Tsuji 2015)

Yukio's reflection on how Astad and he worked together is revelatory:

> Astad created his style with the movement. To me, he can tell the story, not only with the movement, but with eyes, hands and the emotion on his face. So, all I have to do is watch his

---

2 The translation is available on a blog titled Beshno: https://bit.ly/3yRxkUu (last accessed on 5 July 2021).

face and arms and eyes and return the energy to him in a really deep way. And at the same time, he understands, he feels my music and takes it over and we digest and put it out on the stage. We didn't talk about those things, but we understand each other so deeply. That I know. (Int., July 2021)

Yukio's description of following Astad's movements and responding with his music is fascinating.[3] As Yukio played, Astad improvised: 'Slow, slow, slow . . . We fit perfectly. Astad's style is so strong. Almost everything I want to do, to create, fits to his world' (int., July 2021). Entranced by Astad's chakkars, which could go on for nearly 10 minutes, he pondered what they meant to Astad and his spectators. He regarded them as blending into Sufi movements that embody a divine purpose. Through Astad's meditative spinning, 'Turn, turn, turn—he got me into Sufism . . . Now, I'm a Japanese Sufi musician! From traditional shakuhachi music, I started making my own style—Sufi shakuhachi! Astad gave it to me.' Yukio gave Astad credit for 'everyone [spectators and technical personnel] opening themselves, as a group'. He tuned into Astad's dance as reaching 'into nirvana, opening up the channel. That's what we do as artists' (int., July 2021).

Yukio described the synergy of dance and music communicating together for an audience of 200 to 300 people in the Met space where they could see Astad up close. Yukio was always 'on the side. And how closely we produce music and movement together really went to the audience, [that] received the whole energy of Astad, really, in a nice way, I'm sure that happened' (int., July 2021). Although he was the first Japanese musician whom Astad performed with, he was amazed to know how many Japanese friends Astad had and that he had gone to

---

3 In a collaboration with Bharatanatyam dancer Hema Rajagopalan (discussed in Chapter 11), Astad followed, even mirrored, Hema's portrayal of emotion and expression while she danced a padam. Remarkably, Astad was behind her in that segment; he intuitively expressed the emotions conveyed by the nuances of Carnatic music.

Japan in the 1970s, had studied Kabuki and was fascinated by Japanese classical and folk dance styles.

Along with being a flautist, Yukio is a unique percussionist who does not always play the drums but makes drumming and drone-like sounds. Instead of using string instruments such as the cello or bass, he 'makes his own sound on the synthesizers'. In his interview with me, he made a fascinating distinction between the sound of the flute, whose sound 'goes in the air, in space', and that of percussion, which 'ground(s) the space in a certain way'. In *Eternal Embrace*, the two sounds created a fusion of both upward and downward movements, enabling Yukio and Astad 'to create a whole basic [structure]—shakuhachi go in, percussion go in. That's what my music is all about—the energy returns to the dancer, to the actors, with that basic [structure].' Yukio noted that 'sometimes I use Japanese to make the sounds. I make up words by the feeling. And so, in the beginning of *Eternal Embrace*, I use Japanese. Nobody understood!' (int., July 2021).

Astad's mastery of depicting the rasas was the highlight of the collaboration. When I asked Yukio how his collaboration with Astad was different from his work with other dancers or actors, his response was telling:

> Top-of-the-line actors, when they're on stage acting, I can really connect to them because they feel me. I feel them in the same way. With dancers, it's very hard to feel each other. They need just the rhythm and sound. With Astad, he took the deep part of the music. I understand what he wants to express. He doesn't say anything on stage but I can feel it [. . .]. Nobody else [except Astad] can do it. Nobody.

In his younger days, Yukio was a non-traditionalist; he even described himself as a gypsy. I could not resist drawing a comparison with Astad, who in his youth had hitchhiked across Europe, taking ample risks. Yukio's responded: 'Astad took a risk, and he didn't take it as a risk. Because he sees what he wants to do—boom, boom, jump on it. He's so good at making something happen' (int., July 2021).

When *Eternal Embrace* was performed across India, Astad described this collaboration to reviewer Deepa Padmar: Yukio 'created the original music in my presence in accordance to my movements' (Deboo 2016b). Padmar commented that Astad's 'contemporary dance explored the tension between the ephemeral and material worlds', following Bulleh Shah's poem. Astad's movements and facial expressions evoked the life cycle ending in death: 'I intend to take the spectator on a journey of intense emotion through my movements.' He was delighted to notice spectators responding to Yukio's flute music 'blending with Sufi elements. They understood how seamlessly it [music] enhanced the dance [and] is central to the execution of the dance' (Deboo 2016b). A report on *Eternal Embrace* and an interview with Astad in the *Deccan Herald* noted its success in New York City: 'The piece, when performed at the Metropolitan Museum of Art, received a standing ovation, with Astad being touted as "a dancing monk"' (Deboo 2016a).[4]

In my interview with Yukio Tsuji, he expressed great respect and admiration for Astad's creativity in dance and his giving nature during their collaboration. Yukio regretted that their plans to create new work together again did not materialize since Astad passed away before they could enjoy that experience (int., July 2021).

---

4 One viewer at the Met was Astad's friend since the 1970s, Teshter (Tessy) Irani, a Shapur Baug resident, now settled in Queens, New York. She was entranced, appreciating the subtle, almost imperceptible movements of Astad's hands following the music and his face expressing deep emotion. She regretted that 'our country did not appreciate Astad' even as he 'opened our minds to a different dimension' of contemporary Indian dance.

Collaboration with Korean and Indian Musicians
in *Same Same but Different* (2017)

In 2017 Astad danced in another collaborative project: *Same Same but Different*. This was spearheaded by a well-known South Korean music group, Noreum Machi, with artistic director Ju-Hong Kim, traditional percussionists Howon Lee and Hyun-Ju Oh, saenghwang and piri player Gyeongsik Kim, and gayageum player Hyeyeong Oh.[5] This project was sponsored by InKo Centre, the Korea Foundation, Arts Council Korea, Avid Learning and the Royal Opera House, Mumbai. Well known for combining traditional instrumentation with contemporary soundscapes, Noreum Machi mainly uses a variety of drums. The group also fosters collaborations with musicians from across the world. When they were interested in working with Indian artists, Astad worked through Jafer to bring into collaboration the group named Trayam, an ensemble of three critically acclaimed Indian musicians: mridangam player B. C. Manjunath, who has also played in productions of London-based dancer Akram Khan; vocalist and flautist Varijashree Venugopal; and percussionist, composer and music director Praveen D. Rao.[6] These musicians performed with Noreum Machi 'to present an experimental and eclectic soundscape that merges traditional Korean sounds with Classical Indian music, complemented with the stillness and flow of contemporary dance' (Royal Opera House 2020).

Astad was selected to dance in his introspective and meditative style to the music jointly produced by Indian and Korean instrumentalists, providing 'a very still, almost Zen-like counterpoint to the percussion and all the frenzy of the musicians as they built up the tempo' (Jafer, int. with Ratnam, 2021). Jafer recalled Astad discussing this contrast

---

5 The Korean piri is a double-reed instrument while the saenghwang is a free-reed mouth organ. The gayageum or kayagum is a traditional Korean plucked zither with 12 strings, with some recent variants having 18, 21 or 25 strings.

6 A mridangam is a barrel-shaped drum played on both sides; it usually accompanies Southern Indian or Carnatic classical performers.

and how much he enjoyed both tempos in different ways, his 'positive energy' raising the final performance to a high standard. According to Jafer, the ensemble was privileged to work with Astad who had graciously accepted this work from its early stages.

The music ensemble explored the similarities and differences between Korean and Indian performance traditions trying to locate, as Jafer put it, 'that magical shared space'. Would that happen respectfully and without compromise? Jafer added that Astad's 'humanity and empathy to reach out' enabled the group to learn from each other even as they shared their individual skills. Astad's qualities of caring and giving, his 'professional rigour, the stillness which counterpoints movement' all led to 'a tremendously fruitful experience'. Jafer had wished to create an 'interactive-cum-performance space, with Astad's costumes, photographs and with him performing in that space', which did not happen before he passed away (int. with Ratnam, 2021).[7]

Same Same but Different was developed over a year and a half, with the musicians spending three to four weeks in each country. After that, it was presented in South Korea at the Seoul Performing Arts Festival and in India.

Astad danced three pieces in front of the musicians who sat behind him in two rows. He was as much at ease in his first dance to the solo, singular sound of the bamboo flute (without accompanying drums) played in the Carnatic classical tradition, as he was in the second dance to the sound of Korean musicians on the piri and the gayageum. For the finale, Astad danced to the entire ensemble of Korean and Indian musicians. He wore his signature angarkha whose hem kissed the floor in all three dances—the first one in bright orange with silk embroidery on the bodice. The third dance was in a deep blue, full-length costume

---

7 Jafer remained interested in making some version of this plan happen. Astad's family mounted such an exhibition in a gallery in Mumbai on 10 December 2022 to mark Astad's second death anniversary.

whose design depicting cranes matched Astad's bird-like gestures expressed through his fingers and palms, often a slight lift of his shoulders and his face full of emotion (Datta 2020).

This production's young director had brought Astad into the group as a dancer, but Astad's experience of collaboration was not as harmonious as the one with Limb on *Hamlet_Avataar*. Astad was displeased, especially since he had recommended the Indian musicians. He was put in an awkward position of taking 'dictates' from a director who did not first discuss the matter with him. Jafer had to intervene, reminding the director that when artists work together, they need to have open discussions, share ideas and come to agreements, even as the director may structure and put the final presentation together. Nonetheless, the performance was a success. Jafer described Astad's 'superbly controlled, graceful movements' that provided an effective contrast to the rising sound of the drums along with 'the lilt of the gayageum, the mellifluous notes of the flute and the sonorous vocals.' This production had its premiere on 20 October 2017, at the National Theatre in Korea, then travelled to Sarang, the Festival of India in Korea on 21 October. The show toured India in 2019–2020, being performed at the Royal Opera House, Mumbai on 21 February 2020.[8] Astad was quite emotional about this venue since, despite it being in his hometown, he had never performed in the space.[9]

---

8 The performance can be viewed on Royal Opera House Mumbai's YouTube channel: https://bit.ly/3AOYyeP (last accessed 26 August 2024).

9 Astad had worked on another South–South collaboration with Danny Yung, the artistic director of Hong Kong's experimental theatre company, Zuni Icosahedron. Yung had followed Astad's career since the 1980s and had asked him to be involved in a 2016 theatre work. Astad, who has a successful track record of creating work with the deaf, worked as a facilitator for deaf groups in Hong Kong as well as with another local group called Mok Chin. Earlier, in 2007, Astad travelled to Japan to collaborate with musician Keiko Harada, a well-known composer who had worked with Taiwanese dancer-choreographers. Astad felt that Harada and he connected well as artists.

While in South Korea, Astad performed a solo entitled *Liminal: Late October on Jeju Island in South Korea* on 25 October 2017 at Jeju Stone Park. He was attracted to the natural beauty of Jeju Island with its sandy beaches and volcanic landscape. Astad loved to dance almost anywhere, so this outdoor site on Jeju Island was inviting to him with 'a gallery and huge showcase of Korean art, architecture and design, a vast outdoor garden and sculpture park', as noted by Maynard Kirkpatrick, who wrote a lyrical, laudatory review of Astad's performance. It began on a sunny afternoon in a 'unique and challenging setting for any dancer and a challenge that Astad Deboo has succeeded beautifully in overcoming many times in his stellar international dance career' (pers. email, 2017).[10]

In *Liminal*, Astad used the indoor and outdoor space creatively, 'mounting the lip of a vast round pool of water flat to the horizon,' says Kirkpatrick, 'as the skirt of his white costume absorbed the water, and he invoked the spirit of the water with an anointing gesture.' Next, with his feet and hands wet, Astad descended the steps from the fountain, gesturing to the audience to follow him. They passed a potter's field with large earthenware pots glistening in the late-afternoon sun. Astad then waved his audience to the next venue which was 'the opening to the great exhibition hall of the Stone Park'. Now, with the sun tilting and casting elongated shadows on the stones, Astad offered 'tribute to all those modern-day stone-shapers who laboured to create and animate the park from Jeju's abundant inert stone'. Astad animated the stones with his movements, casting long shadows in the light of the setting sun.

Astad performed *Liminal* again at Mumbai's Tamasha, an intimate, experimental performance space. Sanjukta Sharma reviewed *Liminal* as 'a three-piece solo performance about anguish, loss and playfulness that celebrates the flourishes that [Astad] has mastered over 49 years. Deboo is sublime in it' (2018). Sharma notes his signature style with slow, drawn-out and graceful movements, as his limbs 'display[ed] muscular

---

10 My thanks to Astad for sharing Kirkpatrick's review with me via email.

power, rhythmic complexity, full-bodied passion and an astonishingly flexible lower back'. Sharma's review opens memorably with a by-line: 'The dancer is revolutionary in many ways, one being his ability to make his body do what he wants it to.' Her tone is playfully irreverent: 'At 71, Astad Deboo has one hell of a backbend . . . The dancer's spinal column does a lot of work.' In *Liminal*, Astad wore a T-shirt and tights in one section and a flowing black angarkha that he held with one hand. It moved with him as his partner. He told Sharma: 'I am working much more with my back now . . . I work harder to keep myself fit now.'

Astad masterfully uses his body as 'his best tool of expression,' writes Sharma. 'The body does what we want it to, he said—you have to *want* it to do something badly enough and work hard at it.' In ageist Indian society, Astad was a revolutionary whose 'creative idiom is still evolving, which essentially proves that each age group has its qualities and values'. Astad asks why people are afraid of seeing ageing bodies. It is because such bodies are a stark reminder of becoming infirm and unattractive with age. That Astad continued to dance at 71 challenged 'a deeply entrenched Indian view that age means "retirement" or rest or stillness and quietude'. In 2019, Astad had completed 50 years 'as a dance professional. He is trying things he hasn't done before' (Sharma 2018).

CHAPTER 11

Astad's Collaborations with Musicians and Dancers in India and the Diaspora

Collaboration with Indian Rudra Veena Player Baha'ud-din Dagar in *Inter Connect* (2018)

Astad had a special camaraderie with rudra veena player Ustad Mohi Baha'ud-din Dagar, a rapport that enabled them, despite their different genres and approaches, to achieve their shared purpose—to uplift the human spirit—in their co-created work entitled *Inter Connect*. Baha'ud-din Dagar remarked that he had never imagined that an opportunity to work with Astad would materialize. 'He [Astad] reached out first', he said with deep emotion at Astad's remembrance on 10 January 2021 in Mumbai. Baha'ud-din did not know if his musical tradition would work with Astad's dance: 'How to bend the framework? Astad made it sound so simple, making it clear that everyone in the collaborative process would decide equally.' So began their creative exploration on a democratic footing.

From their first meeting, Baha'ud-din was struck by Astad's seriousness about art and his commitment to 'doing it right, without anything on paper, just an idea' to guide him. He was further impressed that Astad knew how to realize that idea in a certain amount of time: 'Professionally, I learnt a lot from Astad. I cannot put it on paper. Astad was a strong influence on my work, even in the way one approaches one's work.' One special aspect of Astad's personality that struck Baha'ud-din was how 'humane' he was to everyone: 'What Astad shared with every person was intimate, a direct contact.' Although he knew Astad for only a couple of years, Astad had left 'a permanent imprint' on his mind—'I miss him in person but he is there in front of us. We cannot erase him.'

Hailing from the illustrious Dagar family of Dhrupad musicians, Baha'ud-din has played across diverse platforms—on television and radio—and for audiences in India and beyond. Astad was deeply attuned to the Dhrupad style of singing from 1990 when he worked with the Gundecha brothers; nearly two decades later, he found an affinity with Baha'ud-din's Dhrupad style in playing the veena. Astad's comparison of Dhrupad music to his dance style is accurate and astute: 'Like my dance, Dhrupad is vigorous one moment and meditative the next' (Swaminathan 2018). Further, Astad compared the Gundecha Brothers' process of 'unravelling the many layers of their music, slowly and steadily' to his own gradual revealing of a dance: 'I too invest a lot of thought into every move and gesture. I like the dance to grow on me and [on] the audience at its own pace' (Swaminathan 2018).

Astad was excited when Baha'ud-din agreed to collaborate with him since the veena maestro was very particular about which artist he played for. Astad narrates the story of their first meeting at a dance conference. The organizer of the conference had asked Astad to create a dance but only gave him a day to do so. Astad asked Baha'ud-din 'if he wanted to jam. The response was tremendous' (Deboo 2018). After that, another opportunity came up from NCPA who would ask Astad for a new work every couple of years. 'I asked Baha'ud-din if he wanted to come on board for my next work', said Astad, 'and he readily agreed.' Together they created *Inter Connect*, which premiered on 30 November 2018 at NCPA's Tata Theatre in Mumbai and was also performed at Mumbai's G5A space on 27 March 2020, marking 50 years of Astad's career.

Inter Connect was performed with Baha'ud-din on the rudra veena, Pratap Awadh on the pakhavaj, Nityanand Haldipur on the flute and

Dhrupad singer Chintan Upadhyaya on vocals. Upadhyaya and percussionist Awadh performed 'in the pure Indian classical technique, in which they are proficient. However, the drummer would normally play on a definite beat, but here I said I don't want a downbeat.' Instead, he suggested pauses between the beats: 'Perhaps tap–pause–tap–tap–pause' (Deboo 2018). Similarly, the veena's sounds would come in gradually, then stop, then re-enter the soundscape.

Inter Connect is a 60-minute work that traces one day from dawn to dusk in the journey of life on Earth. The set and lighting were related to nature with a lit LED screen as a backdrop. At daybreak, the sun rose crimson red, then as the day went on, the light changed to blue, then grey, until dusk and darkness descended with only the stars visible. Astad's minimal movement followed the veena's sound that he describes as 'a slow dissolve like on television from one image into the next. That's how the movements will go as well. I may start off in the centre and gradually I move to the right or left side.' Astad's mudras were particularly prominent in the choreography. Additionally, 'there is an aspect of playfulness . . . I might sometimes respond with quick movement or maybe just with my fingers.' Astad created a mood of reverence while the singer's lines taken from a poem were 'about moroseness and loss, but in the end, there is hope' (Deboo 2018).

The 'Choreographer's Note' on *Inter Connect* is significant not only for this work but for insight into Astad's thoughts on the connection between music and movement: 'I, like many choreographers before me have pondered the eternal question: what comes first, the movement or the music?'[1] While some choreographers may be inspired by the music, others find the music 'to fit within the grammar of their art form'. For Astad, the process of linking movement to music or vice versa 'is entirely fluid'. Music does not simply accompany his movements,

---

1 All quotations from Astad in this and subsequent paragraphs are taken from the 'Choreographer's Note' to *Inter Connect*.

'rather, it is an integral part of [his] creative thinking—a meaningful and engaging ingredient of the entire idiom'. Specifically, for 'the ancient art form of Dhrupad music', Astad wondered: 'Could the identity of each (music and dance) be enriched through the creative process?' Astad linked the two art forms—Dhrupad 'with a structure steeped in antiquity and a glorious tradition along with modern abstract dance movement which is an ever-evolving process firmly entrenched in modernity'. Astad imagined this new union as 'a marriage made in heaven'. Further, he was committed to preserving the integrity of both genres' idiom and structure while allowing for flexibility and adaptability in their presentation.

On the same wavelength as Astad, Baha'ud-din regarded their joint performance as 'a culmination of the old and the new seeking to renew itself whilst maintaining its form. It cannot be looked at as a fusion but a confluence of ideas in the large melting pot'. He elaborated that these ideas are rooted in 'an Indianness that accepts, dissolves and reinvents itself time and again like the concept of the trinities of Brahma, Vishnu and Mahesh where one recreates, sustains and destroys time and again to maintain newness' (G5A Foundation 2020).

Astad recognized the complicated working relationship between a musician and a dancer within which both artists understand that they are 'interdependent'. He says that the dancer and the musician inhabit 'vastly different processes but aspire towards a shared goal to illuminate a thought, a feeling, an emotion [. . .] while maintaining the grammar and integrity of both artists. The "marriage" metaphor for the collaboration goes thus far and no more'. The collaborators may connect on an interpersonal level or through the generic conventions of dance and music.

Astad was aware that music and dance were 'two separate disciplines with separate needs and concerns'. Hence, he regarded *Inter Connect* as 'an ongoing work in progress, a continuous evolution of a work where each discipline will run its course uniquely', within a functioning collaboration, 'with a common goal, to create a new sense of identity'. Such a collaborative process, is, at its root, creative, bringing forth a novel synergistic work that satisfies, even elevates the hearts and minds of spectators. In the profoundly Indian performance of *Inter Connect*, Astad's mudras and rasas created a thrilling experience of dance and music that honoured both tradition and innovation, an intersection embodied by Astad himself.

Collaboration with Bharatanatyam Dancer Hema Rajagopalan in *Inai* (*The Connection*) (2019)

> 'I learned a lot [from Astad]. My art enhanced, my movement vocabulary or even the way of thinking or of approaching a particular aspect [was taken] definitely further. I would say [he] enhanced me as an artist.'—Hema Rajagopalan (int., July 2021)

Hema Rajagopalan grew up in India and has been based in Chicago since 1974. As founder and artistic director of Natya Dance Theatre Company since 1994, Hema is the recipient of the Chicago Dance 2021 Legacy Award which recognizes an artistic leader who has enriched her/his community and made a significant impact on dance in the Chicago–Midwest area. Anita Ratnam, during her interview with Hema on Astad's 74th birthday celebrations on 13 July 2021, noted that Rajagopalan 'has really stamped her unique imprint using her love and knowledge of Bharatanatyam and classical dance arts'.

Hema had the foresight to recognize Astad's talent and to dream of a collaboration. Astad would finally get the opportunity to work with an Indian classical dancer—his life-long wish. 'What he couldn't make happen in India,' stated Anita, 'you [Hema] made it happen in Chicago.' In 2019, Astad and Hema co-created a dance programme aptly entitled *Inai* (*The Connection*) for which Hema assembled a terrific musical ensemble.

FIGURE 37. (RIGHT) Astad receives the Padma Shri from President A. P. J. Abdul Kalam, 2007. *Courtesy Deboo family.*

FIGURE 38. (BELOW) Astad with President Kalam. *Courtesy Deboo family.*

FIGURE 39. (ABOVE) Astad with
President Kalam and *ContraPosition*
dancers and team.
Courtesy Deboo family.

FIGURE 40. (RIGHT) Astad with Krithika
of Clarke School for the Deaf, Chennai.
Rehearsal photo.
Courtesy Ramaa Bharadvaj.

FIGURE 41. (FACING PAGE TOP) Astad
meets Queen Elizabeth II of England at
Buckingham Palace, London, 2 March
2017, at the launch of the India–UK Year
of Culture. *Courtesy Deboo family*.

FIGURE 42. (FACING PAGE BOTTOM) Astad
receives the Birudhu Yagnaraman Living
Legend Award from Krishna Gana Sabha,
Chennai, 2018. *Courtesy Deboo family*.

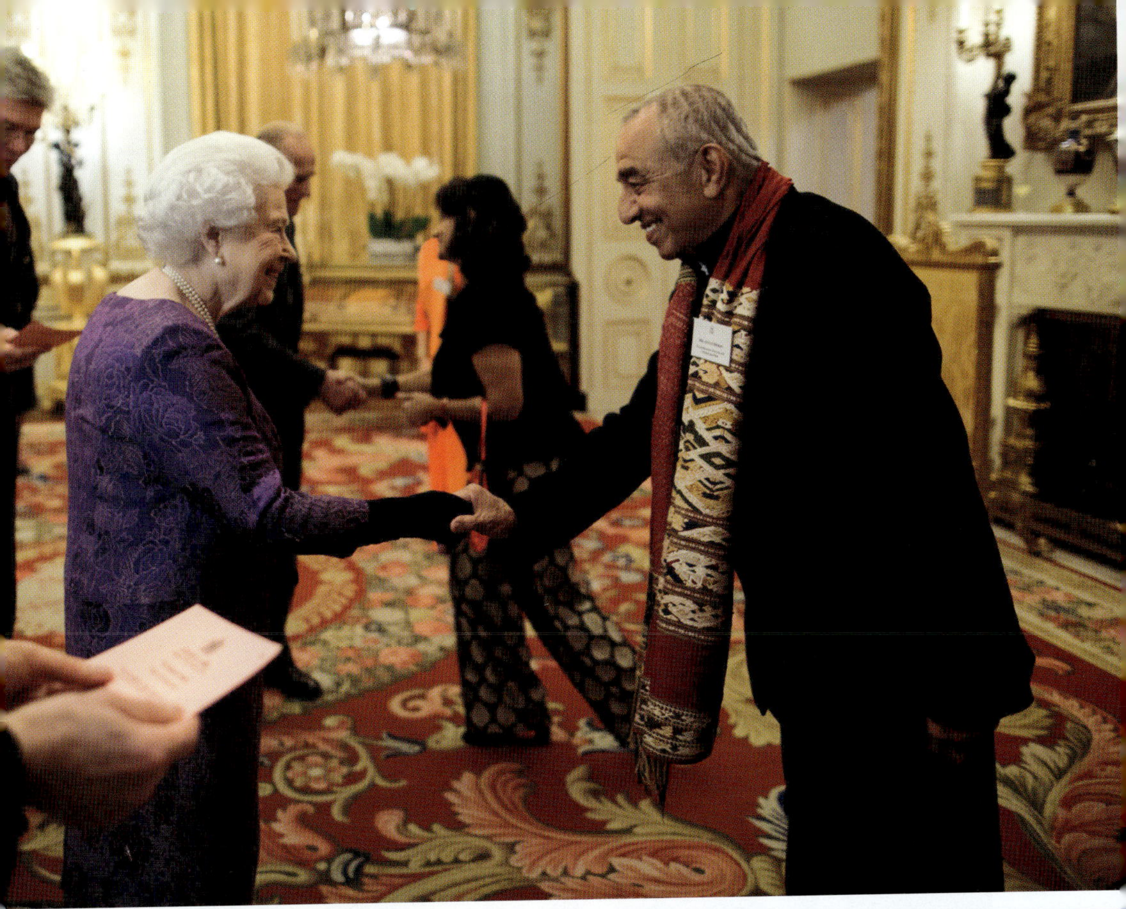

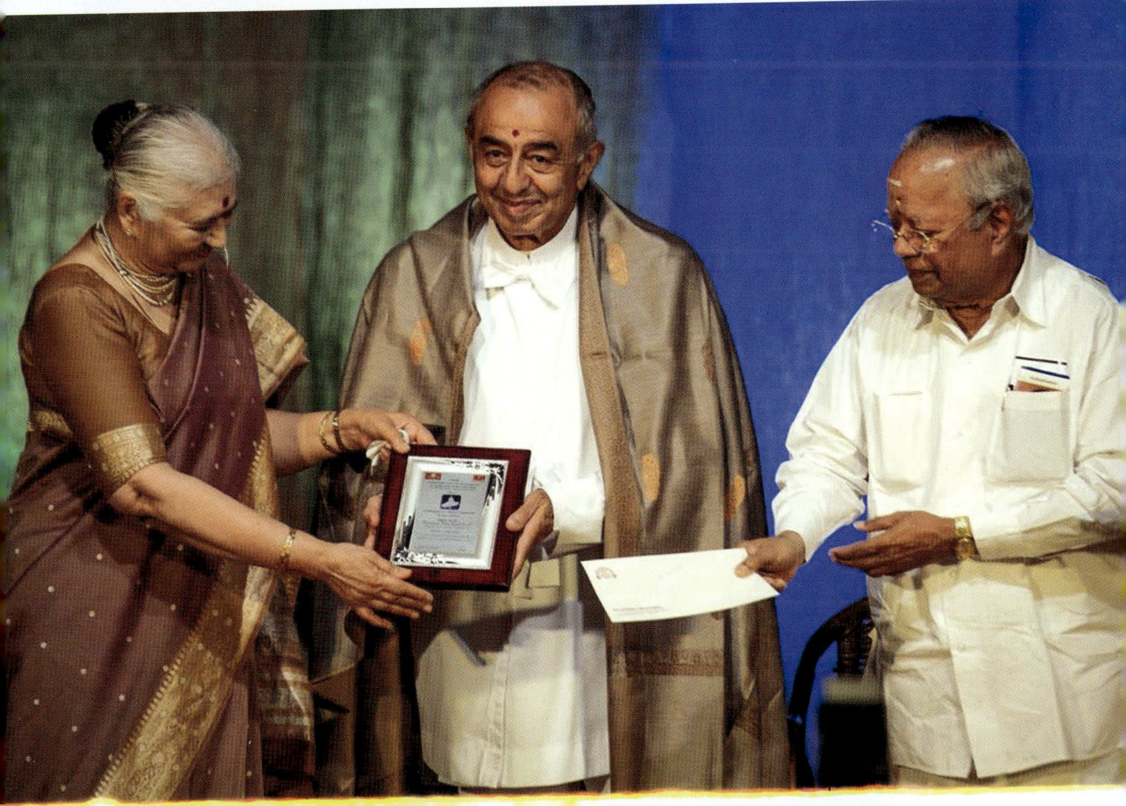

FIGURE 43. (TOP) Astad with Manipuri Pung Cholam drummers. *Courtesy Deboo family.*

FIGURE 44. (BOTTOM) Astad with Manipuri dancers in *Rhythm Divine*.
Photograph by Ritam Banerjee.

FIGURES 45–46. (FACING PAGE) Astad with Salaam Baalak youth in *Breaking Boundaries*.
Photographs by Ritam Banerjee.

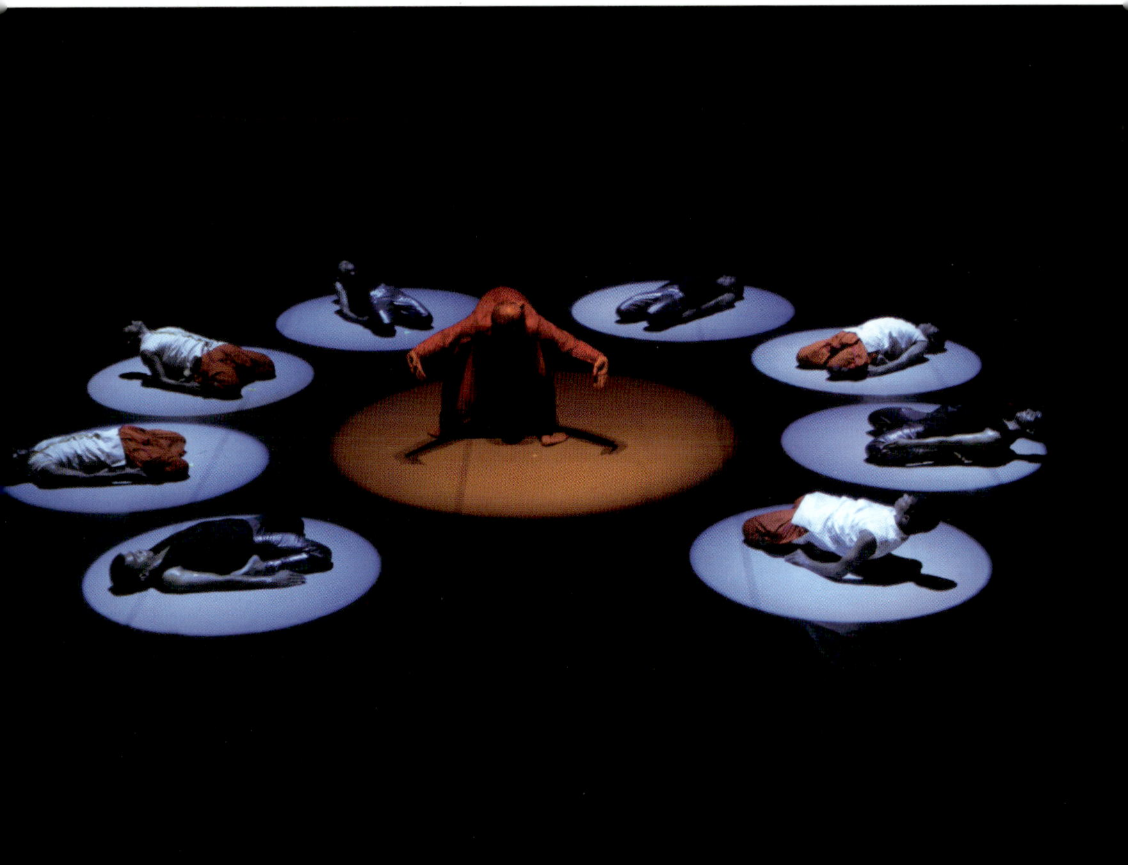

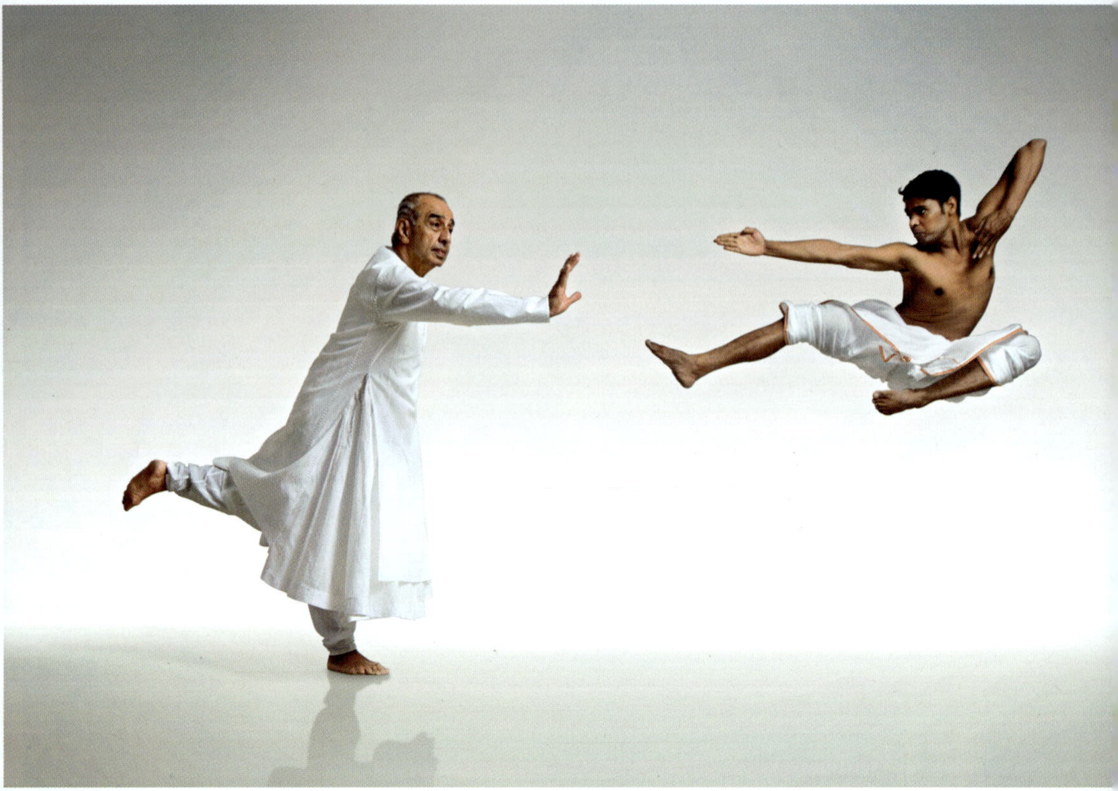

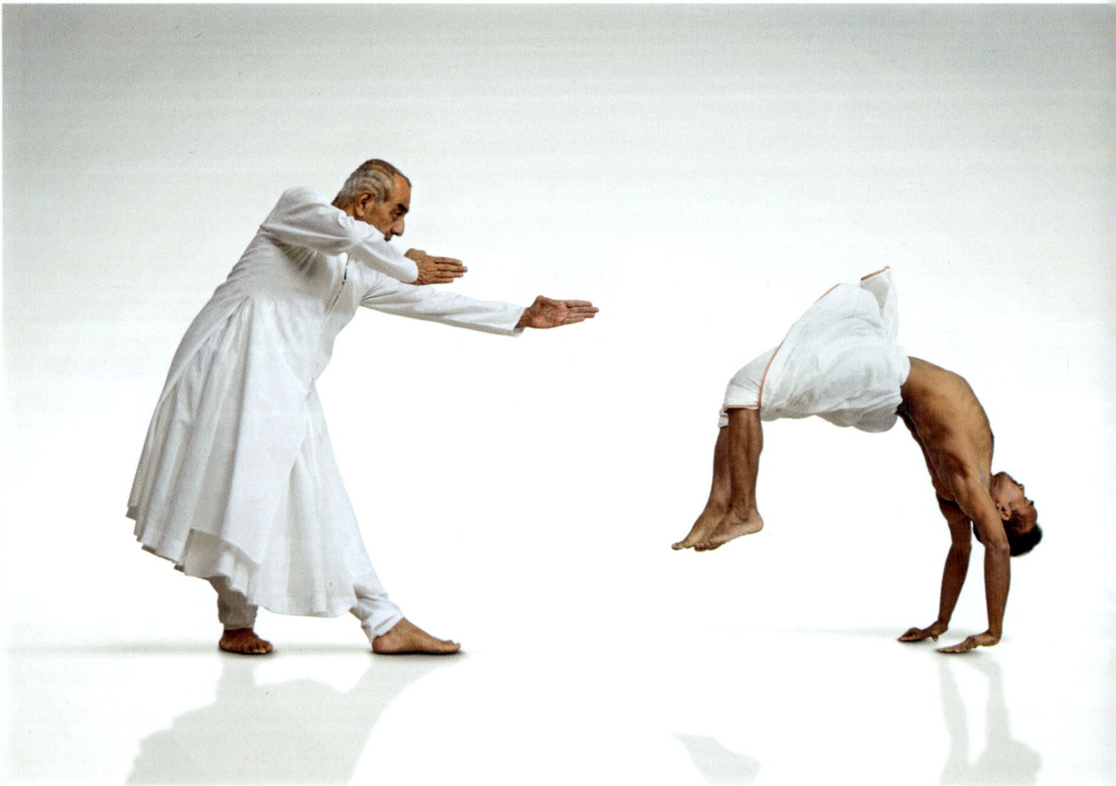

FIGURES 47–48. (FACING PAGE AND ABOVE) Astad with Salaam Baalak youth in *Unbroken Unbowed. Photographs by Ritam Banerjee.*

FIGURES 49–50. (OVERLEAF) Astad with Salam Baalak youth in puppet costume in *Interpreting Tagore. Photographs by Vipul Sangoi.*

FIGURES 51–53. (ABOVE AND FACING PAGE) Astad with Hema Rajagopalan, dancers from her Natya Dance Theatre Company, and Astad's dancer dressed as a large puppet in *Inai* (*The Connection*). *Photographs by Ravi Ganapathy.*

FIGURE 54. (TOP) Astad with Yukio Tsuji in *Eternal Embrace. Courtesy Deboo family.*

FIGURE 55. (BOTTOM) Astad with Korean and Indian musicians in *Same Same but Different. Photograph by Ritam Banerjee.*

FIGURE 56. (TOP) Astad dressed by costume designer Jade Couture. *Courtesy Deboo family*.

FIGURE 57. (BOTTOM) Astad in Mexico. *Photograph by Ritam Banerjee*.

FIGURE 58. Astad in front of Anish Kapoor's sculpture *Cloud Gate*, popularly known as 'The Bean', Chicago. *Photograph by Ritam Banerjee.*

FIGURE 59. Astad on Mehrangarh fort, Jodhpur, Rajasthan. *Photograph by Ritam Banerjee.*

The idea of collaboration arose in 2016 when Hema met Astad in Washington DC. She had been 'intrigued with Astad's work way back when [she] was a young teenager, seeing his photographs and thinking [his dance] is so different.' However, she had not followed his career until after she moved to the US. 'I had seen a lot of his twirling,' remarked Hema, wondering 'what does it do? But it did get me to think meditatively . . . after 2017 Astad used to send me his work . . . it all came organically together. And I thought, why not, why not [collaborate]?' (int. with Katrak, July 2021).

Hema described how this collaboration unfolded from 2016 onwards. In 2017, Shirley Mordine, a modern dancer and founder of the Dance Centre of Columbia College in Chicago, asked Hema to collaborate with her along with another contemporary Indian dancer to 'explore movement vocabulary'. That was how Astad came into the picture. In 2017, Hema and one of her Bharatanatyam style dancers, along with Shirley and one of her modern style dancers from Chicago, met Astad with his two dancers, trained in Astad's style, in Chennai. 'Initially, Astad was very apprehensive,' recalled Hema, 'since we needed a sense of direction as to where, how and what to do [in a project]. I think it was more about workshopping at that time.' They also worked for about a week in Delhi, as Astad had proposed, 'to gather ambience', and give the dancers a chance to get acquainted. Although nothing came from that time together, Hema remembered that Astad 'really wanted to collaborate. He kept asking me to think about it, saying let's do something. And then I got the MacArthur Foundation grant to bring international artists to the US and work with them. And Astad was very, very happy that, at last, he really wanted this dream that he had, to be fulfilled' (int. with Katrak, July 2021).

Astad sought to work with Hema and her students' Bharatanatyam style. Hema had decided not to dance on stage, but Astad encouraged her to perform a padam—an abhinaya dance item—in which he would shadow her from behind. They decided to try this out in rehearsal. Hema of course knew Carnatic music and the lyric's language, plus the padam's overall mood, but Astad, without such knowledge, followed Hema's movements beautifully. Hema described Astad's remarkable prowess: 'Everyone was just awestruck at Astad's weaving whatever I did; it just gelled so beautifully without even my knowing.' What was awe-inspiring was that he could 'emulate [Hema's movements and expressions] without seeing [her]. He was next to me but not really in front of me so that is the beautiful aspect of Astad.' This was, as Hema remarked, 'a really memorable moment' (int. with Ratnam, July 2021).

Hema had come up with the concept of *Inai*, which translates as connection, even embrace. She was inspired by a billboard that she had seen in Europe showing two groups of human beings—'one that just lives, and the other that enjoys and flourishes'. Hema imagined finding 'the bridge', to connect the two groups, and Astad encouraged Hema to develop this idea. 'As a collaborator,' recalled Hema, 'he was extremely generous in allowing me to go to the drawing board and storyboarding. He didn't interfere much' (int. with Katrak, July 2021). Astad made key contributions to the project by including two of his best dancers from Delhi along with two puppets—one large and one small. Astad imagined the large puppet, created by Dadi Pudumjee, as 'a comment-ing person', an idea that excited Hema and her troupe. The inanimate puppets with an animate dancer under them played a significant role in the choreography of *Inai*, intervening in the action as embodying humans, fostering connections and smoothing out tensions.

Another remarkable point in the development process was when Hema and Astad discovered an image of connecting, inspired by the large puppet. They took that 'image to map out and to use as a seed to proceed further'. This image materialized when the two dancers, Astad and Hema, moved together for the first time 'looking at each other, emulating, being inspired by each other's movement'. When they came close together, Astad asked the puppeteer 'with the huge puppet showing a large masculine face to close in'. It was a 'memorable moment', recounted Hema, when she and Astad met each other's gaze with the puppet closing in. Hema interpreted the puppet/ puppeteer as 'a third energy that really made us [Astad and Hema] connect'. She found it inspiring that 'this third dimension gave [Astad and her] the impetus to connect. When we looked at it, we really looked and we turned together towards that huge form, which embraced us with its big arms'. This image of the puppet embracing the two dancers, encouraging them, and then enabling them to connect guided the rest of the choreography in *Inai* (int. with Ratnam, July 2021).

'It was a collaboration,' said Hema to Anita, 'but Astad put his heart and soul into it. It was not a business thing with limits on his time.' Anita added: 'I'm so happy for Bharatanatyam, that you, an artist of your reputation and experience got to collaborate with him and it's so good for the art form to have had just that exposure to what Astad represented. He loved and was so respectful of the classical arts' (int. with Ratnam, July 2021). Hema observed that working with Astad was a pleasure; she never saw him get angry or lose his temper, even with her students. Astad had great respect for Hema, and their collaboration was marked by mutual respect and a spirit of give and take.

Altogether the collaboration involved around 80 days of working together, followed by time spent on the music. The two dancers and Hema's students worked together for 20 days in July 2019 when Astad travelled to Chicago at his own expense. He returned for a month before the show opened in November that year.[2] The music, performed live,

---

2 Before the performance in Chicago, Astad visited Washington DC where he met Deepika Sorabjee, a friend and professional connection who worked with Tata Trusts on arts education. Deepika recalled that she 'could listen to Astad recount stories from the [19]70s till the present . . . . During the pandemic, our chats became longer. I would joke when he called and said, "Hang on let me put on my shoes", as I knew he would be an hour pacing the house [Astad's exercise routine during lockdown] before we both hung up.' Deepika appreciated Astad's diverse interests, so in Washington DC, they went to the David Adjaye–designed Museum

featured Sikkil Gurucharan, a renowned Carnatic vocalist from Chennai, and George Brooks, a saxophone player from California. I was in the audience in November 2019 and particularly enjoyed Astad improvising in response to Brooks' saxophone sounds, creating magic with his uncanny ability to catch the musical nuances. Hema noted that the percussionists 'also loved working with Astad. He was very patient and he learned the rhythmic patterns [of Carnatic music]; he took them in and wanted to understand them (int. with Katrak, July 2021). Here was Astad, a lifelong learner.

The collaborative process was highly congenial—'we sat around, we discussed, we talked about breaking down the walls [between people],' said Hema. She appreciated Astad's 'wealth of knowledge not only in the aspect of the movement vocabulary but also on the thought process [behind the movement].' Astad was also experienced and well-informed about the design aspects of production, offering valuable insights on costuming, stagecraft and lighting. 'He was a walking encyclopedia in terms of knowledge,' said Hema, noting that she has some 'amazing archival footage and videotapes which are really a treasure for [her] because this was the first time [she was] actually collaborating with a contemporary Indian dancer'. What she valued above all were Astad's 'human qualities, his kindness and how he would take care of the dancers': 'Not only did I learn about the craft that I'm so passionate about, but it's also about life skills and how to become a good human being, how to care. So, I miss him a lot' (int. with Katrak, July 2021).

---

of African American History and Culture, had lunch in Georgetown, and walked about. Then, in classic Astad fashion, as 'a caring person', he got a friend to drive them around to view the monuments at night, knowing that this was Deepika's first visit to the city. 'That's the last time I saw him in person and I treasure that night walk, seeing Washington at night, standing across the White House, Maya Lin's Vietnam Memorial, climbing up the Lincoln Memorial (steps)' (int., January 2022).

My interview with Hema ended with her cherished memory of Astad as a caring human being who called her almost daily from Mumbai while she was in Chennai caring for her father after his surgery. That was in December 2019; *Inai* had been completed, but Astad retained his connection with Hema, as he did with other friends, collaborators and ordinary people who touched his life. He was one artist whose 'kind-hearted, moral support I really cherished,' said Hema. 'It was his human touch; it was not about whether he collaborated with me or not. It's more about a person feeling for the other person, his empathy' (int. with Katrak, July 2021).

Astad's collaborative spirit enabled him to achieve amazing performances with his signature choreography, whether dancing with a classical Indian dancer, or to the music of a shakuhachi flautist, a rudra veena player or a saxophonist, a Carnatic vocalist or a Baul singer. Such jointly created works demonstrate Astad at the height of his dance career. He displayed his artistic gifts along with his vast humanity that embraced people, whether in his collaboration with Hema's dancers or with the younger generation of Korean musicians and actors. His ability to remain down to earth and unassuming about his talents put his collaborators at ease. Astad shared his skills with generosity, truth, camaraderie and respect for every artist who crossed his path regardless of their origins. Such a democratic spirit is unusual among artists who reach certain heights of recognition as Astad had done during the last decade of his life. He remained humble and giving, with integrity to his art and to the people he loved.

CHAPTER 12

Collaborations with Costume Designers and Photographers

Astad's dance performances were acclaimed for visual design that included lighting, staging, use of space and his choice of costumes. During his early choreography in the 1970s and 1980s, when enamoured of modern dance with its emphasis on the body, he wore leotards and unitards. From the 1990s onwards, Astad's costume changed to Indian-style long angarkhas, both in sober and bold colours, with churidar-style trousers. Astad was a fashionable man with a riveting stage presence—at times he wore dhotis, short coats and other outfits that created different silhouettes on stage. Astad's collaborations with costume designers have played a major role in his stage presence. His flowing angarkha became an integral part of his performance, often serving as his stage partner as he gracefully twirled, holding one end of it while executing his iconic chakkars.

Anita Ratnam remarked that Astad selected 'a particular silhouette' for each work that came to life with his costume and visual design. Anita noted that on stage, with his floor-kissing angarkha, Astad 'looked much taller than he was in real life; he seemed vast and expansive—even when he was still' (int., August 2021). She contrasted Astad's extravagant stage presence, where his bold-coloured angarkhas added a lush vibrancy, with his deliberately simple offstage attire of white kurta and churidar. Astad carefully selected the colours of his angarkhas—ranging from vibrant pink or yellow to white with white silk thread embroidery or black with gold trim—to suit the work's mood and the stage setting, whether outdoors under a full moon or indoors on a proscenium stage.

The fame of Astad's costumes reached France where a museum, the Centre National du Costume de Scene, which holds a collection of 20,000 theatrical costumes from around the world, was interested in getting a few pieces of his costumes for their collection, reminded Ramaa Bharadvaj. Ramaa added a loving personal note: 'Such was his celebrity. But he wore that stardom as lightly and as gracefully as his stage costume—slip on and slip off! And this is what endeared him to all those who got to know him' (int., August 2021).

Among Astad's costume designers, Archana Shah had a 30-year professional connection and friendship with the dancer. Astad also worked with Jade Couture in Mumbai and Ashdeen Lilaowala in Delhi. Archana, a graduate of the National Institute of Design (NID) in Ahmedabad where she continues to live, shared how surprised she was when Astad met her for the first time at her home and asked her to design a costume for him. Up to that time, she had only seen him in leotards and stretch fabric. 'That was his look,' she remarked, 'a very strong look that suited his minimalist movement.' (int., August 2021; same for subsequent quotes). However, Astad mused about a 'more flowy' costume. As they were both pondering his request, Astad suddenly noticed in the room a painted scroll with a male performer in a bright-red costume with full sleeves. Archana explained that 'there was this painting, Pabuji ki Phad—a painted scroll from Rajasthan, used by a storyteller, normally in villages' (see Map Academy 2022). Traditionally, such a storyteller would stretch out the scroll and narrate the story while dancing, illuminated by a lantern. The audience knew most of the stories, as is common in traditional performances; the excitement lay in the narrator's skill in recounting the tale. Archana thought that this image 'triggered something' in Astad, especially since in this tradition, it is 'normally a male performer dressed in red, wearing a kind of angarkha touching the ground, [of great] length, unlike the angarkhas worn by royalty'.

Inspired by this image, Astad asked Archana to design a costume for him with similar length and flow. I was fascinated to learn this. Angarkhas—translated literally as 'body protectors'—feature ornate embroidery on the bodice. They can be tied with cloth or fastened with buttons near either shoulder. Astad's floor-kissing angarkha soon became his signature costume, putting him in the lineage of Rajasthani male artists and Indian folk tradition as well as in the history of 'our nobility', noted Archana, something she saw was an apt choice by a 'stylish man' on and off stage. But this had nothing to do with Astad's gay sensibility, felt Archana; he did not gravitate to this design for 'anything that was feminine . . . It was something a man wore with great pride— the red and gold that the Rajasthani dancer/storyteller wore.' However, Archana added that 'from day one I knew Astad as a gay man. I never knew that he was discreet about it because he talked about his relationships quite openly at [my] home.'

Be that as it may, Astad's transgressing of gender boundaries is notable—as a male dancer in a long dress, he played with the fluidity of gender identity. This dress did not make him look effeminate, nor was it traditionally worn by male performers to imitate women. This choice of costume differed from the tradition of *stree vesahm*, where a male dancer knowingly—to himself and to the audience—imitates a female, complete with overtly feminine costume, long hair, jewellery and feminine expression and gait.

Historical images abound of Mughal and Rajput men wearing angarkhas. The Mughal version—also called *jamas*—were shorter, reaching just below the knees; they resembled long kurtas. In the Rajput or Rajasthani version, silk or brocade angarkhas were ankle-length, with highly ornate bodices studded with precious stones such as rubies and emeralds. Such male finery caught Astad's fancy, and a match was made between a dancer and a costume designer. Archana said that she must have designed over 30 costumes for Astad. He would willingly come to Ahmedabad for fittings, though, as Archana remarked, 'Costumes became an excuse because he always ended up spending two nights minimum, and the costume work was half a day. So, yeah, it's been many years of friendship. I miss him.' Archana recalled that towards the end of Astad's life, he once arrived in Ahmedabad with several old costumes that needed alteration to suit his changing physique.

But angarkhas were not the only costume that Archana and Astad collaborated on. Archana said:

> We've changed the silhouette so many times—short jackets, dhotis, loose pants, many kinds of long coats because there were times when he wanted a more severe silhouette. He would come up and say, 'Oh, I'm going to dance at the Purana Qila [outdoors with the Fort in the background in Delhi], I need something to match that environment.' Or, 'I'm going to dance at the Bhutanese king's ceremony', or 'I'm doing something at Champaner and this is the kind of monument and this is the kind of dance.'

Archana also described her design for *Inai* in which Astad 'wanted something really simple, in just black. It looked simple though I added much more volume by adding other kinds of panels in it; when he moved, it moved beautifully with him because of the way the panels were cut.'

Archana's insightful comment rings so true for Astad: 'The costume is not like a dress you wear. It needs to perform along with the performer.' Astad was a master at knowing how a costume needed to be weighted, and how it would show the colour on the reverse side as he twirled. 'For Astad, it wasn't just designing a piece of garment; it was a whole' that matched his movement, the particular performance and the space. Archana's clothing store Bandhej provided tons of fabric for Astad's selection. 'Astad had extremely good taste. He was very clear about the kinds of fabric he liked.'

Almost every person who had collaborated with Astad whom I interviewed mentioned that he maintained a professionalism that also included friendship. That's how he was. Archana agreed: 'Astad was a friend. It just so happened that I did a few costumes for him. We spent more time together as friends.' Archana valued Astad's ability to tell stories without criticizing people. As was his way, he had cultivated an independent connection with Archana's husband and her son. Astad 'the foodie with a sweet tooth' was also well known in Archana's household. 'He had to end his meal with an Indian mithai. Once, in earlier times when I didn't know about this, he said, "You don't have mithai?" He wasn't into ice cream and it was okay to have a dessert, but Indian sweets were something he really enjoyed.'

Another costume designer, Mumbai's Monica Shah of Jade Couture, knew Astad as a friend and collaborator for nearly a decade. He opened 'one of our shows at Lakmé Fashion Week with his exquisite talent and signature elegance,' recalled Monica. 'And since then, he has adorned our handcrafted ensembles for his dance performances.' Monica recognized Astad's knowledge and insight about fabric. Since he was 'so rooted in Indian culture, he was very particular about his costume. For him, his ensemble represented Indian crafts and textiles. And he made sure that was represented beautifully and authentically.' This inspired her 'to work towards cultural sustainability and celebrate Indian crafts in a unique way' while working with Astad (pers. email, 14 February 2022).

Ashdeen Lilaowala responded warmly and in detail via email to my many interview questions (2 August 2021; same for subsequent quotes). He was struck with Astad's 'great sense of proportion and colour. He knew exactly what worked for his performances. He could bring life to any costume with his movements. He enjoyed working with colour, and textures to create a visual.' Ashdeen appreciated that Astad could select a colour based on the theme of a work and the environment in which he was performing. 'He could carry a muted white and a fiery orange with the same elan . . . My favourite one sported large crane motifs that were designed in such a way that every time Astad would famously start twirling, . . . it would appear like the cranes had taken flight. In this way, he breathed life into the costumes.'

Ashdeen remarked that as a student at NID, his 'first memory of Astad was seeing a photograph of him taken by ace photographer Farrokh Chothia. In it, he was posing in a blue leotard, framed by dancers in flight dressed in vibrant yellow dhotis.' Ashdeen had cut this photo out from the magazine and 'pinned it on [his] vision board at [his] hostel room—in those days [they] didn't have Pinterest.' Later, Ashdeen saw Astad perform outdoors at NID's amphitheatre, with 'a striking monument in the background'. Ashdeen narrates:

> In the midst of his performance, Astad started to climb the monument. Momentarily he stepped on a loose brick and slipped. A collective gasp was heard from the audience but Astad continued to dance gracefully, completely undeterred. I remember running back to my hostel room to retrieve that photo of him from my board and getting him to sign it.

Ashdeen eventually got to know Astad through his friend Kharmeen in Mumbai. When Ashdeen moved to Delhi, he would often get a call from Astad, 'his deep voice saying, "*Ken chev*, Ashdeen?"' This costume designer echoed the sentiment expressed by so many, that one of Astad's greatest qualities was that he always stayed in touch with people he met all over the world. Ashdeen and Astad would meet up for tea or coffee whenever Astad was in Delhi. He was 'enthralled with Astad's stories of his travels [and] his sense of adventure. Astad's resilience and dedication to his art always inspired [him].' He fondly recollected that Astad was a great supporter, was always willing to help: 'When my label [launched in 2012] was nascent and I didn't want to spend big money on couriers, Astad often carried heavy suitcases full of saris [for Ashdeen's clients] across the country.'

Ashdeen noted 'an abashed sense of Parsiness about Astad', which he believed Astad got from his mother. Meeting her confirmed that

Astad also got his zest for life from her. Ashdeen narrated his favourite anecdote that he always recalled 'with a smile': 'Astad as a globally renowned dancer visited Bombay Parsi Panchayat office with his father for elections. While his father [was] cast[ing] his vote, a group of Parsi ladies who had been sitting bored since morning recognized him and casually asked him, "Mr Deboo jaara dance kareene dekharo ni!" [please dance for us!].' Ashdeen closed his remarks with a loving tribute to Astad:

> [He] had danced in front of kings and queens and fittingly danced with many queens. I imagined that one day, in the midst of one of his performances, the heavens would open their arms and welcome him and he would levitate into the skies twirling and even though that didn't literally transpire, I am sure he is dancing with the Almighty today.

Astad's Collaborations with Photographers

'Astad revealed himself to the world through his photographs. Photography, they say, can bore into a person's psyche and a great photographer can tell you about the subject's personality. [. . .] Across the years, photographers have just loved capturing [Astad's] many moods and his flowing garments and his sparse simplicity because so much of Astad's personality, and actually, his photo sessions were performances of their own.'—Anita Ratnam, at Astad's birthday celebration, 13 July 2021

Astad enjoyed being photographed. Indeed, he was photogenic with a winning smile. He had a special rapport when working with photographers who became friends; some even travelled with him so that they could snap photos of him during performances. Although he could not afford to hire people to shoot or videotape his early performances, Astad worked hard to have a media presence through reviews, interviews and visuals to get himself and his art known to the public. By the

1990s, talented professional photographers—such as Farrokh Chothia, Neelesh Kale, Ritam Banerjee, Shantanu Sheorey, Anil Kumar and Sreekumar Krishnan—wanted to work with Astad. They recognized what a fantastic aesthetic eye he had, not only as a dancer and choreographer but also as a collaborator with photographers.

Farrokh Chothia met Astad through mutual acquaintances, Ratan Batliboi and Sam Kerawalla. Farrokh found Astad to be a good model for a photographer since Astad could himself visualize the desired image. Farrokh had to 'create a different language with photography', so that he could meet the challenge 'of capturing a dancer moving' (int., January 2022; same for subsequent quotes). His camera eye saw Astad combining male and female energies in his dance. He photographed Astad in several works in the 1990s and beyond—including moments with Manipuri dancers leaping high in the air with Astad in mid-chakkar, in *Rhythm Divine*, among many others.

As a fellow Parsee, Farrokh felt 'a natural bonding' with him from the time he met him in the 1990s. He admired Astad's discipline, mental strength and impressive fitness. Astad was known for walking long distances across Mumbai, so he would frequently stop by Farrokh's studio, walking 9 kilometres from Shapur Baug to Dadar, which always amazed Farrokh. Astad had great organizational skills, recalled Farrokh, hence he would set up a photo shoot while remaining 'free flowing' within that structure. He could 'create something from happy accidents', though it was important 'to get out of the way' and let him do his thing—as when he once appeared with his face covered in mud, saying 'Chalo [come on], let's have fun!' As with his other friends, Astad was the one to call Farrokh and keep in touch. During the 1990s, noted Farrokh, interactions among models and photographers were much more fluid and less structured than they are now. Creative people would willingly give their time and talent to collaborate on a shoot. Farrokh lamented that such 'spontaneity has disappeared from the world. People want to know what a gig will get them and the last decade has been influenced by Instagram.'

Farrokh narrated a wonderful memory of going to the terrace of NCPA on 29 September 1998 with Astad, some of the Manipuri dancers and Sushma Reddy, an Indian model and actress who had generously agreed to participate in Farrokh's photography sessions. What resulted was what Farrokh proudly calls his 'ace photo'—Sushma in the middle, her face in profile, glancing to the side with a stunning expression, while Manipuri dancers tutored by Astad jumping high in the air around her—an image he felt was akin to Beethoven's Fifth Symphony.

Two other photographers, Neelesh Kale and Ritam Bannerjee, shared their experience of collaborating with Astad in interviews with Anita Ratnam on Astad's birthday celebration on 13 July 2021.[1] Pune-based Neelesh 'loved to capture bodies, moving bodies in as close to starkness as possible,' says Anita, 'You are a stylist as well, but when you were photographing Astad, there was something very deeply personal.' Neelesh first met Astad around 1995 when he first saw his chakkars on stage and found them 'hypnotic'. After that concert, Neelesh went back-stage to meet Astad and said that he wanted to photograph him—'So, he [Astad] said, "Darling, I don't work with everybody." I said, "OK." He gave me a time and I went to see him.' Neelesh had been working on images of body parts, which Astad liked and hence agreed to give him one shoot. 'When he came for the shoot, I had that impossible triangle [a prop from *Basics*]. The camera was on track, so I told him to sit there. He sat and started doing his thing. I got the picture[s]. Then I processed them, went to him, and showed him the pictures.'

---

1 My thanks to Ratnam for her insightful and perspicacious inclusion of Astad's photographers and her insightful questions about their work with Astad. The sub-sequent quotes by Anita and the photographers are taken from these interviews.

Clearly, Astad was pleased, because they continued working together. Neelesh found him 'an absolute pleasure' to work with and 'learned a lot from him'. As a non-dancer but 'a body person', he differentiated between artists who 'practise art and people who nurture, develop and further enhance arts'. Astad could do both. Neelesh and Astad 'had a pact' on how they worked together: Astad would call and ask for his picture to be taken at a certain time, then for it to be shared on WhatsApp because his 'youth circle were not on Facebook or Instagram'. Many friends recall Astad sending photos on WhatsApp and 'demanding a response'.

Neelesh did a final shoot with Astad in July 2020, when Astad came to Pune but did not breathe a word about his health condition. Neelesh noticed that Astad was getting tired, so they took rests in between work. He instructed Neelesh to post one picture then and another on Diwali. Astad liked the photos. When he called Neelesh to wish him a happy Diwali, Astad hinted that he had sad news, but he would not share it on that auspicious day—'I'll tell you after Diwali'. Neelesh asked if it was anything serious but he simply said that everything was okay. When Astad finally shared his diagnosis, Neelesh 'was completely shaken up. I had no idea about lymph-node cancer'. Earlier, they had planned that Neelesh would stay with Astad for five days in December 2020 to go through the many unprocessed pictures, have him select some, and spend some time with him. That was not to be.

Neelesh admired the rhythm and grace of Astad's body, finding his early works the best when Astad danced on his own and his 'extempore improvisations' were beautiful to see. Each performance would be different 'depending upon his mood, audience, space, lighting, whatever inspired him'. Neelesh compared Astad's dance form to Indian classical musicians who perform without a written score: 'It is not like someone is playing a symphony, which is written down'. Astad could be inspired to improvise by the music or the lighting in his early solo work that lived in the moment and often could not be replicated.

Another stellar photographer, Ritam Banerjee, travelled with Astad to many locations and photographed him extensively. His journey with Astad began at age five when he saw him perform at an auditorium in Jamshedpur. Ritam was 'so influenced and inspired' by what he saw then—even though he did not remember the performance—that he went home and dressed up like Astad, making his 'mother put on a dhoti [on him] and posing in front of the mirror'. His father's pictures from that time reminded him of this incident. Ritam remembered Astad as 'one of [his] super-seniors from Loyola school'.

As a youngster, Ritam always thought that Astad was beyond his reach; he could not even imagine that one day he would shoot photos of Astad. In college, Ritam took photography seriously, he studied photographers like Farrokh Chothia and his images of Astad with Manipuri dancers: 'I was blown away. I just prayed that someday I got an opportunity to take some pictures like those with him.' This dream became a reality when he attended one of Astad's performances at NCPA and

dared to approach and ask him, 'Can we do something together?' Astad being Astad was super-delighted to say yes, without even knowing how good or bad, or even if I was worthy of him. He was Astad, with a heart bigger than I can ever imagine on this planet. So, he embraced me and said let's do something. Then one day he called me up and said, Whenever you're ready.

Astad spoke to Ritam in the latter's native Bengali, because Astad had a special place in his heart and palate for Bengali food. Whenever Ritam's parents visited Mumbai, Astad requested Ritam's mother to cook his favourite Bengali dishes.

Ritam photographed Astad in his small studio in Mumbai very close to Shapur Baug, creating two calendars together and innumerable exhibitions. Astad 'created shows around my pictures,' said Ritam. 'So, my pictures were projected on him and he danced around them in performances at the water festival in Delhi, Ahmedabad, Bombay and several other places.' Once quite suddenly in 2020, Astad asked him if he knew how many countries and cities they had visited together. Facebook told Astad that the number was as high as 20. Ritam had never counted but knew that he was with Astad 'from South Korea to South America, to USA, to Europe. We have even travelled across India.' Ritam recalled that in Colombia,

> there was a festival of the dead, with people masqueraded in the streets. It was a blast. Astad became a child—he started dancing, playing, hugging random people like I was doing . . . we had no inhibitions exploring things beyond the conventional, so what I used to think was impossible, he used to make it always possible in front of my eyes. And that extended my faith in expanding my imagination which helped me grow as a person and as an artist in a much bigger way than I could have ever imagined . . . Astad used to live his dream and he was honest.

This honesty in Astad the artist was evident in his response to Ritam's question: How could Astad keep himself 'excited', 'charged', despite setbacks, when Ritam, half his age, was tired? 'Don't you feel like giving up when people behave the way they do with you? You have done enough, you have nothing to prove, right?' Astad's response was profound and characteristic: 'I have to be honest with myself and I can be honest to the world. Dance is the only thing that God has given me and I have to be honest to it, right? That is the only way I can give it forward.' Astad was 'super-secure deep inside of his self and what he did,' noted Ritam, 'no matter what the outside world thought of him.' Ritam attributed this inner security to 'the experiences he has had. From getting into a ship with goats and cattle to being with the Queen of England. How many people can even think of having such a life? So, that is Astad. I had the closest ring-side view of that life, in a personal form.'

When Anita asked Ritam if Astad had made him 'a better artist, a better photographer', he responded: 'Human being, human being, human being. That is the most important thing.' However, Ritam did discuss what he had learned about shooting dance from Astad:

Photography or any form of art is a very symbiotic association between the artist, the environment, the collaborators. For that to happen, somebody has to be super flexible and open. When I started shooting Astad, I had no clue about dance even though my sister was into dance and I had seen several performances . . . I used to fight with Astad because what I used to think was a good picture as a photographer, he told me that from a dance perspective, it did not work. So, he taught me the form and the grace and the design of his art form. And almost instantaneously, within a few shoots [I picked up what he meant]. After that, he didn't need to tell me anything . . . he had so much confidence and faith in me, and we just went with the flow.

In 2019 in Chicago during Astad's collaboration with Hema Rajagopalan, Ritam 'had this dream of creating something with Anish Kapoor's *Bean* [sculpture]', believing that 'with Astad, Anish Kapoor and Millenium Park, some magic will happen'. As it happened, it was snowing and freezing cold on the day that Ritam had planned to execute his dream. Ritam got cold feet, so to speak, but not Astad, as we hear from Ritam's story:

Astad got up in the morning, and he said, 'You wanted to shoot, right?' I said, 'Yeah, but it's freezing cold and if we go there, I mean, it will be difficult for you to dance, right?' He said, 'Are we meeting for the first time? Don't you know me?' So he gave me a piece of his mind, gave me a hug and said, 'Let's go!' . . . When we got to the *Bean*, he just took off his shoes and started dancing. And it was freezing cold. I mean, with my shoes, with three layers of jackets, I could not move because I felt so frozen. But Astad was not bothered.

This image of Astad dancing barefoot with abandon in the Chicago winter is an image to treasure. Ritam, as photographer, inspired that spirit in the dancer even as Astad 'showed [Ritam] how to dream and live the dream'.

Photographer Sreekumar Krishnan was introduced to me by Ramaa Bharadvaj as someone to interview since he had photographed Astad off stage. Sreekumar had met Astad in Bengaluru in 2016. He was interested in capturing photographs of Astad not in costume but off stage. After spending some hours with Astad, Sreekumar felt that Astad was an artist whose creative spirit was true like that of a child. 'That's what Astad still reminds me—to be connected to the true you', shared Sreekumar. He said he felt privileged 'to know the man behind the dance and the dancer' (int., October 2021; same for subsequent quotes). When he started to shoot, he

> saw the meaning of dance . . . fluid, effortless, simple, yet the air moved to dance with him. He laughed, joked . . . I wanted to catch the elemental Astad. He got on to the desk near the window and started to move, no music. Then the chair. I would ask him for one move as a pose and he took it to another level showcasing the Navarasas in Kathakali format . . . without any airs, he used the long table as the prop, dancing on top, hiding under and then I understood the genius in the man.

Sreekumar noted that Astad would often call him on WhatsApp, 'More so during Covid times, generally to check on me and explore my ideas on future collaboration.' Sreekumar wondered why people like Astad are so rare in this world. Even as a celebrity, Astad made time for Sreekumar who thought of himself as 'an unknown entity'. He dedicated his series of photographs to Astad's memory, saluting 'a man who was more than the dance, for he was the Dance itself.'

In conclusion, Astad's collaborations with costume designers and photographers demonstrate his aesthetic gifts, his visual imagination and his ability to connect to them as a human being. He put in time and effort researching and sharing his vision for each work, its setting, and the appropriate colours and styles with his costume designers, then travelled to them for fittings as needed. With photographers, Astad shared a unique camaraderie, discussing with them the specialized skills necessary to shoot dance effectively and dynamically, to capture a body twirling or leaping and to catch the nuance of a smile or a frown. The story of Astad's life is incomplete without his many memorable costumes and photographs that capture the expansive range of his dance—from the proscenium stage to site-specific works to photos shared by family and friends who cherished Astad's presence at their life events. We journey now to Astad's dynamic collaborations with and transgressions of spatial conventions on stage and crossing boundaries in site-specific work.

CHAPTER 13

Transgressing Spatial Boundaries

'I've never used space as a gimmick. Once I've decided that this is the space that I am going to work with, I try to imbibe it and weave the work around it and not just make it look like a prop. There has to be that participation with the space and for me, the space is also participating with my work.'—Astad Deboo (Shanbag 2010: 26)

Astad's collaborative ad/ventures with the spaces in which he danced, whether on a proscenium stage or in site-specific locations, were a unique aspect of his work from his early choreography onwards. Equally significant was Astad's work 'within conventional theatres', as Sunil Shanbag noted, that face challenges of 'unimaginative theatre design' where Astad created new perspectives, ably assisted by his design team (2010: 16). Ramu Ramanathan, playwright and theatre director, remarks that Astad has boldly broken many confining rules of performance spaces, as he

> was weary of prosceniums, of the traditional stage which reduces all formation to frontal viewing. He tried to unshackle himself from th[ose] narrow walls [. . .]. Which is why he has always been open to site-specific works, be it Champaner, Chandigarh, or a Chettinad home in Chennai. And even the famous dance performance on the Great Wall of China. (2010: 23)

Astad's creative deployment of performance space 'provoked' Sunil to ask several incisive questions: 'What is this space? Is it static and always there, or is it being "produced" even as Astad dances and moves? Is it three-dimensional as we commonly understand it or does he force time into the equation, as Einstein did for the first time?' (Shanbag 2010: 16). For Astad, the performance space was not static and inanimate; he had a reciprocal relationship with it, participating with the space even as the space participates with his work.

Astad was fascinated with performing on heights. For example, in 2004, at the Second Champaner Festival in Gujarat, 'the highlight of the performance', he himself noted, was when he 'danced on this 40-foot high wall, which was 25 feet long'. The challenge of dancing at this site, an old ruin with parts of the structure crumbling, was that the wall was 'undulated', explained Astad, 'and there were stones and bricks jutting out' (Shanbag 2010: 42–43). He described to Sunil how he negotiated the space:

> When I started off, I was perched on a ledge, and then I slowly came down from there and on to the wall. I had seen the space and worked out my piece and then I improvised: I walked, pranced, stopped and looked at the audience . . . it was dark and I was basically just playing with the comfort of my feet. There again I was tempting my audience because there was that risk factor. I nearly came to the edge and they said, 'My God! One slip and he is going to go down.' (Shanbag 2010: 50)

Astad also utilized another area at the site—a platform surrounded by columns—where he gracefully descended from the high wall to the flat surface. He successfully achieved his goal of bringing the space to life. He added another dimension to his dramatic performance by dedicating his dance to the goddess Devi who was worshipped by local people in that area. He complemented the live vocal performance by the Gundecha Brothers with the soundtrack of the prelude to the opera *Carmina Burana*, which, he noted, 'brought a regal feel to the performance. The feel suggested Devi in her domain' (Shanbag 2010: 50).

Astad knew that he had two different sets of spectators on two sides of the wall: on one side, his invited audience formally seated; on the other, the chauffeurs who had brought their 'sahibs and memsahibs' in their cars. Astad made sure that both these audiences savoured his performance. Dressed in black and red, he began dramatically by embodying Devi with a mask. In fact, he heard one of the chauffeurs exclaim: 'Arey! Devi Ma!' Astad's dance was memorably lit—the stage lighting from two angles was complemented by the full moon.

Another of Astad's daredevil performances took place at the National Institute of Design (NID) in Ahmedabad where he 'navigated his dance through staircases and ladders', remarks Sanjiv Shah (2010: 37–38), who has followed Astad's works for nearly 30 years. As an architect and filmmaker, Shah was interested in 'how movements within spaces impacted the use/perception of spaces'. Astad's suspenseful performance at NID took place 'against the backdrop of a small, old and decrepit mazaar [mausoleum] in the lawns' (2010: 37–38). The spectators held their breath in fear as they watched Astad climb the ladder and press his back against the wall, anticipating what would happen next. Shah described the scene:

> When he lifted his leg very slowly, counter to the tempo of the music and came down to rest across the ladder on the ledge, the brick was dislodged and fell; the foot found emptiness and the performance continued, just slightly held back for the briefest of moments. For those watching, an eternity seemed to have passed between the time the brick lost its moorings and Astad's foot found another distant brick to rest on and continue. (2010: 38–39)

Astad does mesmerize viewers when he dances at such dangerous heights, but without such suspense, he says to Sunil, 'the performance would have been very *phika* (bland)' (Shanbag 2010: 49).

The risk factor came into play again with Astad's performance titled *Five Minus Three* at the National Gallery of Modern Art (NGMA) in

Mumbai. He used the museum's five levels and had spectators follow him dancing on both horizontal and vertical planes. Sunil recounts that Astad used the 'spiral staircase running down the middle of the gallery along the bannisters literally—these shiny chrome banisters. And there was a drop of . . . 20–25 . . . 30 feet'. Astad relied on his balancing skills: 'Yes, it looks a bit risky, and looks like I'm pushing the edge. But I don't really want to make it look like a circus act', He told Sunil, noting that he did work out alternative places to find a foothold if something went awry when at a height: 'I looked to see where I could interlock myself. In the NGMA banister, there was another rod which went across and I understood that I could curl my leg around it in case I began to fall off and then begin again from that position. I could then extend myself in mid-air, so I do think of these things' (Shanbag 2010: 49–50).

The audience at NGMA was seated too close to Astad, making it a little uncomfortable; conversely, if an audience was too far away, the impact of the performance would not reach them. In his own words: 'I can feel the audience even in conventional spaces as the dance progresses. I can't really explain how, but I can feel them and I know that now the audience is with me . . . I want the audience to feel the body singing and the music dancing' (Shanbag 2010: 49).

In 2015, Astad danced at the Mehrangarh, a fifteenth-century fort in Jodhpur, Rajasthan, which stands on a hilltop, rising about 400 feet above the surrounding plains. Astad said that he transformed 'the narrow lip of the fort's 30 ft high parapet into his dance dais', admitting mischievously that he caused a lot of stress for the organizers, especially since this was a fundraiser for the non-profit Indian Head Injury Foundation. Astad's goal was 'to make the performance space itself come alive while inviting his audiences to view dance from new angles' (Bharadvaj 2017: 59).

Ramu Ramanathan commented that Astad's well-known dance on the Great Wall of China in the 1990s was simple: Astad and a friend, equipped with a portable music system, a few props and costumes, set off on a walk along the Great Wall. 'This went on for a few hours,' says Ramanathan, '[t]he audience [that followed them] was receptive and the feedback was super.' He asserts that Astad 'uses a totally new language of movement or at best takes parts of our existing vocabulary of Indian classical dance and combines it with other forms' (2010: 23). In a later article in the *Indian Express*, Ramanathan noted that 'Astad Deboo could break free of the stage and do a tandav [divine dance] on the Great Wall of China. He was a citizen of the world, and he brought it home' (2020). Astad performed other site-specific works at festivals in Brazil, France and Norway.

Astad liked performance venues with 'tiered, raked seating' for the audience, as at Mumbai's Patkar Hall, where he did his very first performance after returning to India from his travels in 1972: 'It has a very nice feel', he told Sunil, adding that 'sometimes, the space also gives you a comfort level' (in Shanbag 2010: 50). He also liked NCPA's Experimental Theatre, where he could use the stage and first floor, as well as Prithvi Theatre, where he recalled doing a piece called *The Bomb and After*: 'I had a ladder in the middle of the stage and I came down from the top of it, 16 feet down. Or, when we did *The Ritual* [. . .]. The fact that I could tie ropes to the catwalk and be hoisted up was an advantage.' Astad could make his spectators envision different levels even on a flat stage, being hoisted up, naturally drawing their gaze with him. He states that for his experimental early works, 'the space gave [him] the freedom to present those works in that way . . . it made the performance more effective' (Shanbag 2010: 49).

Astad used height as a partner in his choreography and created exciting possibilities for performance spaces. For instance, he transformed an ordinary space to serve his choreography at the Consulate General of India in New York City that he mentions to Sunil in their conversation in 2010. 'It was a boring space,' he remarked. 'But there was a fireplace and there was a platform and a mirror' (Shanbag 2010: 50). Although this was obviously a lecture space, Astad used the mirror to create a reflection in which viewers could see him and how he used the ledge to come down to the fireplace.

Astad also made creative use of horizontal space as in his early work, *Insomnia*, which portrays a human body unable to sleep—except that in this space, there was no bed to rest on. Rather, Astad's body was suspended, floating as it were between steel rods on which his neck rested at one end and his ankles at the other. Only an illusion of a bed was created with Astad's taut body, the minimal props having been created by Ratan Batliboi.

Dancing in specific sites, Astad favoured 'an exciting space to work in, [one] with character like . . . at the Elephanta Festival, or at Rishi Valley with that one huge banyan tree' (Shanbag 2010: 49). Astad believed that an ideal space for dance would allow 'flexibility', allowing him to transform a large area into a more intimate one with ease. Sunil commented on his experience of lighting Astad in a particular space when Astad was 'keen on breaking that one large space into multiple spaces [. . .] then travelling from one space to another so a kind of corridor is created [. . .] such multiple use of the same space gives each of them a different texture and a different experience' (Shanbag 2010: 43).

Knowledgeable about lighting design, Astad was meticulous about how a performance space was illuminated, ensuring that the stage or outdoor lights highlighted his body and accentuated the expressiveness of his face. He told Sunil that when he dances, his 'body is communicating so the body has to be lit up'. Because of his Indian dance training, with its focus on facial expression, Astad does use his face, 'but not as much as I use my body. I want the stance, the curve and my body to be lit up. Or I want a little rectangle of light to be on me and to follow me.' For him, both how the performance space was used and 'the play of light' were important components 'of the creation of a piece [and its] impact' (Shanbag 2010: 43).

Astad discussed the impact of limited stage access before performances in Indian auditoriums and the technical restrictions imposed by budgetary constraints on how a stage can be used. Given such lack of access, 'one has to rely on one's experience to create a design and choreography,' he said, contrasting this with the opportunities abroad, where an artist can 'rip apart the existing stage' and then 'return it to its original state'. He recalled a 1972 performance in Patkar Hall in which he wanted to have a bath on stage! He told his friend and theatre manager Sam Kerawalla that he would use 'just two mugs of water. But then I had a full bucket and four or five kids all pouring water on me. So, then the water started flowing down and into the audience—not that the audience got wet—and Sam had a fit.' Astad noted how 'today you see performances where the whole stage is flooded! Pina Bausch has done it and also at the Cirque de Soleil—water, water, water! Swimming pool on stage . . . I have wanted to do a piece set in a swamp for a very long time now, but no one will allow it' (Shanbag 2010: 49–50). Such creative freedom runs up against regulations and budgets required for maintaining theatres.

But Astad did have artistic freedom in selecting his performance space, so he played with that space as much as possible to achieve the maximum impact. He described his mental process that began with his first look at a space and imagining 'that a different kind of impact is possible. I know what I need to do in that space.' He added that his confidence in reaching spectators by maximizing the potential of his performance space 'has come through the years. And the fact that I know I'm the manipulator of my own work.' Astad was aware of his capabilities in terms of when and how he could challenge his body in particular performance spaces and when he had to control his impulses. Astad planned improvisation into his choreography, which meant that the length of his performances would vary from one day to the next. He attributes this to his experiences, among others, of Japanese Kabuki and classical Indian dance-drama traditions such as Kathakali. 'I felt the impact of all I saw and slowly it crept into my own work' (Shanbag 2010: 20).

Astad's excursions into unusual performance spaces remain a testament to his courage and dedication to discovering new vistas, both in site-specific and traditional theatrical venues. Sanjiv Shah's comment on this is illuminating:

> I have a sense that Astad, in his work, maybe in life as well, constantly seeks to explore beyond the defined extremities of space that he performs in and are obviously visible to the viewer or bystander. What lies beyond the abyss is what attracts him most, even if it is only he who sees it and dares to look into it. (Shah 2010: 40)

Astad's dialogues with space, time and his body have created captivating dances. As Anuradha Vellat (2020) remarks, his artistic journey has taken place in 'some of the most unconventional spaces like the museum, the street, even the Great Wall of China. To take dance from the proscenium to these locations meant changing the conversation between the dancer and the viewer.' Astad reminded us in his comment to Vellat that when dance is taken outside the usual auditorium 'space speaks . . . the space comes alive. The space itself becomes a part of the performance . . . I am like the spider that catches you into his web.'

Astad's life in dance has indeed caught us—his rasikas—in a web of creativity and his generous heart that gave abundantly to many. Now we conclude our appraisal of Astad's life story in dance with his final bow from this earth as we imagine him continuing to perform and delight all in his otherworldly abode.

Astad's Final Bow—Tributes from the Dance and Media Fraternity

From the jingling of ghungroos in his Kathak classes in youth to his expressive eyes and brows shaped by Kathakali training as an adult, Astad's journey as an artist was exceptional. His extensive travels to educate himself about the world's dance vocabularies, along with music, lighting, costuming, staging and use of space made Astad a unique artist. His body and psyche resonated with a multitude of movement styles from Japan, Southeast Asia, Euro-America, Brazil and beyond. His eclectic knowledge and passion for global soundscapes—ranging from Dhrupad to Brazilian music, from opera to classical Indian and Western music—further enriched his artistry.

Astad loved dance so wholeheartedly that nothing could deter him from his dedication. Indeed, his bhakti to his art and to its truth guided his life as a person and artist. He touched many lives and continues to be missed sorely by family, friends, colleagues and collaborators in theatre, dance and music. *Astad Deboo: An Icon of Contemporary Indian Dance* is my offering as a labour of love to my generous friend and his incomparable artistry. His legacy lives on in the bodies and minds of Salaam Baalak youth whom he trained rigorously in his demanding signature style. Along with propagating his passion for dance and inspiring some of them to become professional artists, he taught them invaluable life lessons of discipline and generosity. With his unwavering democratic and humanitarian spirit, Astad taught these youth, just as he did deaf communities, to always stand tall with dignity. Astad's devout connection to Manipuri dancers for nearly two decades, which created opportunities for them to dance across India and the world, is held close to their hearts even today.

Below, I include many heartfelt tributes by dancers, journalists, audience members and others that poured out as soon as news of Astad's passing on 10 December 2020 was shared by his family. These remembrances would have made Astad smile, if somewhat wryly, since he received recognition for his dance late in his life.

The family announced on social media:

He left us in the early hours of 10 December, at his home in Mumbai, after a brief illness, bravely borne. He leaves behind a formidable legacy of unforgettable performances combined with an unswerving dedication to his art, matched only by his huge, loving heart that gained him thousands of friends and a vast number of admirers. (In *Economic Times* 2020)

The *Economic Times* report also said:

His innovative style of Indian dance may have raised some eyebrows in the 1970s and 80s, but the 1990s saw people embrace this new idiom.

Known for his charitable endeavours, Deboo worked with deaf children, both in India and abroad for two decades. In 2002, he founded the Astad Deboo Dance Foundation which provided creative training to marginalised sections, including the differently able.

Deboo also forayed into other art disciplines like films, choreographing for directors such as Mani Ratnam, Vishal Bhardwaj and legendary painter M F Hussain's *Meenaxi: A Tale of Three Cities*.

One remembrance begins with Astad being invited by curator and Kathak dancer Shovana Narayan to a dance festival at Kolkata's Nazrul Manch in 1995 when 'contemporary Indian dance was still struggling to find a foothold' (Khurana 2020b). Curator Narayan recalls that she had to

> reassure senior dance performers over the inclusion of dancer Astad Deboo . . . 'They said he isn't traditional enough.' But they were talking of tradition as they knew it. Not the tradition that could be evolved or the one that could be interpreted differently, the way a dancer like Astad, who has trained in multiple forms, wanted to present. (Khurana 2020b)

Astad opened the festival when several spectators experienced a 'meditative stance'. Some sceptics 'were converted, others confused . . . at that Kolkata performance, Deboo synthesised Kathak with Kathakali and contemporary styles. The form would never need a name; it was just Astad Deboo's dance' (Khurana 2020b).

Astad's friend and prominent Kathak dancer Aditi Mangaldas, artistic director of the Aditi Mangaldas Dance Company and Drishtikon Dance Foundation, valued Astad's journey. In 'Drishtikon Pays Tribute to Astad Deboo', published in *Narthaki*, Aditi offered this heartfelt homage:

> Astad was a lone crusader, a lone warrior in a very different dance environment. He had such courage that, years ago, he just took off with the knowledge of what he had learned . . . so many of us talk about our great heritage but he thought of the idea of world heritage . . . this man gave India a new language of dance, allowing cross-cultural conversations between various styles.

Aditi shared this further contemplation as a dancer herself:

> What happens to the dance when the dancing body is no more? What happens to the love we shared, when—skin, muscle and bone have disintegrated—dust to dust? Astad, your dance, your humanity, your generosity of spirit and above all your courage and conviction to be the lonely trailblazer on the dance sky, will

forever remain in our hearts and minds. Your dance and your life will inspire and give courage to many generations to come. You are and will always be a part of our living mythology—your 'dance being' had so many stories to share. The heart can only ache . . . and you touched so many. Your friends and fans across the world are devastated. Just a few days ago your voice was positive about your recovery. Just a few weeks ago, we were chatting about your latest photoshoot. Just a few months ago, you shared your brilliant dance film made with your dancers over zoom . . . you are gone. Belief is suspended. I am so, so, so sad. (*Narthaki* 2020)

Sangeeta Rana, director of business development at Drishtikon, shared:

Astad Deboo had an aura that remained in the room even after he left it. I met him for the first time at the British Council . . . what developed over the years thereafter was a friendship and relationship of immense respect for an artist and a gentleman whose passion for his art form was boundless. The next close interaction was in 2009 when Pro Helvetia Swiss Arts Council invited Astad to collaborate with Swiss theatre director and choreographer Thomas Mettler for a project titled 'In Contro'. Astad truly belonged to the world and not just to India. (*Narthaki* 2020)

Thomas Mettler from his home in Switzerland wrote:

I'm truly shaken and so sad. My last solo 'Transitio' was dedicated to Astad! I will remember him as a great, great innovator, a pathbreaking artist, twirling forever with me into eternity . . . what a loss for this WORLD. What a loss for DANCE and the Arts. What a loss for all of US who had the joy and honour to know HIM and to become his friends. (*Narthaki* 2020)

Writing in the *Hindu*, Anita Ratnam (2020) contributed a loving tribute to Astad and his legacy:

Astad Deboo was always able to dance his way through the direst challenges. But sadly, not this time.

My phone registered a missed call from Astad's number on 27 November at 12.13 pm . . . I returned his call. His voice was sombre . . . but in my mind, I knew Astad would dance and find a way through the most dire challenge. After all, this was the imprint of his life—to leapfrog over roadblocks and twirl across continents, to almost stop time with his Zen-like stillness. [. . .]

I was envious of his unique method of movement that had aged like fine wine, just like his body and pedagogy. [. . .]

The last time I watched Astad on stage was at Kalakshetra in February [2020]. It was an Indo-Korean collaboration titled, 'Same Same but Different'. The venue and the moment were serendipitous. I imagined the smile on Rukmini Devi's face as she watched a fellow non-conformist tread the stage at her lovingly created institution. One may think that with their ideology and approach they occupied opposite ends of the dance world, but what they shared was the courage to dream differently.

There will be nobody like Astad Deboo. To call him a friend is a privilege and I am but one of hundreds whose lives he has touched beyond our core disciplines. Smiling and composed in his trademark white kurta and churidar off stage, he can't be forgotten.

Ashish Mohan Khokar (2020), dance historian, archivist and editor of *AttenDance*, offered this remembrance of Astad in *Narthaki* on the day after his death:

His whole life in dance was a quest for an inner urge to express and he traversed the globe many times over. [. . .] His dance was his own. It was like an amoeba, forever evolving a new shape and dimension and no one could state when it was Indian or when international [. . .] He was neither modern nor ancient. He was just him. His music sense was superb and he used works which were new to the palette. [. . .] Astad was the last link between pre-independent India and modern. He tried his best to bridge the dance divide. [. . .] Astad must be remembered as a quiet light that shone and showed the way to many more.

Astad's friend and journalist Madhu Trehan (2020) titled her *Indian Express* tribute piece 'People Took Advantage of Astad Deboo's Talent, Decency':

A friend like Astad Deboo can happen only once in your life . . . how does one come to terms that it could only last as long as his lifetime?

I am angry. I am angry on behalf of Astad Deboo. I should be delighted with all the flowery tributes and eulogies in print and on television. I want to shout, 'Where were you all when he struggled for his livelihood, barely subsisting between work, giving him a pittance for his performances?' [. . .]

I told Astad his attitude was far too obsequious with bureaucrats and impresarios. I said he should be arrogant and kick the furniture around. That's how artists with much less talent than him were treated well. But he was not arrogant and could not even put it on temporarily. [. . .]

Astad was the only friend who never ever judged me. When I moaned on about a problem I had, far smaller than his, he never gave me 'the other side' . . . when I was worried, he never said, 'Don't worry'. He worried with me. His innate compassion overrode everything. He left me wanting to be that kind of friend.

Bharatanatyam luminary Leela Samson, speaking to the *Hindustan Times*, went on to say:

Astad Deboo was always ahead of his time [. . .]. Going back 50 years, I would say he was a shy person. He carved for himself a very personal and also a very lonely journey because he was first among the contemporary dancers in the country. Even there he didn't follow any Western norms. He went about his work in his own way. Whether it was in his costumes or his Sufi dervish-[like twirls], he used his body in a way that was very much himself. (Veigas 2020)

The report quoted another Bharatanatyam exponent Malavika Sarukkai: 'He didn't live in a bubble. He was a person who was concerned about others. He lived with honesty and conviction.' And Swapnokalpa Dasgupta, head of dance programming at the National Centre for the Performing Arts, Mumbai, said: 'His support for young artistes was remarkable. He would frequently come to the NCPA to watch senior and junior performers, attend workshops and discussions [. . .] as for our dance community, this loss is irreparable [. . .] a senior so affectionate and unbiased, a loving soul so giving and sensitive'. Actor Anupam Kher took to Twitter/X to pay tribute: 'World of modern dance has lost a pioneer and India has lost a cultural treasure. Dearest #AstadDeboo it was a privilege to know you. Will miss your art, warm persona, and your infectious smile!' (Veigas 2020).

Soon after Astad's passing, I wrote a tribute, 'A Fond Remembrance . . . and Farewell', for *Narthaki*, reproduced in *Pulse*, *FirstPost* and *Marg Magazine*, in which I said:

Astad Deboo's voice, his memorable chakkars on stage, his prodigious talent in riveting performances, his infectious laugh, his impeccable ability to offer friendship to so many across the world have all been stopped in his untimely passing. This news has shocked and devastated us, his dance fraternity and friends. The Indian dance world has lost one of its most paradigm-shifting and beloved artists.

FIGURE 60. Astad with the author Ketu H. Katrak. *Photograph by Beheroze Shroff.*

Astad was my friend, as he was a friend to many across India and beyond. He had an uncanny ability to cultivate and nurture friendships, keeping in touch with phone calls and visits, even going out of his way. He was loved by so many—artists, and ordinary people with whom he created magical connections both on and off stage. (Katrak 2020)

✳✳✳

With so many loving tributes to his memory, his style, his humanity pouring out across every major print and online outlets in India, it seemed that our country came to a standstill on 10 December 2020. It was somewhat like how time felt suspended when Astad danced and drew us into his magical web. Let us imagine Astad's warm smile that will beam like a star flooding the earth with his special light.

Glossary

abhinaya: A language of gestures used in classical Indian dance to narrate stories and convey emotions through facial expressions, body posture and mudras (hand gestures).

aharya: Jewellery adornment on the face and body used in classical Indian dance.

angarkha: Literally, 'body protector'—an outer garment that protects from heat and is easy to wear. Angarkha is a long, ankle-length robe, with long sleeves, accented at the waist, with an embroidered bodice, at times studded with semi-precious stones or decorated with silver or metal thread. Originates in Rajasthan where folk storytellers wore red angarkhas and carried scrolls from which they would read stories.

bhakta: Devotee, generally in the religious sense.

bhakti: Devotion. In Indian religions, it may refer to loving devotion to a personal God, a formless ultimate reality or an enlightened being.

chakkar: Pirouette, a particularly important aspect of classical Kathak dance.

churidar: Tight-fitting trousers with pleats gathered at the ankles.

dhuti/dhoti: A long fabric wrapped around the hips and thighs with one end brought between the legs and tucked at the waist.

gamaka: Ornamentation used in the performance of North and South Indian classical music, both vocal and instrumental; embellishments done on a note or in between two notes.

ghagra: Long skirt usually worn by women.

ghungroo: ankle bells used in classical Indian dance.

Guruvayur: Traditional Indian pedagogical system in which a student stays with the teacher (guru) and is immersed in studying the art form along with learning life skills from the guru.

jugalbandi: Indian classical duet performed by two soloists—two musicians, or a dancer and a musician.

mudra: hand gesture used in classical and contemporary Indian dance.

Navarasas: The nine primary human emotions that form the aesthetic underpinning of Indian classical dance and theatre performance—*shringara* (love), *bhayanaka* (fear), *hasya* (laughter), *bibhatsya* (disgust), *veera* (valour), *raudra* (anger), *karuna* (compassion), *adbhuta* (wonder), *shanta* (peace). The first eight were enunciated by Bharata Muni in his *Natyashastra* (200 BCE–200 CE); the ninth was added by later scholars. An even later addition to the list is *bhakti* (devotion).

nritya: Indian dance movement patterns in different rhythmic cycles rendered by the dancer's limbs, as well as the neck and eyes.

padam: An abhinaya dance item in a traditional Bharatanatyam repertoire to accompany a song set in a specific mood.

rasa: Literally 'essence, or taste' in Sanskrit; a concept central to the Indian classical arts that refers to the aesthetic essence of a musical or performance work, evoking a particular emotion or feeling in the audience. (See *Navarasas*)

rasika: An arts appreciator, one with rasa (emotion), an artistic sensibility and an open heart.

rudra veena: Stringed instrument with a long tubular body (like a sitar) made of teak wood and metal, with two dried or hollowed pumpkin gourds on both sides. It originates in North India. It is played with plectrums (a small tool used to pluck the strings) worn on the index and middle fingers of the right hand.

List of Interviews

For this volume, interviews with Astad Deboo's friends, family and collaborators were conducted by Ketu H. Katrak via phone, email, Zoom and WhatsApp, and in some cases by Anita Ratnam. A chapter-by-chapter list of these interviews is as follows.

Preface. Sunil Shanbag, via email, July 2021.

Ramaa Bharadvaj, via email, August 2021.

Anjali Patil, via Zoom, 16 February 2022.

Shankar Ramakrishnan, via Zoom, 22 February 2022.

Chapter 1. Gulshan Deboo and Kamal Antia, via Zoom, 30 June 2021.

Cawas Deboo, via phone, 28 June 2021.

Vidhya Gajapathi Singh, via email, 16 July 2021.

Yasmine Stafford, via email, 4 July 2021.

Shernaz Cama, via email, 14 August 2021.

Orville Domingo, via phone, 16 July 2021.

Ashok Chirayath, via phone, 7 July 2021.

Shanoo Bhatia, via email, 14 July 2021.

Xerxes Antia, via Zoom, 24 June 2021.

Danesh Antia, via WhatsApp, 7 June 2022.

Chapter 2. Jeelu Billimoria, via email, 28 June 2021.

Jeelu Billimoria and Deena Vakeel, via email, 24 August 2021.

Rohini Desai Mulchandani, via email, 26 June 2021.

Kharmeen Ginwalla, via email, 30 July 2021.

Soli Surti, via WhatsApp, 4 August 2021.

Bharti Patel, via email, 5 July 2021.

Yezdi Unwalla, via phone, 19 July 2021.

Prabha Rao, via email, 6 February 2022.

Phainie Xydis, via email, 13 May 2022.

Chapter 4. Sunil Shanbag, via Zoom, 1 July 2021.

Ratan Batliboi, via Zoom, 5 July 2021.

George Michell, via Zoom, 5 July 2021.

Uttara Coorlawala, via Zoom, 20 August 2021.

Chitra Sundaram, via Zoom, 12 August 2021.

Anita Ratnam, via Zoom, 6 August 2021.

Rani Nair, via Zoom, 21 June 2021.

Chapter 5. Dadi Pudumjee, via Zoom, 8 July 2021

Chapter 6. Malavika Sarukkai, via Zoom, 3 August 2021

Alarmel Valli, via Zoom, 15 August 2021

Aditi Mangaldas, via Zoom, 21 August 2021.

Vikram Iyengar, interviewed by Anita Ratnam, 13 July 2021

Deepak Kurki Shivaswamy, interviewed by Anita Ratnam, 13 July 2021.

Chapter 7. Astad Deboo, in person, October 2005.

Satya Achayya, via email, 6 July 2021.

Mary Ann Whitten, via email, 29 October 2021.

Chapter 8. Chakpram Narendra Singh, via Zoom, 25 August 2021.

Chapter 9. Swapnokalpa Dasgupta, interviewed by Anita Ratnam, 13 July 2021.

Shamshul, via Zoom, 11 August 2021.

Chapter 10. Rathi Jafer, via email, 19 March 2018.

Rathi Jafer, interviewed by Anita Ratnam, 13 July 2021.

Yukio Tsuji, via Zoom, 11 July 2021.

Chapter 11. Hema Rajagopalan, via Zoom, 6 July 2021.

Hema Rajagopalan, interviewed by Anita Ratnam, 13 July 2021.

Deepika Sorabjee, via email, 5 January 2022.

Chapter 12. Archana Shah, via Zoom, 18 August 2021

Ashdeen Lilaowalla, via email, 2 August 2021.

Farrokh Chothia, via Zoom, 9 January 2022.

Sreekumar Krishnan, via email, 8 October 2021.

Neelesh Kale, interviewed by Anita Ratnam, 13 July 2021

Ritam Bannerjee, interviewed by Anita Ratnam, 13 July 2021.

Works Cited

AHANTHEM, Chitra. 2015. 'Astad Deboo and the Dance of Rebellion in Manipur'. *Rediff News* (13 January): https://bit.ly/3WZUFLQ (accessed 12 December 2023).

ANDRADE, Carol. 2017. 'About a Dream'. *Freelibrary* (1 June): http://bit.ly/-3SE5SAX (accessed 12 December 2021).

ARORA, Shveta. 2020. 'Astad Deboo's *Unbroken Unbowed* Channels Gandhi but Reflects the Present'. *Kala Upasana*: https://bit.ly/4cy2ez2 (accessed 21 August 2024).

ARTAUD, Antonin. 1958 [1938]. *The Theatre and Its Double* (Mary Caroline Richards trans.). New York: Grove Press.

BANA, Aban. 1984. 'Astad Deboo: A Peacock in Full Bloom'. *Society* (April): 84–89.

BAPTISTA, Marcell. 2005. 'Amazing Grace!' *Mumbai Mirror* (26 September), n.p.

BATLIBOI, Ratan. 2010. 'Defining Zero Space' in Anmol Vellani (ed.), *Beyond the Proscenium: Reimagining the Space for Performance*. Bangalore: India Foundation for the Arts, pp. 51–58.

BHARADVAJ, Ramaa. 2017. 'Astad Deboo: Pilgrim, Pathfinder, Protagonist'. *Marg* 68(4) (Special Issue: Contemporary Dance in India) (June–September): 52–61.

BHASKAR, Ranjith. 2002. 'The First Step in a Circle of Feeling'. *Narthaki* (June): https://bit.ly/4dHan4X (last accessed 14 August 2024).

BRITISH LIBRARY. 2022. The Buggery Act, 1533. British Library: https://bit.ly/-47rMWJS (accessed 25 July 2022).

CAMA, Shernaz. 2016. 'Threads of Community: Zoroastrian Life and Culture'. *Wire* (12 May): https://bit.ly/3FRBNpR (accessed 25 July 2024).

CHAITANYA, Krishna. 1987. 'Indian Dance: Naïve Longings for Winds of Change'. *Sangeet Natak* 83 (January–March): 5–13.

CHATTERJEE, Madhusree. 2012. 'Exploring New Terrain: Living and Breathing Tagore'. *Spectrum: The Tribune* (13 May): https://bit.ly/46T6l7y (accessed 21 August 2024).

CHOKSI, Sharavati. 2004. 'Style without Sound'. *Chennai City Express* (9 December), n.p.

COORLAWALA, Uttara Asha. 2016. 'East–West Dance Encounter (1984)', in *The Routledge Encyclopedia of Modernism*: https://bit.ly/3z2aBVS (accessed 31 August 2024).

———. 2021. 'In Memoriam: Astad Deboo, 1947–2020'. *Seminar* 738 (February): 82–83.

DATTA, Sravasti. 2020. 'Veteran Dancer-Choreographer Astad Deboo Says Much More Can Be Done to Present Dance Shows'. *Hindu* (12 March): https://bit.ly/4fWQcSH (accessed 26 August 2024).

DE, Aditi. 2004. 'Challenging Beats'. *The Hindu* (28 November), n.p.

DEBOO, Astad. 1995. 'I Am Still Exploring . . .'. Interview by Anjum Katyal, Biren Das Sharma and Sreejata Guha. *Seagull Theatre Quarterly* 8 (December): 24–47: https://bit.ly/40x1pBU (accessed 26 August 2024).

———. 2003. 'Creating Endless Possibilities' in Sunil Kothari (ed.), *New Directions in Indian Dance*. Bombay: Marg Publications, pp. 118–30.

———. 2016a. 'I Feel Dance Is Serious Work'. Interview by Ranjitha Menon. *Deccan Herald* (21 December): https://bit.ly/47xlDy0 (accessed 26 August 2024).

———. 2016b. 'Of Subtlety and Sufism'. Interview by Deepa Padmar. *Hindu* (15 December): https://bit.ly/3Xh2Qod (accessed 26 August 2024).

———. 2017a. 'India Still Lacks a Platform for Contemporary Dance: Astad Deboo'. Interview by Sangeeta Barooah Pisharoty. *Wire* (2 March): https://shorturl.at/ewJZ7 (link no longer active).

———. 2017b. 'When I Met the Queen of England'. As told to Archana Masih. *Rediff News* (2 March): https://bit.ly/4f6BCHT (accessed 26 August 2024).

———. 2018. 'One Man's Footprint on Contemporary Indian Dance'. Interview by Emmaly Wiederholt. *Stance on Dance* (26 November): https://bit.ly/-3SzpFBF (accessed 26 August 2024).

———. 2020. Interview. *Aroop: A Journal of Arts, Poetry, and Ideas* 4 (Special issue: 'Failure'): 159–68.

———, and Yukio Tsuji. 2015. 'Behind the Scenes of the Moroccan Court Music Series: Astad Deboo and Yukio Tsuji's *Eternal Embrace*'. Interview by Julia Rooney. *The Met* (29 September): https://bit.ly/478Rhms (accessed 26 August 2024).

Deccan Herald. 2009. 'Now, Street Kids Break Boundaries'. *Deccan Herald* (15 April), n.p.

Economic Times. 2020. 'Dance pioneer Astad Deboo Passes Away at 73, Tributes Pour In'. *Economic Times* (10 December): https://bit.ly/4cIClg1 (accessed 31 August 2024).

G5A FOUNDATION FOR CONTEMPORARY CULTURE. 2020. 'Inter Connect | Astad Deboo X Bahauddin Dagar': https://bit.ly/3XiValc (accessed 26 August 2024).

GOKHALE, Shanta. 1990. 'Looking for a Niche at Home'. *Times of India* (24 November), n.p.

GOKHALE, Veena. 1988. 'Brij Serenades Astad Deboo'. *Mid-Day* (16 December), n.p.

GOPINATH, C. Y. 1979. 'Astad Deboo: Watch Him Move'. *Debonair* (January), n.p.

India Today. 1978 [2015]. 'Astad Deboo Takes Bombay Dance Scene by Storm'. *India Today*: https://bit.ly/47aucjl (accessed 31 August 2024).

INKO CENTRE. 2014. 'Hamlet_Avataar: An Indo-Korean Theatre Production'. *Focus* 27 (October): 9–11.

JOYAIN, S. 2019. 'Photo Special: Astad Deboo Celebrates Gandhi in *Unbroken Unbowed*, in His 50th Year on Stage'. *Indian Express Indulge* (29 November): https://bit.ly/3WRZIO5 (accessed 21 August 2024).

KATRAK, Ketu H. 2011. *Contemporary Indian Dance: New Creative Choreography in India and the Diaspora*. Basingstoke, UK: Palgrave Macmillan.

———. 2020. 'A Fond Tribute . . . and Farewell'. *Narthaki* (10 December): https://bit.ly/3XbglEL (accessed 31 August 2024).

———. 2021. 'Interrogating the "Nation" in Contemporary Indian Dance in India and the Diaspora'. *South Asian Review* 42(2): 169–91.

KHOKAR, Ashish Mohan. 1995. 'Dancing like Dolphins'. *Times of India*, n.p.

——. 2020. 'Obit/Tribute'. *Narthaki* (11 December): https://tinyurl.com/-ycx4x48u (accessed 31 August 2024).

KHURANA, Suanshu. 2020a. 'Astad Deboo Passes Away: He Talked with Every Muscle in Body—and with His Stillness'. *The Indian Express* (17 December): https://rb.gy/k7rlaz (accessed 31 August 2024).

——. 2020b. 'Being Minimal is Harder'. *The Indian Express* (20 January): https://bit.ly/4dPKWyL (accessed 7 September 2024).

KOTHARI, Sunil. 2012. 'Astad Deboo Dance Foundation's *Interpreting Tagore*'. *Narthaki* (8 May): https://bit.ly/3SZxQq9 (accessed 21 August 2024).

LAL, Shrimati. 1990. 'Dance Macabre'. *Times of India* (30 September), n.p.

LECHNER, GEORGE, and Jamshed J. Bhabha. 1984. 'East–West Dance Encounter'. *NCPA Journal* 13(2): 5–7. Republished on *Narthaki*, 2016: https://bit.ly/-3Z1QZM4 (accessed 31 August 2024).

MAHESH, Chitra. 2002. 'Stepping Beyond the Aural Realm'. *Hindu MetroPlus* (11 June), n.p.

MAP ACADEMY. 2022. 'Pabuji ki Phad': https://bit.ly/3T5PxEC (accessed 26 August 2024).

MASIH, Archana. 2017. 'When I met the Queen of England'. *Rediff News* (2 March): https://bit.ly/3FRaJHq (accessed 26 August 2024).

MEHTA, Sejal. 2005. 'When Silence Makes Music'. *Femina* (21 December), n.p.

METTLER, Thomas. 2016. *Incontro (2009/2010)*. Vimeo: https://rb.gy/5jus4b (accessed 26 August 2024).

NAGARAJAN, Raju. 1977. Profile of Astad Deboo. *Kayhan International*, Tehran (7 November), n.p.

NAIR, Rani. 2024. 'An Evening with Astad': https://bit.ly/3z223yl (accessed 21 June 2024).

Narthaki. 2020. 'Drishtikon pays homage to Astad Deboo'. *Narthaki* (20 December): https://rb.gy/kghie8 (accessed 31 August 2024).

News Desk. 2020. 'Jamshedpur remembers choreographer and former Loyola student Astad Deboo'. (10 December 2020): https://bit.ly/3QT20L6 (accessed 10 January 2022).

News India Times. 2018. 'Indian-American Dance Company Gets Prestigious MacArthur Grant'. *News India Times* (15 November): https://shorturl.at/-aUV68 (link no longer active).

PATEL, Bati. 2013. *My Kahaani.* Self-published, Mumbai.

POLICHETTI, Kayleen. 1985. 'The Golden Days of Dance Are Here'. *Span Magazine*, pp. 44–47.

PUDUMJEE, Dadi. 2020. 'Astad Was a Genius Who Could Never Sit Still'. *Indian Express* (13 December) Available at: https://bit.ly/3FX6nOV (accessed 2 August 2024).

RAMANATHAN, Ramu. 2008. 'Waah Ustad Waah!' *India Perspectives* (April–May), pp. 57–67.

———. 2010. 'Making It New', in Anmol Vellani (ed.), *Beyond the Proscenium: Reimagining the Space for Performance.* Bangalore: India Foundation for the Arts, pp. 19–26.

———. 2020. 'Astad Deboo Could Shock Tradition and Yet Remain Open to Collaborations'. *Indian Express* (14 December): https://rb.gy/lv0sv2 (accessed 25 October 2022).

RATNAM, Anita. 2020. 'Astad Deboo: The Last Twirl'. *Hindu* (10 December): https://tinyurl.com/2m3jrd5b (accessed 20 August 2024).

———. 2021. 'Amazing Astad'. Narthaki Official on YouTube: https://bit.ly/-3yQfHo5 (accessed 31 August 2024).

REDIFF NEWS BUREAU. 2001. 'Dance for Astad!' 2021. *Rediff News* (13 July): https://bit.ly/4ghkxeU (accessed 7 September 2024).

ROYAL OPERA HOUSE (Mumbai). 2020. 'Same Same but Different': https://-bit.ly/3MnL5xj (accessed 26 August 2024).

SALAAM BAALAK TRUST. 2024. 'Performing Arts': https://bit.ly/3WVqCoa (accessed 20 August 2024).

SAWHNEY, Anubha. 2002. 'Astad Deboo: In Step with Life'. *The Times of India* (28 April): https://bit.ly/3SuZITL (accessed 24 July 2024).

SHAH, Sanjiv. 2010. 'Beyond the Edge', in Anmol Vellani (ed.), *Beyond the Proscenium: Reimagining the Space for Performance.* Bangalore: India Foundation for the Arts, pp. 31–40.

SHANBAG, Sunil. 2010. 'Conversation with Astad Deboo', in Anmol Vellani (ed.), *Beyond the Proscenium: Reimagining the Space for Performance*. Bangalore: India Foundation for the Arts, pp. 14–16, 17–31, 41–50.

SHARMA, Sanjukta. 2018. 'Astad Deboo's Astonishing Backbends'. *Voice of Fashion* (29 November): https://bit.ly/4dCcKX9 (accessed 26 August 2024).

SHARMA, Vichitra. 1980. 'The Deboo Phenomenon: Combining Western and Indian Dance Rhythms.' *Contour* (March), n.p.

SOMESHWAR, Savera. 2002. 'Dancing the Deaf Way'. *India Abroad* (9 August), n.p.

SS. 1995. 'Dancing with the Dolphins'. *Daily* (3 September), n.p.

SWAMINATHAN, Chitra. 2018. 'Astad Deboo Never Fails to Surprise.' *Hindu* (12 April): https://bit.ly/3AOuEr4 (accessed 27 August 2024).

THOMAS, Maria. 2018. 'Timeline: The struggle against Section 377 Began over Two Decades Ago'. *Quartz* (6 September): https://bit.ly/3sxB3mR (accessed 25 July 2022).

TREHAN, Madhu. 2020. 'People Took Advantage of Astad Deboo's Talent, Decency'. *Indian Express* (16 December): https://tinyurl.com/494wa988 (last accessed 31 August 2024).

UCHIL, Shraddha. 2016. 'Astad Deboo to Perform with Manipuri Drummers in Paris'. *Mid-Day* (22 September): https://bit.ly/3XdE6Mz (accessed 20 August 2024).

VEIGAS, Vanessa. 2020. 'Astad Deboo Dies; Artistes Say India Has Lost a Cultural Treasure'. Hindustan Times (10 December): https://bit.ly/475n2N7 (accessed 31 August 2024).

VELLAT, Anuradha. 2020. 'The Enchanting Web of Astad Deboo: The Making of the Master'. *Hindu* (23 January): https://bit.ly/3SwZStQ (accessed 2 September 2024).

VENKATARAMAN, Leela. 2009. 'Peerless', review of *Breaking Boundaries*. *Hindu* (1 May), n.p.

VENKATARAMAN, Leela. 2019. 'Understanding Dancer Astad Deboo: The Lonely Crusader, Still an Enigma'. Asian Age (15 August): https://bit.ly/4g7rUW8 (accessed 2 September 2024).

Further Reading

This list of articles demonstrates Astad's efforts to maintain a media presence, especially during the 1970s and 80s, when he did not have large audiences for his performances. It is useful for readers to see that along with dance, he had ventured into theatre, film, fashion and extensive travels, many of which were featured in popular magazines such as Debonair, Society *and* Film World. *Astad's family kindly granted me access to the personal archive of news and features that he had maintained over decades until he passed away. Most of the pieces mentioned below are from that archive; I have included as much bibliographic material as available on the clippings.*

Ketu H. Katrak

ADVANI, Vinod. 1986. 'French Critics praise Debo's performance in Paris'. *Sunday Observer* (27 April), n.p.

ANANTH, Rukmini. 1982. 'Enjoyable Performance by Astad Deboo'. *Times of India* (May 1), n.p.

BANERJEE, Arnab. 2004. 'Deboo Matches Steps with Sufi Strains'. *Hindustan Times: HT City* (March 27), n.p.

BARSI, Sheela. 1980. 'Deboo's World'. *Sunday Standard* (19 October), n.p.

BHATTACHARYA, Jayatsen. 1993. 'Body Language'. *Telegraph Weekend* (18 September), n.p.

Bombay: The City Magazine. 1980. 'Making Waves'. *Bombay: The City Magazine* (March), p. 62.

CHOKSI, Sharavati, 2004. 'A Flawless Performance'. *Chennai City Express* (11 December), n.p.

Contour. 1980. 'The Deboo Phenomenon'. *Contour* (March), n.p.

Daily. 1983. 'Dancer's Wanderlust'. *Daily* (7 November), n.p.

———. 1986. 'Till divorce do us part'. *Daily*, n.p.

DASGUPTA, Shougat. 2002. 'The Journey to Find Home'. *Tehelka* (3 November), pp. 49–50.

Debonair. 1973. 'Astad Deboo's Concept of Fashion' (cover story), pp. 45–46.

DEBOO, Astad. 1989. 'Interview' with Annahita P. Limki (cover story). *Mahila Weekly, Rathestar* (March), pp. 5–6.

DUTTA, Pronoti. 2011. 'Reinterpreting Tagore with Street Children'. *Times of India* (28 September), n.p.

Film World. 1980. 'Dancin' Feet'. *Film World* (October), n.p.

Free Press Bulletin. 1986. 'Deboo Performs with Russian Artiste'. *Free Press Bulletin* (9 January), n.p.

Gentlemen & GFQ. 1982. 'Jazz-M'Tazz' (cover story). *Gentlemen & GFQ* (August–October), n.p.

India News. 1994. 'Dance Performance by Astad Deboo', Kennedy Center, 20 October). *India News* (1 November), n.p.

India Today. 1979. 'Gyrating Around the World'. *India Today* (18–30 November), n.p.

JATHAN, Dhyanesh. 2005. 'Spellbinding Performance'. *Week* (9 January), n.p.

Kaiser-e-Hind (English Edn). 1980. 'Astad Off to Europe, America'. *Kaiser-e-Hind* (October 19), n.p.

KARKARIA, Bachi J. 1988. 'Astad Deboo's Cultural Revelation in China'. *Times of India*, n.p.

KAUR, Harpreet. 2002. 'Personality: Sound of Silence'. *Jetwings* (October), pp. 40–44.

KOTHARI, Sunil. 'Power of Movement'. *Statesman* (18 September), p. 4.

Maharashtra Herald. 1985. 'Deboo's Art of Creative Dance'. *Maharashtra Herald* (22 December), n.p.

MENON, Shankar, S. 1980. 'Astad Deboo Arrives'. *Financial Express* (20 April), p. 5.

Metropolis. 1993. 'Ustad Astad'. *Metropolis* (25–26 December), n.p.

MICHAEL, Patrick. 1979. 'Astad Deboo: The Body Is My Temple'. *Onlooker* (1–15 January), p. 50.

Mid-Day. 1979. 'Discomania night'. *Mid-Day* (5 September), n.p.

——. 1988. 'Astad Deboo's Disquietude'. *Mid-Day* (May 27), n.p.

——. 1988. 'Fusion of East and West'. *Mid-Day* (21 December), p. 28.

Parsiana. 1978. 'Body Language. Deboo: Ideas in dance form'. *Parsiana* (March), p. 15.

PESTONJI, Meher. 1991. 'Vicious Cycle'. *The Afternoon Despatch & Courier* (6 December), n.p.

RAMNARAYAN, Gowri. 2002. 'Tradition and Modern Juxtaposed'. *Hindu* (4 January), n.p.

RODGERS, Debbie. 2002. 'Theatre of Dance'. *CityExpress* (16 February), n.p.

ROY, Niraj. 1989. 'Deboo Storms the Dancing World'. *National Herald* (13 July), n.p.

SARMA, Ramya. 1991. 'Battle for Dance'. *Times of India* (26 March), n.p.

SETH, Nikki Ty-Tomkins. 1982. 'Dance'. *Times of India* (2 May), n.p.

SHETTY, Gopal. 1988. 'Astad Deboo's Disquietude'. *Mid-Day* (27 May), n.p.

SIDHWA, Shiraz. 1987. 'Now, India's Most Expensive Disco'. *Sunday Observer* (New Delhi) (19 July), n.p.

SINGH, Suhani. 2009. 'Dance Expansion Plans'. *Timeout Mumbai* (18 September– 1 October), p. 65

——. 2011. 'Man of the Whirl'. *Timeout Mumbai* (25 November–8 December), n.p.

SOOFI, Mayank Austen. 2013. 'Some Tagore Twists'. *Livemint* (11 February): https://bit.ly/3MB0avC (accessed 7 September 2024).

SRINIVASAN, Sumitra Kumar. 1987. 'Astad Deboo—Profile of a Modern Dancer'. *Namaskar:Inflight Magazine of Air-India* 7(4) (July–August): 10–17

——. 1987. 'Dance Review: Quintet—Deserves to Be Danced All Over India'. *Mid-Day* (2 May), n.p.

——. 1988. 'A Textured Grace'. *Indian Post* (26 May), n.p.

SUBRAMANYAM, Arundhati. 2004. '"Tanz der Saris", Dance Workshop with Astad'. *Timeout Mumbai* (10–23 September), n.p.

——. 2009. 'Astad Deboo: Rhythm Machine'. *Timeout Delhi* (2–15 October), n.p.

SUREKHA, S. 2011. 'Dance like a Man'. *Mid-Day* (25 November), n.p.

TAY, Malcolm. 2003.'What Is There to Celebrate?' *Asian Week* (21 November), n.p.

Times of India. 1986. 'Astad to Perform for Bolshoi Ballet'. *Times of India* (12 January), n.p.

VAJIFDAR, Shirin. 1988. 'Visionary Experiment'. *Indian Express* (28 May), n.p.

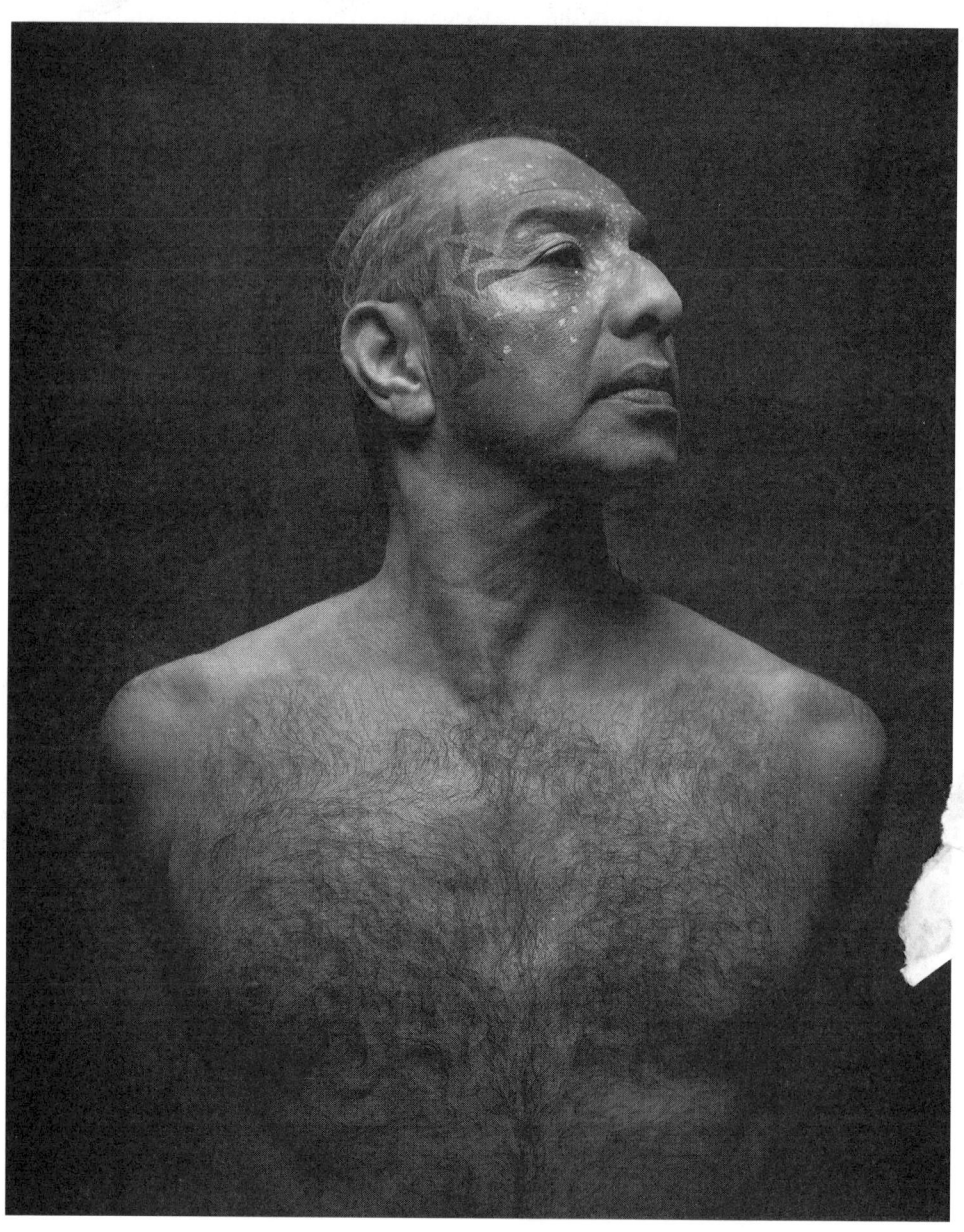

FIGURE 61. Astad bust pose. *Photograph by Farrokh Chothia.*